STRATEGIC COPY EDITING

STRATEGIC
COPY EDITING

John Russial

THE GUILFORD PRESS
New York   London

© 2004 The Guilford Press
A Division of Guilford Publications, Inc.
72 Spring Street, New York, NY 10012
www.guilford.com

Printed in the United States of America

This book is printed on acid-free paper.

Last digit is print number: 9   8   7   6   5   4   3   2   1

Library of Congress Cataloging-in-Publication Data

Russial, John
   Strategic copy editing / by John Russial.
        p.   cm.
     Includes bibliographical references and index.
     1-57230-926-1 (pbk.)
     1. Copy-reading.   I. Title.
   PN4784.C75R87 2004
   808'.06607—dc22

                                                    2003017715

Acknowledgments

Few copy editors are "naturals." We learn how to edit copy in school and on the job. And like many other journalism students, I probably would not have chosen a career in copy editing had it not been for a teacher who pointed out that I seemed to be pretty good at it and that I liked the work. That professor was Bob Sullivan, who taught copy editing at Lehigh University in the '60s and '70s.

Much of what I've learned about the craft since my college days and many of my views on copy editing practices stem from my experience as a copy chief at The Philadelphia Inquirer in the '80s and early '90s. The Inquirer was, and is, a model for how newspapers should be copy edited, and I owe my former copy desk colleagues and supervisors a large debt of gratitude for what I learned on the job. Other newspapers have very good copy editors, but few treat their copy editors with as much respect as The Inquirer does. Much of the credit for creating that trusting environment belongs to Gene Foreman, the paper's former managing editor, who now teaches at The Pennsylvania State University in University Park.

I'd also like to thank the professionals and professors I've met through the American Copy Editors Society. ACES is the premier training organization for copy editors in the United States and is the strongest voice in support of copy editors' interests. I have learned much about the profession from the leaders and the members of the group.

Two people who contributed more directly to this book were reviewers Frank E. Fee Jr. of the University of North Carolina at Chapel Hill and Malcolm Gibson of the University of Kansas. They offered many excellent suggestions. They made a lot of nice catches too. So did the copy editor for The Guilford Press, Philip Holthaus, who worked on the manuscript. Reviewing the mistakes I missed in proofreading confirmed my suspicion that everybody needs a copy editor, especially a copy editor. I'd also like to thank Kristal Hawkins of Guilford for her encouragement and for her help in moving the manuscript through the publication process.

In addition, Carol Ann Bassett and Tim Gleason of the University of Oregon School of Journalism and Communication read parts of the manuscript and provided extremely helpful criticism and suggestions. Finally, I'd like to thank my students, whose questions often lead me to question my own opinions about what copy editors should do.

Contents

1

Introduction
What Do Copy Editors Do?

Copy editors deal with words—and with people. They are expected to focus on details such as grammar and punctuation, and they should be capable of addressing broad issues of content and focus. They need to have more advanced computer skills than most people in the newsroom, and they should have visual skills that enable them to see how text and images work together. Copy editors can be the "glue" that cements relationships between sometimes warring factions in the newsroom. Their greatest asset is their ability to think critically and to criticize constructively, and these skills are best employed by editors who respect and are respected by others in the newsroom. The best copy editors think strategically—they have the tools, but more important, they know how and when to use these tools.

Many talented word editors downplay the important human dimension of their craft, and as a result they are not as successful or productive as they could be. Ignoring people skills often leads to unnecessary friction between editors and writers and gets in the way of producing the best story possible. The purpose of this text is to look carefully at editing skills and people skills. Editors who develop both sets of skills—who are good wordsmiths as well as good communicators, negotiators, colleagues and critical thinkers—are in great demand. In this text, therefore, I define *editing* as a set of language and critical thinking skills as well as the ability to

1

interact professionally and productively with others in the organization. Moreover, editing is the strategic application of all those skills.

I also assume that editing can be done well, even under deadline conditions, but that how well it can be done is always constrained by time, staffing and other institutional considerations. This approach—both practical and strategic—reflects the editing process at some of the most-respected newspapers in the country.

In most editing instruction, one tacit assumption is that perfection is within reach. This book, grounded in three decades of newspaper copy editing and teaching experience, sets perfection as a goal but is written from the perspective that the time pressures involved in news editing make perfection unattainable. The prudent goal is to do as good a job as possible in the time available and to become better at managing time and setting priorities. These are keys to becoming a better editor. A fundamental skill in deadline environments, one that is seldom taught, is knowing when good enough *is* good enough. Editing is decision-making, and one important skill is knowing when to stop editing.

Another focus is on strategies to meet the goal of high-quality editing. All copy editing texts provide examples of poor editing and flawed headlines and demonstrate how to improve them. As any editor knows, fixing is a big part of the job, and this book will discuss many examples of writing that needs fixing. It also will deal with coaching, which operates at a different level and uses a different logic. The broader goals of this book are to foster critical thinking about the process of editing, to discuss strategies of editing and to examine the received knowledge that has long been a part of editing education. For example, rather than simply say, "This is the rule that most newspapers follow," I ask: "Does this rule serve a purpose? Is it still valid?" One simple example is the rule long followed by many newspapers that headline writers should not split thoughts that belong together. I would argue that this rule on "splits" should be retained because keeping related elements together makes headlines clear and readable. Another example is the rule that some editing instructors and editors follow about not "padding" headlines. They argue that auxiliary verbs and articles are typically unnecessary in newspaper headlines and waste precious headline space. I agree that sometimes such words are unnecessary, but in many cases, the articles and auxiliary verbs are necessary for headline readability and clarity. These two considerations can be more important than saving a character here and there or awkwardly forcing another idea into the mix.

The themes in this text arise from my experience as a professional copy editor, most of it on the copy desk at The Philadelphia Inquirer, a newspaper widely known as one of the best-edited papers in the country. They also come from my 10 years as an editing teacher and my occasional work in consulting and coaching. A third area that provides a backdrop for this book is research. I have studied and written about editing and newsroom change for more than 10 years.

Most of my views on editing stem from newspaper copy editing, but their application is broader. They are appropriate for editing on the Web, and many of the ideas and strategies should have a home in any type of editing in which print information is presented.

MEDIA CONVERGENCE AND SPECIALIZATION

The buzzword in journalism education these days is "convergence," a word that defies simple definition. Many media scholars and professionals define *convergence* as the tendency for different media forms—print, radio, television, online—to coalesce into one. Others think of it as an approach to publication or presentation—that media organizations should strive to disseminate information in whichever form makes most sense at a given time. An example is Tribune Co., the parent of the Chicago Tribune, WGN television and radio, cable TV operations and several Web sites in the greater Chicago market. "Convergence," to the Tribune Co. might mean that a story broken by a Chicago Tribune reporter would get to the public first via broadcast, cable or the Web, which are more timely, and only later in the newspaper, which operates on a daily rather than on an up-to-the-minute deadline schedule.

The need for specialized editors in specialized media industries might be overtaken by convergence at some point. Print editors then will have to understand their craft as it applies to electronic media and multimedia as well. For the near term, however, print-editing issues are distinct enough to require their own elaboration. Electronic media do have lessons to offer print, and there are common issues across media boundaries, but video editing is quite different from print editing in the tools and techniques editors actually use. The differences are striking enough and important enough to write a book aimed at a print audience, particularly print journalists who work in deadline-based environments.

As for the Web, for the time being, it is largely print on a screen because of bandwidth limitations and because business models and technologies have not been developed that make true online presentation of multimedia information viable to more than a narrow slice of the online public. News organizations have been experimenting with online multimedia forms for at least five years, but those forms—primarily video and audio clips—are not yet fundamental to the message, as they are in traditional broadcast news media. They are digital sidebars—available to users who have an interest in them and the patience and level of access needed to see and hear them without unacceptable delays. That situation may change, but I believe—and I track this issue closely for my students' sake—that it will not change substantially for at least several years and perhaps not for several more.

Others will disagree with me on this point. For example, several universities are shifting to a generic, even a multimedia, approach to journalism education to prepare students for a multimedia future.[1] Many others are considering carefully whether they should change. Practice with multimedia forms is a good idea for journalism students in all media areas, but I believe the jury is still out on whether the schools that have moved the fastest are too far ahead of the curve. The Web is here to stay, but whether it will supplant traditional news media or whether television will become the locus of convergence are unknown at this time, despite the overconfident predictions of futurists. The dot-com crash of the last two years has further muddied the picture. Research that colleagues at two other universities and I have conducted on the practice of editing and on the teaching of editing at accredited schools suggests that my view is consistent with the beliefs of most faculty members who teach editing.[2] Other work I have done strongly suggests that these views are similar to those held by editors in the newspaper industry on the whole.[3] There is great demand in the newspaper industry for students who have print-based skills, and there is yet little demand in print newsrooms for copy editors with skills in multimedia editing and presentation. There are journalistic Web sites, such as CNN and MSNBC, that rely on multimedia information as well as text and photos. But for now, print-editing skills are more fundamental to Web editing, as the background of so many Web editors strongly suggests.

A PHILOSOPHY OF COPY EDITING

A typical news organization has many positions with the word "editor" in the title. There are, for example, city editors and features editors, design editors and photo editors, managing editors and copy editors. This book is written for copy editing students and copy editors, but the nature of the work copy editors do is not well understood, and many editors who are not called "copy editors" spend a significant portion of their time copy editing.

The practical definition of copy editing—in effect, what copy editors do all day—varies by type and size of publication, and to some degree by organizational culture. At a small newspaper, say a community daily of 15,000 circulation, copy editors wear many hats. During a typical workday, they edit stories, write headlines and design pages. Some also act as department or desk editors, choosing wire stories, updating stories with new information, assigning stories to reporters or helping reporters shape their stories. A smaller number are responsible for photo editing, graphics and digital image adjustment. Some prepare stories for the paper's Web site. Copy editors at papers of this size typically work with a variety of computer applications, such as a front-end text-processing system and a pagination program such as QuarkXPress. Some use Photoshop and perhaps even a graphics program such as Freehand or Illustrator. Some do HTML coding.

At the other end of the spectrum, the largest metropolitan dailies, copy editors typically are responsible for two tasks: editing copy and writing headlines. They work on a front-end editing system and typically do not use any computer applications other than online archives and the Web. At those papers, other editorial tasks are done by specialists such as section editors, page designers, photo editors, photo technicians, Web producers, and so on. In general, the larger the paper, the greater the specialization, but some small and midsize papers structure the job the way large ones do and a few relatively large papers define copy editing more as their smaller counterparts do.

Some publications, because of tradition or management philosophy, limit the responsibility of copy editors in the realm of word editing. At those papers, copy editors are expected to check accuracy; ensure that grammar, spelling, usage and punctuation are correct; keep an eye out for potentially libelous statements; and write headlines. Questions about a story's focus, logic, organization or fairness are handled by other editors. At other papers, including most of the best-edited publications, copy editors are encouraged to pay attention to all of those matters—the broader issues as well as the more detail-oriented ones. This approach not only benefits the news organization, it benefits the copy editor as well, enabling him or her to develop and employ a range of skills that he or she can use across a wide variety of news positions.

Copy editors best serve the publication and its readership by looking at the text-editing portion of their craft holistically—by paying attention to the broader issues of fairness and focus as well as to the more narrow ones of grammar and punctuation. It is true that other editors are primarily responsible for the broader issues; it is also a given that such problems often will be missed. Copy editors can provide a safety net for the newspaper if they are allowed to do so, and this book assumes that a copy editor's responsibilities range from the very narrow to the very broad in the area of word editing. Beyond word editing and headline writing, a copy editor's duties depend on the degree of specialization a newspaper can afford.

The overall structure of this text is based on a related idea: that copy editors work on a number of levels. Editing well means being able to focus on different levels at the same time—in effect, to see not only the forest and the trees but also the branches, twigs and leaves, and sometimes even the veins in the leaves. The best editors do not lose sight of one level while they are immersed in another. At the narrowest focus, editors make sure the commas are in the right places. At the broadest level, they may play many roles, sometimes on the same story. They might be supporter or critic, good cop or bad. They must be detectives, and occasionally they might be confessors. They need to develop the skills to help writers say what they want to say, and as Ron Patel, a former Sunday editor from The Philadelphia Inquirer, used to say, they need to be able to "hear the music" of the story.

Some issues cut across all aspects of copy editing. For example:

Editing is about rules. Copy editors must ensure that writers follow rules of grammar, punctuation, usage and style. They must pay attention to the headline and caption rules that most papers follow, and they must see that rules specific to a given publication, or even a section of a publication, are followed. Copy editors have no greater love of rules than others in the newsroom. But because copy editors are the last line of defense, the "palace guard," they often are tarred as comma-chasers or petty bureaucrats slavishly dedicated to the letter of the law. Some copy editors, unfortunately, behave in that stereotypical way. Good copy editors are wordsmiths, not word police. Editing is about following rules, but it also entails occasionally breaking them and questioning them when they don't seem to help or they fall out of date. Good copy editors maintain a respectful but critical stance toward rules.

Editing is about making choices. It is about deciding what's OK and what isn't, what's worth pursuing and what isn't, what needs to be checked, what should be checked if there's time and what doesn't need to be checked at all.

Editing is about critical thinking. It's about analyzing and questioning. Copy editors are not automatons; their most valuable skills are their ability to think independently and to examine critically. Newspapers serve readers well when they encourage copy editors to be "readers' representatives."[4] When copy editors look at stories as a thoughtful, critical reader does, they have the best chance of finding the problems readers might find, asking the questions readers might ask, and raising the same sorts of concerns readers might raise. Maintaining that stance is sometimes difficult; copy editors, after all, work alongside reporters and editors who have already approved the story. Office politics and personalities can get in the way of independent criticism, but there is no better way of ensuring quality than focused, constructive criticism.

Editing is about working together to provide the best-possible journalism. It's about respecting others and insisting on respect from others. It's about learning when to hold one's ground and when to back off. It's about balancing the sometimes-conflicting goals of different groups of professionals—for example, the word versus the visual experts.

Editing is about balancing perfection and pragmatism. Top editors might say they want perfectionists on the copy desk, but what they really need are committed, skilled pragmatists. Copy editing is about blending skill and common sense.

Editing is about ethics. It's about ensuring that stories are fair, that all sides are heard, that questionable assertions are questioned and that the accused have the opportunity to respond. In doing so, copy editors are much like reporters. Ethical issues underlie headline writing as well. The headline is often the only part of a story that a reader sees, and copy editors should write headlines that are fair and accurate, that preserve important qualification and attribution and that do not hype the story. Editing is about a belief that fairness and balance serve everyone's interests best.

In short, editing is about both skills and strategies.

A FINAL WORD

This book focuses on strategies to deal with each level of editing and to balance the often conflicting demands of different levels. Chapters 2–6 deal with editing copy, starting from the more detail-oriented issues and working up to broader ones, cumulatively, as I do in my editing classes, but realizing that all the levels are important and that one must not ignore any of them. Chapter 7 is a detailed discussion of people skills and how to solve problems. Chapters 8–12, which deal with writing headlines and other display type, also move from the simple to the complex, from straightforward news headlines to multi-element packages that require integrative and visual thinking. The book discusses page design in Chapter 13, and it talks about the editing of infographics, but not their creation, which is a highly specialized skill. This lack of discussion about the more visual aspects of the craft should not be considered a comment on their importance. The ability to think visually is a fundamental skill for editors at all levels, and many college-level editing classes include such issues. In my opinion, students should use a good design text, such as Tim Harrower's "Newspaper Designer's Handbook."[5]

Chapter 14 looks at change in the newspaper industry and what it means for copy editors. Chapter 15 explains how copy editors can continue to learn and grow in their field. Chapters end with a section on tips and strategies that can help.

This text does not include a discussion of wire editing, that is, selecting stories from wire services, or working as a department editor, such as a city or features editor. With rare exception, students do not become wire editors or department editors at the beginning of their careers. Newspapers do, however, offer excellent opportunities for students to enter the field as copy editors, and even novice copy editors are expected to know how to edit copy well and write good headlines. The training and techniques involved in wire editing and department editing differ enough from place to place that training in these areas is best left to individual newspapers. Working as a journalist means lifelong learning.

I spend more time on certain areas than other texts do (e.g., logic, precision and people skills), and I spend less on some topics than others do (e.g., spelling and style). Other references that should be part of a student's or a journalist's library—a good dictionary, a stylebook, a grammar reference and an atlas or gazetteer—deal with those subjects in more depth than any textbook can.

Throughout the text, I make some claims or offer opinions that other editing instructors and editors might disagree with. When I do so, I mention it and attempt to explain my reasons. Some of my ideas might be considered more "liberal" than traditional practice, such as discarding the rule on headline "padding." Others may appear too conservative to some, such as my belief that excessive electronic manipulation of headline type can generate bad headlines and bad habits in headline writers. Disagreement can be healthy, and I would urge instructors to use these issues as points of discussion in class.

2

Mechanics
The Nuts and Bolts

WASHINGTON—Stock market losses amounting to about 30 per cent of it's $1 billion endowment have forced the Freedom Forum to close four international offices.

The offices are in London, Buenos Aries, Hong Kong and Johannisburg. The foundation, which encourages world press freedom, also will close its First Amendment Center in New York.

Charles Overby, the chairman and chief executive officer, said the organzation's emphasis during the next several years would be on moving from its Arlington, Virginia Headquarters, to a site on Pennsylvania Ave. near the Capital.

The foundation did not disclose how many of their 285 workers would be effected, but it did say that all full-time employes would be offered buyouts.

How many style, spelling and punctuation mistakes do you see in the preceding story? I count 13 (see end of chapter), but even if you counted fewer, you probably noticed most of them. And, if you are like most readers, the mistakes probably caused you to pause for a moment.

The "simple" mistakes—typos, spelling errors, grammar errors, usage errors, style errors—make a publication look unprofessional, but that's not the whole story. The bigger problem is that they are distracting. They make the reader pause for an instant if only to think "That's not right" or "That doesn't look right." Sentences and paragraphs should flow freely, carrying the message, the news, the story without obstruction. The simple, careless mistakes are little barriers to fluidity, and like rocks in a stream they divert the flow. In a stream, rocks slow down the flow and provide habitat for aquatic life. In reading, they merely block the way, delaying comprehension. Moreover, such mistakes detract from a publication's credibility, according to a comprehensive study by the American Society of Newspaper Editors.[1]

I call this area of concern the level of "mechanics"—the nuts and bolts of wordsmithing. It's the bedrock of copy editing. The rest builds atop it, and for this reason it is very important to pay close attention to this level. There are other, more important, areas of copy editing, such as ensuring accuracy and fairness and filling holes in stories. But skill in the mechanics of editing is a necessary condition for good copy editing.

GRAMMAR AND USAGE

If you want to become an expert grammarian, that's fine. It might come in handy someday. But many excellent copy editors cannot cite chapter and verse about grammar without consulting a textbook or reference book. Moreover, most of the time, they have no need to do so. They might not be able to distinguish a gerund from a participle more than 50 percent of the time. But they know grammar on a pragmatic level—they know what's correct and what isn't, what works and what doesn't. If you ask many of them how they can spot a mistake, they'll say, "It doesn't sound right." Grammar is an academic pursuit for a few scholars, the grammarians, and they often disagree and sometimes even change their minds on what is correct and what isn't. For journalists, grammar is a practical concern, a means to an end. The end, of course, is clarity in expression. The good news is that one does not need to become a grammarian to become an expert at spotting grammar problems. The number of common mistakes is manageable.

Grammar is logical. It is a system of rules that makes a language predictable and understandable. Subject and verb must agree in number; disagreement, because it is illogical, is distracting, if not downright annoying. Proper word usage also helps comprehension. The use of *who* or *whom* follows a logic that is not difficult to grasp in most examples. Word order is important for comprehension, and a dangling modifier simply does not make sense. Following are some areas that copy editors should pay particular attention to, because, unfortunately, writers often don't.

AGREEMENT

Disagreement is one of the most common errors both in student work and in professional journalism. Disagreement in number occurs between a pronoun and its antecedent or between a subject and its verb. A typical problem is treating a collective noun as a plural. In American English, most collectives are singular. Under that guideline, the following sentences are incorrect:

> A new *coalition* of small-business owners said *they* supported an initiative that would raise the minimum wage to $7 an hour.

> *Napster* never copies a single music file; *they* merely provide links between users.

> *Washington State* has never beaten Stanford, and the closest *they* came was a 5-point loss in 1998.

In the first example, the noun *coalition* should take the singular pronoun *it* rather than the plural pronoun *they*. In the second example, *Napster*, the music-file-sharing Web site, is singular in the first clause; the singular verb *copies* is correct. But the pronoun that refers to *Napster* shifts to the plural *they* in the second clause, which is illogical. If it is singular in the first reference, it must be singular in the second. The same holds for the third example. *Washington State* takes a singular verb in the first clause, but it becomes a *they* in the second. In British English, the opposite is true. Nouns such as *team*, which take singular verbs in the United States, take plural verb forms in British publications.

Agreement problems also tend to appear when sentences have compound subjects or multiple verbs or when subject and verb are separated by a phrase or clause.

> As the election approaches, the usual *complaints, nonsense and posturing* that *surrounds* the candidates and their campaigns have returned.

Complaints, nonsense and posturing should have a plural verb; they are separable issues, and thus demand a plural subject. Notice that the final verb in the sentence, *have*, is correct. Moreover, it sounds right. If *have* is correct, *surrounds* cannot be right, because it is singular, and both verbs must agree because they have the same subject.

Agreement can be a problem between two sentences, as this passage shows:

> If *a voter* fails to return a ballot during two consecutive general elections, *his or her* name is dropped as a registered voter. *They* will not receive any more ballots until *they* reregister.

Recasting the sentences makes the pronouns consistent and eliminates several other wording problems:

> If *citizens* fail to return ballots during two consecutive general elections, *their* names are dropped from the list of registered voters. *They* do not receive ballots until they reregister.

PARALLEL CONSTRUCTION

Elements of a sentence that act as a series must be consistent. Consider the following example:

> Jeremy is the picture of aggressiveness in three sports. He likes battling for rebounds against taller players, crunching tailbacks as soon as they hit the line of scrimmage and to smash tennis volleys right at his opponents.

The series is not parallel. *Battling* and *crunching* are consistent parts of speech, but the third, *to smash*, is not. It should be *smashing*. Lack of parallelism is a readability problem; it is jarring.

WHO/WHOM

Some writers and even some usage experts feel that *whom*'s days are (or should be) numbered.[2] I advise learning the rule about *who* and *whom* because the distinction is followed by most publications and probably will continue to be followed for a long time. The next examples reflect common problems with *who* and *whom*:

> A 15-year-old boy, whom authorities said had escaped from a halfway house in Marion County, was taken to the county juvenile detention center.

> A student who she befriended in college had a profound effect on her life.

The difference is one of case—whether the word in question is in the subjective case (acting as a subject) or the objective case (acting as an object). Subjective requires *who*, objective requires *whom*. The best tip is the same advice English teachers have been giving their students for decades: mentally recast the sentence so that you can replace the *who* or *whom* with a pronoun, *he* or *she, him* or *her, they* or *them*. Then it's easier to determine which is correct.

In the first example above, recasting yields "authorities said *he* had escaped. . . . " *Who* is correct. In the second example, recasting yields "she befriended *her*." *Whom* is correct. All *who/whom* mistakes can be spotted and corrected this way.

THAT/WHICH

Grammatically speaking, in American English, the word *that* is used in essential clauses or phrases. The phrase that follows *that* should be essential, or crucial, to the meaning of the sentence. The word *which* is used in nonessential clauses or phrases. The common mistake is using the nonessential *which* in place of the essential *that*:

> The car *which* is parked illegally belongs to the professor; the other one belongs to the student.

The clause *which is parked illegally* is crucial to the meaning of the sentence—if you eliminate that clause, the sentence does not make the sense the writer intended. The sentence should read:

The car *that* is parked illegally belongs to the professor; the other one belongs to the student.

Some writers change the second *that* in a sentence to a *which* because they want to avoid using the same word twice. For example,

The car *that* is parked illegally belongs to the professor; the one *which* is parked behind it belongs to the student.

That usage doesn't make sense. Two *that*'s don't equal a *that* and a *which*. The sentence should read:

The car *that* is parked illegally belongs to the professor; the one *that* is parked behind it belongs to the student.

A less-common mistake is using *that* instead of *which*:

It's a bird. It's a plane. No, it's a pterodactyl, *that* is neither a bird nor a plane.

The sentence makes the sense the writer intended if you end it after the word *pterodactyl*. The rest of the sentence is fine to add, but it's not essential. If you want to include the additional information, you should write:

"No, it's a pterodactyl, *which* is neither a bird nor a plane."

The pronoun *that* is sometimes incorrectly used to refer to people. For example,

Serena and Venus Williams are the first sisters *that* competed against each other in the tournament final.

That should be *who*.

LESS/FEWER

Less wood has also meant *fewer* sawmills and wood plants, which has resulted in *less* jobs.

If you can count the items, *fewer* is correct; if the quantity does not lend itself to enumeration, such as quantities of sand, sugar and wood, *less* is correct. In the previous sentence, *less wood* and *fewer sawmills* are correct. *Less jobs*, however, is incorrect. One can easily count jobs; *fewer* is the right word. My guess is that the writer did not want to say *fewer* twice in close proximity. The editor's job is to point out that if *fewer* is the right word for *sawmills*, it has to also be the right word for *jobs*. The editor might also point out that the sentence could be rewritten more clearly:

> *Less* wood has also meant *fewer* sawmills and wood plants; one result is *fewer* jobs.

EFFECT/AFFECT

Most of the time *effect* is a noun. Nearly all of the time *affect* is a verb. *Effect* occasionally is used as a verb, as in *to effect change*, but that usage is uncommon. About the only place one ever finds *affect* used as a noun is in psychology textbooks, where *affect* (pronounced AFF-ect) is a term that means feeling or emotion. The following examples reflect the common problems.

> "I'm not here just to coach basketball," the coach said. "I want to have an *affect* on basketball."
>
> Officials worry that raising the price of an education could *effect* lower income residents who need a community college the most.

In the first sentence *affect* should be *effect*, and in the second vice versa. Some writers never learn the distinction, so copy editors need to watch for these errors, which make a publication look unprofessional. Which of the following sentences incorrectly use *affect* or *effect*?

> 1. The teaching hospital won a grant to help continue its study of Parkinson's disease, which effects about 1 percent of Americans over age 65.
>
> 2. Jane said a Vietnam veteran who she met in Washington had a profound affect on her life.
>
> 3. The affects of flooding in the East will be felt by consumers at Thanksgiving.

4. Its unclear how the labor shortage will affect the high-tech industry in the "Silicon Forest" area of the Northwest, the industry group spokesman said.

The first three use the wrong word. The last uses *affect* correctly, but *its* is incorrect. The word should be *it's*.

MODIFIERS

The dangling modifier is endemic in American journalism. One can find examples in publications ranging from the smallest weekly to the largest daily, from e-zines to mass-circulation magazines. Why? Perhaps because writers get bored with subject–verb–object sentence structure and try to vary the order. What too often happens then is a sentence that is out of step with itself and sometimes trips up readers.

The following sentence appeared in a garden-section story about ornamental kale, a leafy vegetable that was developed for looks rather than taste:

"Born in the garden, horticulturists bred these vegetables for ornamentation."

The sentence is incorrect unless the horticulturists were Cabbage Patch Kids. Kale varieties, not horticulturists, were "born in the garden." With dangling modifiers, the meaning is seldom at issue, but common sense and sentence structure are. After perhaps pausing for a chuckle, one can figure out what the writer meant to say. Humor is fine in writing meant to be humorous; in anything else, it is a distraction. Here's an example about a band called Radiohead and another about actor Robert Downey Jr.'s troubles with the law:

Led by the eerily beautiful voice of Thom Yorke and vaguely reminiscent of Pink Floyd, Rolling Stone magazine described Radiohead's "Kid A" as a "space-rock opera."

Hours after his release, "Ally McBeal" producer David E. Kelley issued a brief statement saying Downey had been fired.

Rolling Stone might have a "voice," but not an eerily beautiful one. The writer of that sentence needs to start over. The second example is much worse. It says, literally, that Kelley was released, when Downey's release was the point. The fix is simple:

> Hours after Downey's release, "Ally McBeal" producer David E. Kelley issued a brief statement saying the actor had been fired.

Here are two examples that aren't as funny, but they are distracting:

> Denser than a winter fog, even taillights aren't visible in high-desert dust storms.

> As Los Angeles mayor, Tom Bradley's appointments were controversial.

Taillights are not denser than a winter fog; the dust storms are. Bradley was the mayor, not his appointments. The solution is easy. Cover up the part of the sentence that follows the modifying phrase. If the next word is not the noun to which the phrase refers, recast the sentence. And save the reporter some embarrassment.

> In high-desert dust storms, which are denser than a winter fog, even taillights aren't visible.

> As Los Angeles mayor, Tom Bradley made some controversial appointments.

Another common problem is the misplaced modifier:

> As the colder weather moves in, drivers need to watch for deer along roads and highways that are moving to lower elevations, wildlife officials say.

Roads and highways do not move to lower elevations, except in landslides. But deer often do. The solution in that case is recasting, or, better yet, eliminating "along roads and highways." It's unnecessary because we assume that drivers are using roads and highways. Here's another example:

> Since 1984, Mr. Jones has been pastor of Sublimity Baptist Church, a stately white temple on a hill whose soaring steeple has been a beacon for folks living near this town since 1843.

Does the hill have a soaring steeple or does the temple? Obviously it's the latter, but the placement of the modifier creates a momentary pause because it invites ambiguity. Recasting the sentence solves the problem. Making one sentence into two is another approach.

A related problem is the *non sequitur*, a phrase or clause that doesn't follow logically. Newspapers run many obituaries, and obituary writers sometimes produce non sequiturs when they get tired of simple biographical statements, such as "He served in the Marines and was a Vietnam War veteran" or "He was a Mason and a Shriner." For example:

> Born in Skokie, Ill., Mr. Smith worked for many years as an audio technician with National Public Radio.
>
> Born in Pennsylvania, Russial has seen far too many non sequiturs in his editing career.

Being a Pennsylvania native has as little to do with spotting non sequiturs as being an Illinois native has to do with audio skills. The beginning and the end of a sentence should have something to do with each other.

SPELLING

Spelling in English is a challenge, as syndicated newspaper columnist and wordsmith James Kilpatrick points out periodically. Unlike some other languages, English has many words that sound the same but are spelled differently. The same letter or letter combinations may be used to create different sounds, often depending on other combinations of letters in the word, but sometimes almost arbitrarily. The oddities of the English language, Kilpatrick says, stem from its polyglot roots: English has borrowed liberally from many other languages. The result is a richness of words and meanings, but the wealth comes at a price. As many international students, not to mention native speakers, know, spelling in English is as much an art as a science. Elementary and middle schools spend a great deal of time encouraging (if not forcing) students to memorize spelling words. Spending the time on reading might be wiser.

Some people are naturally good spellers and others are not. Those who aren't shouldn't despair. Even mediocre spellers can become good copy editors if they learn to recognize words they don't know how to spell.

Step 2 is to look those words up. Copy editors who have a knack for spelling are a step ahead; they can edit more quickly. But as a practical matter, it is probably not worth the time poor spellers would have to invest to become good spellers. It is a far better use of one's time to become an efficient user of the dictionary. Spelling is the easiest element of writing mechanics to check. And it might offer one of the biggest payoffs in credibility. One of the six major findings in the American Society of Newspaper Editors' credibility study was that people see too many factual, spelling and grammar errors in the newspaper.[3]

Spell-checkers will flag most spelling problems, but they can be abused. Spell-checkers cannot catch the wrong word spelled correctly. Here's a fragment of one of many cautionary verses professors show journalism students:

> I have a spell-checker
>
> That came with my PC
>
> It plainly marks for my revue
>
> Mistakes eye cannot sea . . .

It's easy to dismiss this point as silly. A spell-checker might not catch those incorrect words, but who would make such mistakes? Unfortunately, many writers do, and it's the reason professors show the silly verses. The wrong word appears often in student writing as well as in professional writing, possibly because of an overreliance on technology. The following sentence has three "spelling" mistakes, two of which will slip through a spell-checker:

> Farber brought the *compliant* in the county circuit court, using a county *ordnance* prohibiting dogs "from acting in a *viscious* and dangerous manner."

The problem with spelling is not so much the words that always have been difficult to spell, such as *vicious, accommodate, concomitant, commitment, parishioners, minuscule* and *separate.* Spell-checkers will pick them up. It's the misuse of *pouring* for *poring, lead* for *led, effect* for *affect, sight* for *site* and the like.

When spell-checking software becomes sophisticated enough to flag the wrong word in context, the tools will be much more useful. But don't hold your breath—that day is a long way from tomorrow. The danger of spell-checkers is that some people come to rely on them instead of careful proofreading. A second danger emerges when writers or editors blithely use search/replace functions or give the spell-checker carte blanche to fix the "misspelled" words it flags. Software is not the equal of human intellect yet, and it probably never will be. Good copy editors use computers to augment their skills but never use them as a replacement.

The misspelling of proper names is also a serious problem, not just in newspapers, whose time is sharply constricted by daily deadlines, but also in magazines, which have more time, and even in books, where it used to be rare to find any mistake. Cutbacks in publishing budgets have led to much less quality control at all levels of publishing processes. The result is that copy editors have to be extra-vigilant.

> The software company, which is based in Berkley, Calif., has sales offices in Singapore, Luxemburg, Ottawa and Macao.

How many of those cities are misspelled? Two: Berkeley and Luxembourg. If you are unsure, you can check them quickly in a dictionary, gazetteer or atlas. Sometimes the error is more subtle:

> Great Valley Medical Center has begun a new program to play "Brahm's Lullaby" at the birth of every new child.

If you are familiar with classical music, you'll know that the composer's name was *Brahms*, not *Brahm*, and that the reference should be Brahms' Lullaby. If you aren't sure, look it up. The more you read and the more widely you read, the less time you'll spend chasing down such references. Incidentally, you should strike the word *new* from the sentence in both places. If the hospital has begun a program, that means it is a "new" program. If a child is born, it's certainly a new one.

TYPOS

Typographic errors are not the same as misspellings. But, from a reader's perspective, they might as well be. An editor (or a reporter) can catch the majority of typographic errors by doing a spell-check, but many typos, including some of the worst ones, will not be caught that way. Here's an example that was posted to a journalism discussion list in 1997 by an editor from a Washington state newspaper:

> "This reminded me of a typo that got into our paper almost a year ago. I think it was a weather story and instead of '*snow*' the writer (just once) missed the right key and it became '*snot*.' It was obvious what was meant, but we had all sorts of people calling us about it. One guy called us for three days straight asking if there was any more '*snot*' in the forecast and whether or not he needed to take an umbrella with him."

The editor related this anecdote to point out that readers are sometimes too critical. They might not be so critical, he said, if they realized how many tens of thousands of words newspapers process each day in conditions that often work against careful checking. He is right, but news organizations will never be able to persuade readers to ignore such mistakes. Readers believe newspapers should not make them. The only solution is to spell-check *and* to proofread carefully.

STYLE

Style, in the journalistic sense, can be tedious and arbitrary, but it is absolutely necessary. Style has to do with consistency of usage, spelling and other matters throughout a publication, independent of writers. Most smaller newspapers (i.e., most newspapers) treat the Associated Press Stylebook as a bible and create their own style supplements for local names and places that are not covered in the AP manual. Large metropolitan dailies often have their own full-service stylebooks and use the AP Stylebook as a supplement.

Different styles are used in different areas of journalism. Most newspapers use AP style, which tends to be concise, sometimes even telegraphic. Space historically was at a premium in telegraph reports and in newspapers, and AP style reflects those roots. Abbreviations and numbers are used liberally in AP style. Other journalistic media, such as magazines, use more broad-based styles such as those of the University of Chicago and the Modern Language Association (MLA). A comparison of the entries on numbers shows how styles differ. In AP style, whole numbers below 10 are spelled out; 10 and above take figures. In Chicago style, whole numbers from one through ninety-nine are spelled out. And the entry in the 1999 version of the MLA stylebook begins, "If you are writing about literature or another subject that involves infrequent use of numbers, you may spell out numbers written in one or two words and represent other numbers by numerals." So *two hundred* would be correct.[4] All three styles have many exceptions to the general rule, and the exceptions are not consistent among styles.

Style, in other words, can be arbitrary. In AP style, for example *back yard* is correct for the noun and *backyard* is correct as an adjective. One could easily argue that *back-yard* is a more appropriate adjective. In terms of comprehension and readability, it really doesn't matter whether you write *11 players* or *eleven players*. Both are clear in context. But *11* is correct in AP style, *eleven* in magazine style. Newspapers write *Descartes'* philosophy, and magazines write *Descartes's*. A newspaper will say "Manassas, Va., was the site of a famous Civil War battle," whereas magazines and books will say "Manassas, Virginia, was the site . . . "—spelling out the state name rather than using the abbreviation. AP retains a traditional set of state abbreviations, using upper- and lowercase—for example, Calif., Ore. and Okla. Some other styles have shifted to the two-letter U.S. Postal Service abbreviations (CA, OR and OK). AP allows these only with full addresses, including ZIP codes.

Sometimes AP style appears to make little sense. Why, one might ask, is the title *City Editor* uppercase when used before a name but the title professor isn't? Go figure.

What does matter is consistency. If one story says *11* and the next says *eleven* in a similar context, a publication looks unprofessional. If one says *Fort Bragg* and another says *Ft. Bragg* (*Fort* is correct in AP style), the publication looks unedited. Moreover what looks unprofessional often is distracting, getting in the way of the message. If you disagree, read a few amateurish newsletters—their style discrepancies are annoying.

The use of numerals is one of the most confusing aspects of AP style. It may seem as though there are more exceptions to the rule than cases in which the rule is followed. For example, ages take figures (a *6-year-old boy*), many sports terms take figures (a *par-5 hole*, a *5–4 record*, a *score of 7–5*), as do references that invite measurement or calculation (*the new model gets 4 more miles per gallon, but he drove four miles*). The exceptions become second nature after a while. Less experienced editors will need to look them up until they become familiar with them.

Stylebooks offer more than style—the AP Stylebook, for example, includes a wealth of easily accessible facts and the most common grammar and usage issues, though its indexing can be confusing. Besides explaining how to punctuate a series of items and to list a legislator's party affiliation, the stylebook explains what a *convertible bond* is and tells you that *colt* refers to "a male horse 4 years old and under." You won't, however, find that explanation under *colt*, unless you realize that it is in the horse racing section in Sports Guidelines. Or unless you use the new online version of the style guide, which is searchable. A search for *colt* turns up that explanation as well as references to Colt, the gun manufacturer.

Copy editors often spend too much time searching for facts or spellings of proper names in other references when the stylebook itself includes many of those references. Is it *Sun Belt* or *Sunbelt?* Is the "o" in *Ouija* uppercase, and is the word spelled correctly? Is it the *Mason–Dixon* or *Mason Dixon* line, or is it *Line?* Does CDC stand for *Center* or *Centers* for Disease Control, and is it acceptable to use the abbreviation on first reference? All are in the AP Stylebook. The stylebook tells you that *Sierra Nevada Mountains* is incorrect because *sierra* means mountains and that *Shariah* is the strict Islamic law.

Style, usage and other elements of mechanics can be a source of friction between copy editors and reporters. The reporter accuses the copy editor of rigidity or of trampling on the reporter's voice for pointing out that long titles should follow the person's name rather than precede it, that the word *include* is properly used only when the items that follow are part of the total or that *livid* is not the right word to describe a red face. Such animosity is unnecessary and unfortunate. Copy editors don't invent style, and they seldom set style policy unilaterally. Disputes about style often mask more fundamental issues about what level of editing is appropriate, a situation that varies from publication to publication. Disagreements should be discussed openly, not waged by proxy battles over style points or "voice." Voice is individual; style is institutional. Voice has to do with the way a person writes: the choice of words, patterns in sentence construction and other specific, even idiosyncratic, choices that place a writer's mark on a story.

Style is organic. It changes to reflect changes in society, technology, culture and other aspects of modern life that journalists cover. The AP Stylebook had no entry for *Internet* in 1986, even though the Internet had been used by scientists and researchers for years. In 2002, the stylebook included an eight-page Internet Guide, including entries for technical terms that did not exist a decade ago, such as MP3 and DSL.

Meanings and connotations change. The word *Negro*, once commonly used in racial identification, now should be used only in titles of organizations and quoted material, according to the AP manual. The term *black* is preferred. The "courtesy title" entry has changed substantially over the years as social usage and etiquette have changed.

Style is a living thing, but sometimes it seems as though it is barely breathing. In 2002, AP finally changed its entry on *teen-age* to *teenage*. The original rationale for spelling the word *teen-age* was to avoid confusion with *teenage*, a plant so rare that it not defined in some dictionaries but apparently has long been known to the AP style committee. Another change allows the use of *host* as a verb; many newspapers were ignoring the prohibition anyway. Despite the glacial pace of some modifications, on balance it is probably wise to avoid changing style too rapidly. Fad words and terms enter and exit the language like shootings stars, and it pays to wait and see whether they make a mark before fixing them in style.

A benefit of the widespread use of AP style is that news reporters and editors typically do not need to learn a different style when they change jobs. If they move to a very large newspaper, they probably will have to learn to refer first to the newspaper's in-house stylebook, then to AP's. Most of the rules will be the same.

Style consistency is important, but there's a caveat, one that is reflected in the two overriding rules laid out at the beginning of The Philadelphia Inquirer's style manual:

1. Use common sense.
2. Trust your ear.

The two rules aren't an excuse to do what you will, but they sometimes offer a useful corrective. Style rules should not be broken—unless you have a good reason. Good reasons are typically in short supply.

PUNCTUATION

Punctuation is the source of far too many sloppy errors in publications. Middle-school language arts teachers who believe in teaching the basics delight in pointing out these mistakes, much to the chagrin of editors and reporters. Again, the issue is credibility. Professionally edited publications should not be riddled with comma errors. A well-educated readership will notice punctuation mistakes and will think less of the publication.

Like style, punctuation is institutional, and like grammar, it is logical.

There are good reasons to use commas in certain situations and semicolons in others. For the most part, punctuation follows the same logic across the range of print publications, though there are some arbitrary differences in different systems of style. The AP Stylebook, for example, differs from Chicago and MLA style on the serial comma.

> The cell-phone ban in Springfield is similar to local ordinances passed in communities in New Jersey, Ohio and Pennsylvania.

The previous sentence would be correct in newspapers; in most magazines and books, a comma would follow *Ohio*. AP style does use the serial comma to avoid ambiguity if an integral element of the series required a conjunction:

> I had orange juice, toast, and ham and eggs for breakfast.

Also, AP style calls for the serial comma before the last conjunction in a series of complex phrases:

> The main issues before the agency are whether breaching the dams will increase the number of young salmon that reach the ocean, whether the electrical power generated by the facilities is replaceable, and whether the economic impact on the farming and shipping industries is manageable.

Paragraphing is very different in newspapers than it is in magazines or books, leading to some unusual punctuation rules. For example, quotations that run more than a sentences or two are often broken into separate paragraphs in newspapers for visual reasons—to avoid masses of unbroken type. Here is the appropriate passage from the AP Stylebook under "Running Quotations":

> "If a full paragraph of quoted material is followed by a paragraph that continues the quotation, do not put close-quote marks at the end of the first paragraph. Do, however, put open-quote marks at the start of the second paragraph. Continue in this fashion for any succeeding paragraphs, using close-quote marks only at the end of the quoted material."

If a quote ends a paragraph, but continues to the next, another rule applies.

COMMAS

Commas are important for comprehension, and incorrect use of them can lead to momentary confusion, sometimes even a change of meaning.

> After the pickup truck rolled over several pedestrians stopped to see whether they could help the driver.

Most readers will stumble on that sentence, and many will go back and re-read it. With a comma after *over*, they can see the meaning at a glance and move on. In the following sentence, a comma is unnecessary:

> Pacemakers are commonly used to stimulate a slowed heartbeat in humans, and sometimes contain a defibrillator device to correct irregular heartbeats.

Independent clauses joined by a coordinating conjunction, such as *and* or *but*, take a comma. Such clauses, which could stand on their own as sentences, take a semicolon if there is no conjunction between clauses:

> The holiday falls on a Tuesday, and many workers will take Monday off.

> The holiday falls on a Tuesday; many workers will take Monday off.

Here are two examples of another often-abused comma:

> The school's copies of "One Flew Over the Cuckoo's Nest" have pictures of the movie on the cover, said Eileen Babbs, who is the wife of close Kesey friend, Ken Babbs.

> Well-known novelist, Stephen King, has suspended work on "The Plant," an experimental online novel.

Unless the writer Ken Kesey had only one close friend, which is very un-likely, the comma before Ken Babbs is incorrect. Even then, the sentence would be clunky. It would be correct to write "close Kesey friend Ken Babbs" or "a close Kesey friend, Ken Babbs." Or, "a close friend of Kesey's, Ken Babbs." Stephen King is not the only well-known novelist. Therefore, the commas are incorrect. Correct versions include "Well-known novelist

Stephen King has suspended . . . " or "A well-known novelist, Stephen King, has suspended. . . . " One might even drop the *well-known* because if he is well-known, people don't need to be reminded.

Newspaper reporters make this comma mistake often and in a variety of ways, perhaps because they don't want to "slow down" the flow. The real issue, though, is not flow; it's meaning. The proper use (or proper absence of the comma) signals the correct meaning.

> Ann's husband Jim is an insurance underwriter.

This sentence needs commas around Jim because Ann has only one husband.

> Ann's former husband Jim had quit his job in insurance to become a fly-fishing instructor.

The sentence is correct if Ann has more than one former husband. It needs commas if Jim is the only one. A more rare comma mistake, but a more serious one, is the case in which meaning is changed. Consider the following sentences:

> The Democrats say the Green Party candidates will lose the county elections.

> The Democrats, say the Green Party candidates, will lose the county elections.

Such problems are rare because context usually flags what's incorrect, but they can happen. Here is a subtle example of a change in meaning that a comma causes in a story about the challenges of being a female ranch manager:

> She can now walk into most local parts stores and be treated with respect, but she becomes irritated with agricultural salespeople, who call at 5 a.m. and hang up after learning she is a ranch manager.

The commas before *who* literally means that all agricultural salespeople are rude and sexist. That's not what the writer intended to say. The manager is irritated at the minority of salespeople who do act that way.

SEMICOLONS

The misuse of commas where semicolons are appropriate seems to have become more widespread in journalism. Print journalism probably offers more opportunity to abuse this rule than other types of writing because of the extensive use of quotations and relatively short clauses. For example:

> "That was the worst decision of my life," he said, "all that I can think about is all of the opportunities I missed."

> "Every year we vote on the same issues, they just look and sound different," he said.

> "I see a light at the end of the tunnel, it's probably a mirror," she said.

The problem is known as a "comma splice," because it splices, or joins, two clauses that it really should not be connecting. In all three cases, a semicolon is considered correct. Newspapers tend to follow the rule that independent clauses require a semicolon, unless they are very short.

POSSESSIVES MISTAKES

Everyone has heard of the common mistake or using *it's* for *its*, or vice versa. What is surprising is how often the mistake appears in published work. The following sentence illustrates both problems. *Its* should be *it's* and *it's* should be *its*.

> Economists said *its* too soon to tell whether the state's recent tourism decline will create long-term hardship for *it's* residents.

In the city where I live, a yard-work company has the following slogan painted, rather nicely but mistakenly, on the back of one of its trucks:

> Tree-trimming in all it's branches

A similar problem occurs with apostrophes less frequently in the following: *her's*, *their's*, and *your's*. No such words exist. They are *hers*, *theirs* and *yours*.

Another typical misuse occurs when a possessive is mistakenly used instead of a simple plural:

> "We came from a rural environment, but we didn't act like the Walton's," Abigail said.
>
> At various times a stagecoach stop, a train stop and a home, the building was in poor shape when the Wilson's bought it.

In both cases, the apostrophe is incorrect. In practically every city in the United States, you can find a sign on a shop, a restaurant, a market, an office or a commercial vehicle that makes this mistake. The topic comes up occasionally in online discussion groups, such as the list of the American Copy Editors Society. And sometimes it strikes very close to home. A copy editor from an Ohio newspaper pointed out that a sign leading from her newsroom to the production area reads: "Employee's only."

TIPS AND STRATEGIES

Practice does eventually make perfect at this level of editing. The more you edit, the more you'll be able to spot such problems. But here are a few tips that can help speed up the self-improvement process:

• Prudence pays off. I find it helpful to think of the process of editing like I think of riding a bike in traffic. I assume drivers are going to make mistakes. Every time a car overtakes me near an intersection, I assume it will make a right turn across my path. It seldom happens, but when it does, my prudence pays off, and I don't get brushed or knocked down. It may sound pessimistic, but a similar strategy can help in copy editing. Most copy is correct, but if you assume that there are mistakes, chances of finding them increase because you'll be paying better attention.

• Don't count on the Web. Try an experiment: misspell the name of a place and look it up it in one of the major Web search engines. You will find a surprising number of pages with the name misspelled. The Web offers many excellent references, including dictionaries, encyclopedias and other pages with meticulously checked reference information, but it also readily yields thousands of pages that have spelling mistakes. The prudent copy editor (or reporter) will not automatically rely on the Web; the source must be trustworthy. Besides, it's often faster to use hard copy references.

Many publications also have online archives, also with search engines. The same danger exists, because misspellings make it into the archive and sometimes remain uncorrected.

• Keep your eye on the ball. Part of becoming a better editor is to recognize the pitfalls that human nature encourages and make allowances for them. For example, mistakes often come in pairs. In creating assignments in copy editing, I often place two mistakes near each other, sometimes in adjacent words. I find that many students will find the first error, perhaps a blatant typo, and in a self-congratulatory glow skip right past a more serious second mistake, such as a misspelled name. Professional copy editors do the same thing. Read every word and hold your applause until the end.

Another common problem is to let your guard down when you approach the bottom of the story, particularly on stories written in the inverted pyramid form. The least important and often least interesting facts are at the bottom of a traditionally written news story. Copy editors, like other readers, might find their attention flagging at that point. That's when errors sneak through.

• Learn reporters' strengths and weaknesses. All journalists should pay attention to mechanics, but, as any professional copy editor knows, some writers are better than others at this level. Pay attention to the conditions under which stories are written. Stories written hastily and stories that are breaking and need to be updated quickly tend to have more mistakes. The same is true on the copy desk. When a copy editor is facing deadline and has too many things to finish, mistakes can slip through. A copy chief or other copy desk supervisor who pays close attention to the conditions on his or her desk will have a better chance of backstopping the copy editor.

• Share your expertise. A copy editor who notices a reporter making an error consistently can help that reporter by mentioning it and explaining why it's wrong. An added benefit is that the copy editor will not have to spend so much time fixing the reporter's stories and can concentrate on other important matters. The trick here is knowing when and how to point out such problems. The wrong time is when the reporter is busy trying to finish another story or heading out the door at the end of the day. The wrong way is to nag or be shrill. That worsens the stereotype of the copy editor as the newsroom scold. A better time is when both copy editor and reporter have some time, and a better strategy is to talk about what's good about the reporter's writing as well as what can be improved.

• Learn to sweat the small stuff early in your career. Do yourself a favor. The larger and more prestigious the paper, the more attention it generally pays to issues of mechanics. I spent five years copy editing at a midsize paper in Pennsylvania that was fairly well edited for its size. When I took a job at a much larger paper, I realized quickly that I was not up to speed at spotting and fixing errors in mechanics. The larger, more prestigious paper had much higher standards, particularly regarding grammar, punctuation and usage.

One way to improve is to build a library of reference works—and study them. Here are a few:

"The Careful Writer," by Theodore M. Bernstein
"Words on Words," by John B. Bremner
"Working with Words," by Brian S. Brooks, James L. Pinson and Jean Gaddy
"The Elements of Style," by William Strunk Jr. and E. B. White
"The New Fowler's Modern English Usage," by H. W. Fowler
"When Words Collide," by Lauren Kessler and Duncan McDonald[5]

There are many Web sites devoted to grammar and usage issues. A Web search will turn up hundreds. One site aimed at copy editors is "The Slot" (http://www.theslot.com), created by Bill Walsh, a Washington Post copy editor. Another is "Words on Words" (http://www.copydesk.org/words), the resource page of the American Copy Editors Society

Another way to become more adept at spotting mechanics problems is to review proofreading changes made by more experienced copy editors. Seeing the changes they make in copy you've already read will sensitize you to the areas where you need work. If you don't understand why a change was made, ask. If your grammar, punctuation and usage are shaky, take some time to learn them well. It is worth the time spent, because it is more time-consuming to constantly look up problems in those areas than it is in spelling.

Here's the corrected version of the story from the beginning of this chapter:

WASHINGTON—Stock market losses amounting to about 30 percent (**not per cent—AP style**) of its (**not it's**) $1 billion endowment have forced the Freedom Forum to close four international offices.

The offices are in London, Buenos Aires (**not Aries**), Hong

Kong and Johannesburg (**not Johannisburg**). The foundation, which encourages world press freedom, also will close its First Amendment Center in New York.

Charles Overby, the chairman and chief executive officer, said the organization's (**not organzation's—typo**) emphasis during the next several years would be moving from its Arlington, Va., headquarters (**not Arlington, Virginia Headquarters—AP style is Va.; use a comma after Va., and headquarters is a generic term, not a title**) to a site on Pennsylvania Avenue (**not Ave.—AP style**) near the Capitol (**not the Capital**).

The foundation did not disclose how many of **its** (**not their**) 285 workers would be affected (**not effected**), but it did say that all full-time employees (**not employes—AP style**) would be offered buyouts.

One could argue that the lead could be recast to make it active rather than passive, but that's another story.

Care with mechanics is vital for credibility. The study mentioned earlier in this chapter concluded that newspaper credibility is lower than it should be for a variety of reasons. One of those—the one listed first—is mistakes, both in what I'm calling mechanics and in accuracy, the topic of the next chapter.

3

Accuracy

The following excerpt is from an e-mail message a talented student sent me at the end of a prestigious summer copy desk internship at a metropolitan daily in the Midwest:

> "At every paper I've worked at, reporters are responsible for verifying the facts in their story (names, statements of fact, numbers, etc.). I expected to have to do a certain amount of fact-checking, but copy editors [here] are responsible for double-checking all facts in stories and all proper nouns. If something is wrong, it's great that you caught it, because you're the one who'd get in trouble if an error got into the paper—not the reporter.
>
> "This is really time-consuming . . . and they make a big deal about how you can't just rely on one source, and you're not just supposed to use the Internet. This leads to a lot of resentment—I feel like reporters don't take responsibility for fact-checking a lot of the time, and rely very heavily on us to do it for them.
>
> "It's also frustrating when you absolutely can't verify a fact. They also push you to call the reporter before you change almost ANYTHING. Even when you have multiple sources (which you have already determined are far more reliable than the reporter) telling you the right answer. And then you call the reporters and they're often irritated you bothered them. If they call you back at all. Sometimes I feel like I'm doing battle. I like editing wire stories because I don't have to deal with talking to staff reporters."

Is the student copy editor out of line in her end-of-internship "rant," as she called it? I don't think so.

JUST WHO IS RESPONSIBLE?

Accuracy is the responsibility of everyone who handles a story. Copy editors can verify names, addresses and many facts in a story if they have enough time. But, in the last instance, it is the reporter who must bear most responsibility for accuracy. It has to be this way. As the primary collector of information, the reporter is in the best position to ensure the accuracy of names, places, dates and other factual elements of a story. Some reporters fail to understand this concept, and some news organizations behave as though accuracy were the sole responsibility of the editing staff, particularly copy editors. Such an approach is counterproductive. For one thing, placing the burden for accuracy entirely, or even primarily, on editors is inefficient. Some checking is fine; double-checking every fact in a story is too time-consuming for daily news organizations. Reporters have direct access to sources and source material; copy editors often don't. And, as the student suggested, such a policy can encourage bad habits among reporters. Reporters can come to expect the copy desk to do the basic checking that they themselves should do automatically. Errors, not to mention ill will, can easily follow.

THE COPY EDITOR'S ROLE

So if the primary responsibility for accuracy is the reporter's, what is the copy editor's role? One of the most important of a copy editor's many jobs—and one of the most difficult—is to provide a safety net for accuracy. The copy editor's responsibility is quality control. The responsibility is heavy, because a copy editor typically is the last person to read the story. If a copy editor misses an error, the mistake is on doorsteps all over town. But that does not mean a copy editor can, or even should, check all facts. That isn't the copy editor's job.

One could argue that because other editors are primarily responsible for a story's focus, organization, flow and fairness, a copy editor's time is best spent fact-checking and proofreading. Copy editors indeed must provide an important level of fact-checking, but they have much more to offer; they cannot spend as much time fact-checking as, say, a magazine fact-checker would. A newspaper that fails to provide its copy editors with the authority and support to critically examine levels beyond mechanics and accuracy is wasting its talent and not serving its readership very well. Some of the best-edited daily newspapers in the United States—a group that includes The New York Times, The Philadelphia Inquirer, The Dallas Morning News and The Boston Globe—have built their copy desks according to this belief.

John Bremner, the legendary professor who taught editing at the University of Kansas, used to tell his students, "If your mother says she loves you, check it out!" It's a line that often has been repeated by editing teachers. But professional copy editors know that checking everything is impossible under daily deadlines. Tight deadlines constrain the level of checking that can be done. Even magazines that employ fact-checkers publish inaccuracies.

Copy editors often feel that they have the most to check in the least amount of time. And, like the intern, they sometimes find themselves caught in the middle, responsible for accuracy but unable to ensure it unless they drop everything else. Publication pressures should not keep copy editors from making important checks, but fact-checking is only one of the duties of copy editors. They must try to balance the need to check with the need to move on to other important copy editing, headline writing and page design tasks. Under deadline pressures, copy editors cannot act as book or magazine-article fact-checkers. But they can assume an important role. They can help safeguard accuracy.

To be good at this game, though, requires a well-developed sense of what needs to be checked and what doesn't, what can be checked quickly and what can't. Skilled copy editors make those calculations on every story they read, and they make them faster than a computer could. What makes copy editors worth their weight in platinum is a keen ability to spot what needs to be checked and to spend those precious minutes in a way that will have a substantial payoff. Which facts in a given story need to be checked? This is the real question, and the answer is one that copy editors work hard at answering, and refining, throughout their careers.

News organizations should strive for complete accuracy, but they also need to realize that complete accuracy is impossible in an institution that faces the pressure of daily, sometimes hourly, deadlines.

Reporters are fallible. Sometimes they misunderstand their sources. Sometimes the sources are wrong, and sometimes reporters don't double-check what those sources tell them. Sometimes they get busy and fail to check facts. Sometimes they get lazy and fail to check facts. Sometimes they just get it wrong.

Editors are fallible too. The assigning editor—the city editor, perhaps—might hurriedly recast a paragraph and inadvertently introduce a mistake. He or she might make an assumption and introduce an error. Or add a name and fail to double-check the spelling or the person's title. Copy editors make mistakes too, and they sometimes introduce errors into copy.

Given the combination—fallible and often overworked reporters and editors—is it any surprise that accuracy issues are near the top of reader concerns?

AN APPROACH

As a general rule, check any fact that seems wrong to you. This may seem to be circular reasoning, or perhaps a cop-out, but it isn't. An editor's best allies are instinct and common sense. Trust your instincts, but at the same time continue to refine them. The key is to develop a heightened sense of "what seems wrong." Of course, "what seems wrong" will differ from person to person, and "instinct" depends in part on a copy editor's store of background knowledge. For this reason, many copy editing pre-employment tests include a general knowledge section, and the prestigious Dow Jones Newspaper Fund internship program includes such material on its nationwide test every year. Journalism students who are interested in a wide variety of subjects, or perhaps are trivia buffs, often fail to realize that reading widely and remembering what you read are extremely valuable assets in copy editors.

Good copy editors tend to be information sponges, and they soak up facts in many ways. Some are public television and Discovery Channel devotees. Others are Weather Channel junkies. Some develop expertise in areas such as astronomy, baseball, court systems, fly fishing, genres of literature, guns, psychology, Russian history or zoology. Good copy editors have a knack for remembering facts—or at least recognizing them and remembering enough to know what they should look up.

A story mentions that a recent advance in satellite imagery has enabled researchers to detect a 10-foot bulge in the Earth's surface on an inactive volcano's flank. You double-check, because 10 feet doesn't sound right. A 10-foot bulge would be detectable by less sophisticated methods, perhaps even by eyesight. Moreover, you know from other reading that satellite imagery is able to detect much smaller variations in topography. And you remember from that Geology 121 class you took to fulfill a science requirement that significant earth movement can be measured in inches or less. You check and find out that 10 feet should be 10 inches, still a significant difference in geological measurement, but nothing like 10 feet.

While reading an obituary years ago, for example, I came across a sentence that mentioned that the deceased had served in the U.S. Air Force in 1944 and '45. That date raised a flag; I knew the Air Force did not become a separate branch of the armed forces until sometime after World War II, though I did not know the actual date. My father, a bomber pilot during the war, always talked about the Army Air Corps. That was the pre-war name of the service that became the Army Air Forces in 1941. A glance at the AP Stylebook or an encyclopedia shows that the U.S. Air Force would not become a de facto entity until 1947 and would not be formalized as a separate branch under U.S. law until 1951. Some encyclopedias are available online, making it easier to look up such facts.

A flood story from the Upper Midwest mentions that the Red River is expected to crest above flood stage in Grand Forks, N.D., on Sunday and in Winnipeg, Manitoba, almost 150 miles north, several days later. That doesn't sound right. During floods, the crest moves downriver, and you know that few rivers in the United States flow north for long distances. A glance at the map shows that the Red River indeed flows north; it empties into Lake Winnipeg. The story does make sense. Did you waste your time looking it up? I'd say no. It was a good bet based on what you know. And now you know more.

Once I came upon a passage in a story about a bicycle racer that mentioned that he used a 22-gear bike. As a longtime bike commuter and weekend cyclist, I happened to know that was impossible, or at least highly improbable at the time. Road racing bikes had two or three chainrings and usually seven or eight cogs. The number of gears is the number of chainrings times the number of cogs. It could be 21, 24 or even 27, if the bike happened to have nine cogs, but it couldn't be 22. Not every copy editor will know that, or would be expected to know that. But nearly everyone has ridden a bicycle and has some sense of how the gears operate. A reference to 22 gears should raise a question. It just doesn't sound right.

Bottom line: It's important to read widely, to remember things, and to know where to look things up quickly.

AREAS OF CONCERN

Here are a few general areas of accuracy problems:

1. Names

News stories are full of names—of people, places, organizations and events—and there isn't time to check all of them unless a newsroom has people falling all over one another. But is it vital that papers get names right. Readers sometimes have long memories and hold grudges even longer. Many will remember mistakes made in the names of their family members in obituaries for decades. It's important to develop a sense of which ones might be wrong. Inconsistencies are easy. At least one has to be wrong, and there's even a small chance that both are wrong. Pay particular attention to unusual spellings that you don't recognize and names of famous people that don't seem right. The more you read, the more you'll learn to recognize potential problems with names.

Although there always have been unusually spelled names, these days, it seems, parents have become much more creative in naming their children, and *Caitlyn, Caitlynne, Katelyn* or even *Kate-Lyn* just might be correct. Here are a few commonly misspelled names:

Volkswagen, *not* Volkswagon
Procter & Gamble, *not* Proctor & Gamble
Centers for Disease Control, *not* Center for Disease Control
Cincinnati, *not* Cincinnatti
Groundhog Day, *not* Groundhog's day (an AP style point)
Laundromat, a capitalized trade name, *not* laundramat.
Magna Carta, *not* Magna Charta
Novocain, *not* Novocaine
Philippines, *not* Phillipines
Plexiglas, a trade name, *not* Plexiglass
Qantas, *not* Quantas
Sheetrock, *not* Sheet Rock
7-Eleven, *not* Seven-Eleven

Plenty of other names are tricky. Many copy editors know them by sight; if you don't, they're easy to look up. Quite a few are included in the AP Stylebook.

2. Geographical References

Is it *13th Street* or *13th Avenue?* Mistakes in street names, city names, addresses, compass directions and the like are legion. And they are embarrassing cracks in the facade of a publication's credibility.

Checking any street names you are unfamiliar with is a good percentage bet. In fact, it's a good idea to glance at a map whenever you have a story based in a community you are unfamiliar with. It's helpful for a copy editor to have a sense of the "lay of the land," where the mountains are, what rivers flow through the community or nearby, how big the town or city is. Be careful, though, about local names. Often there are discrepancies between maps and city directories or between maps and local phone books. Some local maps show streets that do not exist (a street might have been planned but never built). Creating and maintaining a local addendum to the AP Stylebook on regional place names can be a blessing.

Also, every community has its own problem spellings. In the Portland, Ore., metropolitan area, there is a suburb spelled *Milwaukie*, not *Milwaukee*, as the major Wisconsin city is spelled. *Pittsburg* is a medium-size city in the San Francisco Bay area and a small city in Kansas; *Pittsburgh* is the biggest city in western Pennsylvania. It's *Reading, Pa.*, but *Redding, Calif.*, and *Paterson, N.J.*, but *Patterson, N.Y.* Is it *Berkley* or *Berkeley*, Calif., *Wellesley* or *Wellesly*, Mass.? The second "e" is correct in both cases.

3. Historical References and Dates

These facts are extremely easy to check and very easy to get wrong when you don't check. Columbus might have sailed the ocean blue in 1492, but when did Captain Cook first sight land in the Pacific Northwest? When did Marx write "The Communist Manifesto" (and wasn't Engels a co-author?). When did the Three Mile Island nuclear accident happen, and in what year did the Vietnam War end? The Cuban Missile Crisis was in 1962, the space shuttle Challenger exploded in 1986, and the Exxon Valdez ran aground in 1989. A copy editor's best friend in these matters is The World Almanac. Dictionaries, compact encyclopedias and trustworthy Web sites are other handy sources.

4. Scientific and Medical References

Is the speed of light 186,282 miles an hour or a second? And do you round it to 186,000? Are the drugs called *proteus* or *protease* inhibitors? And are they used to fight AIDS or Alzheimer's disease? Is it *Alzheimer's* or *Alzheimers'*?

Many scientists and researchers do not hold newspapers and other general news periodicals in high esteem. They sometimes criticize publications, often with merit, for inadequate reporting, for trivializing or ignoring major stories, for overplaying minor findings as "breakthroughs" and for failing to qualify statements or assertions as carefully as scientists do. Misstating facts, particularly facts that can easily be checked in standard reference works, does little to improve that reputation.

5. Numbers

Specific problems with numbers are treated in the following chapter, but it's worth mentioning them in the context of accuracy as well.

The best strategy for copy editors (not to mention reporters) is a simple one: Always do the math. Calculate whatever you can, even if you're pressed for time. There are so many math errors in newspapers that it's difficult to think of a situation when checking the math is time wasted. Many stories that are printed contain numbers that don't add up because no one—the reporter, the assigning editor or the copy editor—did the math.

DETECTIVE WORK

Good copy editors also develop what might be called a sixth sense for accuracy. They approach stories much as detectives would. They are always looking for clues (or cues). They base their investigation on what they know about news, what they know about the subject and what they know about the reporter. Good copy editors learn reporters; they remember each reporter's strengths and weaknesses. They know who is meticulous about names and who isn't, who can't spell, whose brain works faster than his or her fingers. All of this knowledge is useful; it can save time by helping an editor decide what to check and what to let go. But copy editors should not get lulled into a false sense of security—even a meticulous reporter can make mistakes.

Here's an example, based loosely on an actual story, that illustrates the idea of copy editing as detective work:

ASTORIA, Ore.—Electrical power was restored Tuesday morning on a cruise ship with 1,200 people aboard 80 miles off the Oregon coast after a problem with an electrical generator disrupted heating, lighting, ventilation and other ship systems.

The generator aboard the Intrepid was brought back to operation at 6:10 a.m., about three hours after power went out, said Coast Guard Petty Officer Jonathan Smythe.

The Intrepid was bound for San Diego and was under way, he said. The 720-foot ship was never in danger and no Coast Guard aid was requested, Smythe said.

A passenger using a cell phone called 9-1-1 to report problems.

"The passenger was a little panicked," Smythe said. "The 9-1-1 operator called us. We contacted the vessel, and the captain told us he was confident the problem would be repaired and that they were not in danger and did not need any assistance."

Nelson Bly, 55, a retired newspaper reporter aboard the Intrepid, said that the power outage was an inconvenience and that the crew did not do a good job of communicating with the passengers.

"We haven't heard anything from the bridge, other than that they lost power," he said. "One of the crew members told me that this sort of thing had happened before but the outage lasted just a half hour."

He described the weather as windy and "crystal clear . . . you can see some little towns on the shore."

Bly said he was with a group of 50 that visited Baniff National Park in the Canadian Rockies, then boarded the ship in Vancouver, B.C., for a cruise to San Francisco.

The Intrepid, a 52,000-ton luxury liner, was built in 1992 and used on cruises to Alaska in the summer. It left Portland late Monday after a scheduled stop, Bly said.

He said the power went out minutes after the ship left the mouth of the Columbia River at Astoria, about 50 miles northeast of Portland.

The story has a few simple accuracy problems. For example, the spelling of the park is *Banff*, not *Baniff*. If you don't recognize the name, check it in an atlas or gazetteer. In the last paragraph, "northeast" should be "northwest," as a quick glance at a map confirms. There is a possible inconsistency in the route of the ship: The top of the story says it was bound for San Diego, and the bottom says Bly was with a group bound for San Francisco. Perhaps the ship was scheduled to stop in San Francisco and then proceed to San

Diego, but it's worth a question to a reporter. Also, 55 is a little young for a journalist to be retired; that's probably worth a question too.

The other problem is a bit more difficult to catch, but the story offers clues. A copy editor who approaches each story as a detective has a better chance of solving the puzzle. The lead says power was restored when the ship was 80 miles from the coast. The second paragraph says power was restored in three hours. Bly said the ship lost power minutes after leaving the mouth of the river. Those facts add up to an inconsistency. A ship wouldn't drift 80 miles in three hours. In fact, a fast ship can barely cover 80 miles in three hours under full power. Bly also said he could see towns along the shore. Unless a passenger is in the crow's nest and the towns are pretty far up hillsides, it is unlikely that a person could see shore even on a "crystal clear" night. The curvature of the earth limits your view to much less than 80 miles. And the Coast Guard spokesman said a panicked passenger used a cell phone to call 9-1-1. Do cell phones usually operate on a ship 80 miles from shore? These clues do not add up to a ship 80 miles off the coast. The ship, as it turns out, was only 8 miles from shore. The extra "0" was a typo that if printed becomes an inaccuracy. Good copy editors don't just catch the easy ones—the Baniff's. They read critically, constantly asking themselves: Does it makes sense? Are the facts consistent? Do they add up? An editor's common sense is one of his or her most useful tools, and using it on every story will keep it sharp.

In this story, one might argue, the misstated fact is not that important. What's the big deal whether it's 80 miles offshore or 8? The reader still understands that a cruise ship carrying many passengers lost power somewhere off the coast. True, some inaccuracies are more serious than others, but inaccuracy is inaccuracy, and all erode credibility. Moreover, this inaccuracy is not trivial; a large ship adrift 8 miles from shore is a greater immediate threat to coastal communities (and itself might be in greater danger) than one 80 miles out.

Incidentally, British Columbia is spelled out in AP style, not abbreviated, as in the third-to-last paragraph.

TIPS AND STRATEGIES

• Always check phone numbers—call them. Many news organizations require reporters to make this check and note that they have done so. Double-checking on the copy desk is a good idea—it takes only a few seconds. Publishing incorrect telephone numbers is a credibility-destroying triple play. The mistake annoys readers who reach the wrong number, it doesn't help the organization or individual who was supposed to be called, and it often infuriates the unfortunate organization or individual who gets the calls intended for someone else. In all cases, the target of wrath, ultimately, is the publication.

• Look up Web site addresses before you publish them. It is very easy to make a mistake in Web addresses, particularly those that have unusual internal characters, such as underlined spaces and hyphens. Checking Web addresses is very easy at most publications. Most editors have Web access on the desktop these days.

• Know your community. Many journalists, including copy editors, move around, especially early in their careers. In a new community, spend some time driving and walking around. Become familiar with the major streets, the geography, the parks, the churches, the schools and other points of interest. You will catch many more mistakes if you are familiar with the community, and you will provide a backstop for reporters who might move around more than copy editors do. A few enlightened newspapers give new staff members guided tours of their communities. Most don't, but you can do it yourself.

• Know one another. Copy editors often develop expertise in several areas. A good *slot*, or copy desk supervisor, knows the strengths of each member of the desk. A good copy editor also knows. Who, for example, reads Scientific American or Horticulture magazine? Who knows the difference between Mozart and Mendelssohn and who knows what "music" 13-year-olds listen to these days? Who is an expert cook, an Olympics junkie or an avid gardener? Who was an English lit major, and who is most comfortable with statistics? Who reads history for relaxation? Who has kids? Who is a Catholic? Who grew up in New York City? A good slot can expand the power of the desk by learning which reporters have what expertise—beyond their beats—and asking them for help.

• Don't be cowed by reputation ("He's a Pulitzer Prize winner; he must be right"). A reporter's reputation should not lead copy editors to drop their guard, and a reporter's position should not be used in a newsroom to create an aura of untouchability. Some newsroom managers exacerbate the prima donna problem—they take the path of least resistance and either subtly or openly discourage editing of the self-styled stars and squeaky wheels of the newsroom. A particularly sensitive area is the editing of columnists. Columnists are given a great deal of latitude in what they say and how they say it. They are given no latitude in accuracy. Fact errors in columns often resonate louder, because columns tend to have high readership. Hands-off policies in editing columnists help nobody. The readers suffer. Such policies also can reinforce bad behavior on the part of writers and build resentment among copy editors. For copy editors faced with working in such an environment, a good suggestion is to take it slowly—to not raise a fuss but to build trust with writers and their editors one catch at a time. Many of the best reporters truly appreciate good copy editing. Even prima donnas will come around eventually.

• Don't ease up. Don't drop your guard when you edit the best on the staff. Good reporters and writers deserve good editing. In fact, one could argue that because they do such a good job regularly they deserve to have their occasional lapses caught before publication more so than the reporter who is lazy or sloppy about facts. I always felt worse about missing a mistake in talented, careful reporters' stories. I felt that they deserved better and that I let them down.

• Pay attention to the sentence level. Often inaccuracy creeps into a publication because it is lost in context, or because editors paying very close attention to the level of mechanics fail to keep the level of accuracy in mind. I have demonstrated this at least a dozen times in editing classes by asking students to catch errors in a series of sentences that have style, punctuation, spelling and grammar mistakes, followed by this one:

> In the Old Testament story, Moses took two of each species aboard the Ark.

Often, nobody catches the fact error. They worry about whether *Old Testament* and *Ark* should be capitalized or whether the comma after story is necessary. They fail to see the obvious. It was Noah, not Moses. Miss one like this, and the letters pour in from Bible-school children.

• Learn your way around standard reference works, such as the World Almanac, the World Atlas, a regional road atlas, a city map, a compact encyclopedia, the Congressional Directory, the Trade Names Directory, the Physician's Desk Reference (known as PDR), Jane's Fighting Ships and Lloyd's Register of Shipping and Jane's All the World's Aircraft.

• Be wary of the Internet. The Web is an almost unlimited source of information, but it is also a source of much misinformation. For example, there is a famous quote often attributed to former U.S. Sen. Everett Dirksen: "A billion here, a billion there, and pretty soon you're talking real money." If you search for "Dirksen and billion" on the Web, you'll find many, many references to the quote. If you search for "Dirksen and million," you'll also find many, many references to the quote, but with the word "million" instead of "billion." You can also find many references to the quote that are not worded the same way. And if you keep looking, you'll learn that an organization called the The Dirksen Congressional Center tried and failed to authenticate the quote.[1] It's a cautionary tale about trusting what you see in print—or on the Web.

• Look for advice. Frank E. Fee Jr.'s "44 Tips for Greater Accuracy" (http://www.unc.edu/~ffee/teaching/accuracy.htm) offers a wealth of tips about ensuring accuracy. A column by Chip Scanlan of The Poynter Institute called "Getting It Right: A Passion for Accuracy" (http://www.poynter.org/column.asp?id=52&aid=17939) discusses the issue and provides links to several other Web pages that focus on accuracy problems.

• Take special care with late-breaking stories and big events. News reports coming in from all sides on a major disaster or crime are almost always inconsistent. Death and injury counts change quickly. Early reports often are incorrect and almost always are incomplete. One reporter or news service might have later information than another. The graphic done an hour ago no longer agrees with the latest story. Information in such cases is usually sketchy at best. Emergency and police officials are often wrong about details.

• Return to sender. Occasionally, the best approach is to pass the story back to the reporter to check the facts. This, obviously, can create problems between editors and reporters, and copy editors need the support of their supervisors to make this strategy work. But on occasion, if a story is so riddled with sloppy reporting and inadequate fact-checking, tossing it back to the reporter may improve the paper in the long run, even if it means the story must be held for a later edition or until the next day. The improvement comes through consciousness-raising—a reporter is made to understand the hard way that basic accuracy is in his or her court.

4

Precision
and Language

> The difference between the almost-right word and the right
> word is really a large matter—it's the difference between the
> lightning bug and the lightning.
>
> —MARK TWAIN

Twain was prone to exaggerating, but his point is apt. If the levels of
mechanics and accuracy are the bedrock, words are the foundation. And
precision in choosing words helps the foundation fit together tightly. At
this level of editing, the focus is still through a microscope but at a lower
level of magnification. Precision—saying exactly what you mean—is the
issue, and problems at this level manifest themselves in many ways. Writers
who use the wrong words give readers pause, probably even more so than
writers who make mistakes in grammar or spelling. Word choice can influence a reader's perception of a sentence, a story, sometimes even a publication. A loaded word might invite readers to conclude that the publication is not fair to an individual or a group. A gratuitous adjective used to
describe a woman might lead readers to think a publication is sexist, or an
ill-considered phrase suggesting that an older person's achievement is ex-
traordinary might inadvertently tar a publication as "age-ist."

Precision, oddly enough, is not always an all-or-none proposition. If
the issue is numbers, or math in general, the great likelihood is that some-

thing is either right or wrong. But even in terms of numbers, there can be shades of imprecision. A number or a statistic, say an average, might be precise, but it might not be the best choice to illustrate a point. If the number of instances is low, an average can be misleading. When it comes to words, precision is typically a matter of degree. Gross imprecision is always a serious problem, but more subtle shades of imprecision can hurt as well.

THE WORD LEVEL

Some imprecise terms are known only to a few readers—and to copy editors. For example, it is imprecise to say that two cars *collide* when one strikes another from behind, though most members of the reading public are probably not aware that the word has such a narrow meaning. The term *rear-end collision*, though imprecise, is commonly heard in speech. The word, however, refers to objects that are moving toward each other, such as a northbound and a southbound car hitting head-on.

Similarly, there is a technical difference between *convince* and *persuade*, though many people use them interchangeably in everyday conversation. As the AP Stylebook indicates:

> You may be *convinced that* something or *of* something. You must be *persuaded to do* something.

Between is the correct word when talking about two people; *among* is correct for more than two people. Two brothers divided the cake *between* themselves. Three sisters divided it *among* themselves.

Unique is not the same as *unusual*; therefore it is imprecise to refer to a performance or a piece of art as *very unique*. *Unique* is not a matter of degree. Moreover, copy editors need to be extra careful when a story says something is *unique*. It often isn't, and if so, *unique* is inaccurate. The same is true for *first, biggest, smallest, fastest,* and the like.

The word *myriad* often appears as a noun, such as in the phrase *a myriad of ideas*. It is most properly used as an adjective, as in *myriad ideas*. A flag on shore should not be described as flying at *half-mast*, even though people often speak that way. That usage is proper for ships and naval stations, according to the AP Stylebook. Otherwise, flags are flown at *half-staff*. If you take an unpaid leave for a month, you don't *forego* your salary; you *forgo* it. *Forego* means to go before, not to give up.

Most members of the reading public might not know the difference between *enormity* and *enormousness*. A Los Angeles Times service story referring to downhill skier Picabo Street's comeback after an injury made the mistake on the day of the 2002 Olympic downhill final:

> Street's strong personality and young-won fame has not always endeared her to teammates, or coaches, yet there is no getting around the enormity of what she has done and, perhaps, is about to do.

Careful writers and editors simply do not call something a "great evil" (the definition of *enormity*) when they mean to refer to the magnitude of the accomplishment. They do not say *fortuitous* for *fortunate*. They do not use the word *staunch* as a verb, as a major newspaper did in a report about executive pay:

> Financial leaders such as Federal Reserve Chairman Alan Greenspan are calling for accounting changes to staunch the flow of stock-option giveaways to executives.

Staunch is an adjective, used in constructions such as a "staunch supporter." The verb is *stanch*, meaning "to stop," as in "to stanch the flow of blood." A careful editor might also ask why a writer would want to use the word *stanch* in that sentence in the first place. *Stanch* means to stop; Greenspan was not calling for the elimination of stock-option perks for executives; he was trying to "limit" or "reduce" them. *Stanch* is imprecise in this context.

The verb *loathe* should not be used when the adjective *loath* is meant, as in the following sentence:

> Even if PBS President Pat Mitchell wished the flap over Rukeyser's show had never taken place, PBS management is loathe to second-guess station managers.

Careful writers and editors do not use the word *margin* when the precise term they need is *ratio*. The misuse can often be found in wire service reports at the close of the daily stock-trading session:

> On the New York Stock Exchange, advancing stocks outnumbered losers by a margin of 3–2.

The context in this sentence makes it clear that the intended concept is *ratio*. *Margin* is the difference between two numbers. *Ratio* represents the relative size of two quantities. With thousands of different stocks trading hands, the difference between gainers and losers cannot possibly be 3 to 2, but the ratio certainly can be. The same mistake can often be found in election stories:

> Mayor Richard M. Daley won a fifth term by more than a 5–1 margin over his closest challenger.

Again, it's a ratio, unless only six people voted, and if that were the case, it would be a margin of 4.

The word *range* is another quasi-mathematical term that often is loosely used or misused. It properly refers to elements that can be measured along some dimension. The following two sentences correctly use the word:

> Adult coho salmon range in size from about 2 to 6 pounds.

> Fly-fishing aficionados can find a range of moving water in the state, from tiny spring-fed creeks to broad, powerful rivers.

The following two are incorrect, because there is no obvious dimension of comparison:

> Jenny took classes ranging from literature to chemical engineering.

> The produce offered by the cooperative farm ranges from cabbage to beets to Hubbard squash.

Sentences that misuse *range* can easily be recast using wording such as *a variety of* or *including*.

Some imprecision in choice of words is obvious to a greater number of readers. The difference between *concrete* and *cement*, for example, is familiar to anyone who has mixed cement with sand and rock to make concrete—not the majority, perhaps, but more than a handful.

Some words are simply egregiously wrong and can be spotted by many readers: *affect* instead of *effect*, *its* for *it's*, *poured* for *pored*, *hoards* instead of *hordes*. Fox News Online certainly meant *its* when the Web site posted a notice looking for interns "to join it's editorial production team." One would hope its interns will know the difference. Chances are good that basketball star Michael Jordan *bore down* in the second half, not *bared down*, as the AP reported in a lead during the 2001 basketball season. If Jordan had removed his uniform, *bared* would be correct.

Some imprecision may appear harmless, and relatively speaking, it might well be harmless. The proper term is *Canada goose*, not *Canadian goose*, but the meaning is clear nonetheless. In the sentence "Hurricane Jane caused an estimated $30 million in damages in the Carolinas," readers will understand the meaning even though the correct word is *damage*. *Damages* are assessed in a civil court proceeding. Context often yields the correct meaning even when a word or phrase is imprecise. But credibility dies the death of a thousand nicks, scrapes and cuts. The correct words should be used, and words should be used correctly. Good editors realize that there is no reason to use the wrong word when the right word is at hand. The AP Stylebook has many examples of words that often are misused, and well-edited publications insist on making those distinctions.

Imprecision also can flow from grammar or usage errors:

> Tate's volunteer causes have included a leadership role in the Metropolitan Affordable Housing Corp., which over the last seven years has bequeathed the metropolitan area with about 200 new apartment units for low-income tenants.

The sentence is too wordy, but the chief problem is the verb. An ear tuned to the pitch of English can tell that "bequeathed . . . with" simply doesn't sound right. A glance at the dictionary confirms why. *Bequeathed* is a transitive verb; it requires an object. Even if the dictionary allowed the use of *bequeath* as an intransitive verb, it's still jarring enough that a good editor's antenna will go up. Moreover, one could argue that *bequeathed* does not carry the correct meaning; it means "to pass on or to hand down property," typically by way of a will. The writer of that sentence was seduced by a $2-word, when a 25-cent word or two would have captured the meaning without distortion. Perhaps the agency had "built 200 apartments and donated them," or it had "bought and donated 200 apartments." Good editors can stanch the flow of seductive, but somewhat imprecise, $2-words.

Verbs of attribution are fertile ground for imprecision. Some writers dislike the word *said* so much that they will go to any length, including to the thesaurus, to find other verbs of attribution. Some simply want to vary the attributive verb to avoid repeating the verb *said* throughout the story. Verbs such as *explained, announced, remarked, commented, expressed,* even *stated* may be used—sparingly—if the connotation they carry is appropriate. They do carry connotations. *Remark* as a verb, for example, suggests that a source did not carefully prepare the comments. *Announce* has a ring of formality, meaning "to proclaim or declare." Similarly, *state* means "to declare" and often conveys strong conviction. *Explain* means "to elucidate or define." The problem occurs when such verbs are blithely used to replace the word *said* in contexts where their connotation is not on the mark. In any reasonable calculation, a hint of repetition trumps a suggestion of misuse every time. *Said* remains the best four-letter word in a journalist's lexicon.

JARGON

Some reporters fall into the trap of writing the way their sources speak. It's no surprise. Reporters, like other people, tend to pick up patterns of speech from those they spend time with. A careful editor will save them from their own excesses. Here's an example:

> Six years ago, the deputy district attorney was tasked with prosecuting child-abuse cases.

The dictionary allows *tasked* as a verb, but people do not speak that way unless they work for a government agency or have a tin ear. This sentence would be better written as "Six years ago, the deputy district attorney began prosecuting . . . " or, if an agent is important to the meaning, "Six years ago the chief county prosecutor assigned the deputy district attorney to prosecute child-abuse cases." Either revision also eliminates the unnecessary passive voice. Government, the military and high-tech business are three sources of impenetrable jargon, but other areas are prone to it as well. Most of it is unnecessary.

Some imprecision erodes credibility instantly. If you doubt this assertion, write a caption that identifies a goose as a duck in a paper that circulates in farm country. Then run for the high ground as the flood of calls, letters and e-mails pours in from readers who say their 6-year-old can tell the difference. This error, which might seem to be imprecision to the writer is seen as simple inaccuracy to a knowledgeable reader. Other examples of imprecision might not be picked up by readers but will be by sources. A *sanitary sewer collector* is not the same as a *storm sewer collector*. A police officer knows the difference between a *pistol* and *revolver*, or between an *automatic* and a *semiautomatic* weapon, and writers who confuse them look as though they haven't done their homework. Reporters need to maintain credibility with their sources as much as they do with their readership, and careful copy editors can help them.

LOADED WORDS

Another area of imprecision is the use of words that say more than they should. Words can connote as well as denote, invite conclusions as well as explain or describe. "Loaded words" can raise fairness or legal concerns, but they also represent imprecision.

The difference between the following two sentences is subtle but real:

> James Smith claimed that he did not embezzle the funds.
>
> James Smith contended that he did not embezzle the funds.

The verb *claimed* carries with it a shade of doubt, a hint that we might not believe the speaker. The verb *contended* is more neutral and thus more appropriate in contexts in which the intention is not to cast doubt on the speaker. In most journalistic writing, reporters do not strive to cast doubt on the speaker, and editors should be vigilant so that the paper does not inadvertently do so. Other verbs of attribution carry similar baggage. The dictionary defines *admit* as "to acknowledge, confess" and gives an example: to admit the truth. *Admit* contains shades of both *acknowledge* and *confess*. *Acknowledge* is more neutral if the admission is not a confession.

Adverbs and adjectives can lead to similar pitfalls.

> The politician stubbornly denied that he had met with the bookmaker.
>
> The politician steadfastly denied that he had met with the bookmaker.

Stubbornly casts doubt; *steadfastly* is more neutral. Or don't use either word.

Nouns also can carry unwanted connotations:

> American Airlines disclosed a scheme to lure new customers.

Scheme can connote sneakiness or underhandedness. The word *plan*, which is neutral, would be a better choice. *Announced* would be a better choice than *disclosed*, unless the element of secrecy conveyed by *disclosed* is appropriate.

Sometimes whether a word is loaded depends on the reader. For example, *pro-life* is a term used by groups that oppose abortion. That usage irritates people who support a woman's right to abortion because it suggests that they are *anti-life*, a label they strongly dispute. A solution used by some publications is to allow the usage in direct quotes but to find another way to describe the position outside of quotes. Such issues should be addressed through an in-house style guide if the AP Stylebook is silent.

Even a seemingly innocuous term can appear biased. A judicial *reform* movement in Pennsylvania a couple of decades ago created headaches for copy editors. Who could possibly be anti-reform? Many people and groups in the community supported the *reform* proposal, which sought to depoliticize the selection of judges by making the positions appointive rather than elective. Others, however, disagreed, arguing that the proposal was not a *reform*, because it shifted power from ordinary citizens, who could vote for judges, to politicians and special interests. One person's reform can be another's step backward.

Connotations are particularly troublesome in situations of conflict. On the international scale, one person's *freedom fighter* or *patriot* might be another's *terrorist*. On the local level, copy editors need to take care so that the words used do not reinforce stereotypes. Consider the following:

> Negotiators for Local 10 of the American Federation of State, County and Municipal Employees demanded a 10 percent increase in each year of a two-year contract, and the company offered 5.

Readers are used to hearing about union *demands* and company *offers*. How would it sound reversed? The union offered to settle for 10 percent, but the company demanded that the workers accept 5. By saying, without reflection, that a union *demands* and a company *offers*, a story invites readers to conclude that the union proposals (naturally) are unreasonable and the company's proposals (naturally) are reasonable. That might be true in some cases, but it is not true in others. A good principle to follow in choice of words is evenhandedness. Treat people or groups equally, unless there is good reason not to.

BIAS AND SENSITIVITY

Applying the same principle of evenhandedness would eliminate most references that appear biased, whether the bias is based on sex, race, national origin, sexual preference, age, region of the country or another inappropriate criterion. Blatantly biased wording is no longer as common as it once was. Decades ago, news reports included phrasing such as "Police were looking for a Negro male who robbed. . . ." Today it is rare to see a suspect's race reported in a crime story unless it is part of a detailed description of someone police are looking for. But more subtle forms of bias continue to appear, such as a story whose wording suggests it is highly unusual for a member of a given race, or, say, a woman to have achieved or accomplished something.

In 1993, Hillary Clinton testified before congressional committees about health care. She had been named by President Clinton to head a health care task force and appeared before Congress to promote the president's health plan and answer questions. Here is the lead of a New York Times story on her testimony:

> WASHINGTON—Hillary Rodham Clinton invited Congress to join her and President Clinton to "give the American people the health security they deserve" as she captivated and dominated two usually grumpy House committees Tuesday.

And, several paragraphs later:

> So taken with her presentation were the members of the House Ways and Means Committee that they applauded as she left, a virtually unheard-of tribute. They were plainly impressed that she had handled the dozens of issues they raised with detail and conviction, and without notes from advisers.

The next day, in a news analysis, Delia M. Rios of Newhouse News Service pointed out in a column that the underlying tone of the coverage irritated groups such as the National Women's Political Caucus. Certainly, it was atypical for a president's wife to testify before Congress on complex policy issues. That was newsworthy. But gushing about how she had handled the issues "without notes from advisers" went over the line. Hillary Clinton's performance was not unusual for a professional woman, indeed a lawyer, which she is. Characterizing it that way is sexist. Moreover, it is difficult to imagine a news lead referring to Bob Dole, George Bush or a Wall Street lawyer as "captivating and dominating" a congressional committee. Asking whether the story was evenhanded, whether it treated a professional woman as it would have treated a professional man with similar credentials (other than the obvious tie to the president) would have turned up the problem before it was published.

The problem can appear in headlines too:

Female botanist wins Nobel Prize

One way to identify potential problems is to ask how it would look if the word *male* were substituted:

Male botanist wins Nobel Prize

That would be silly. Isn't it just as odd or gratuitous to use the word *female?* It is not unheard of, or even unusual, for a woman to be a botanist. Men and women should be treated evenhandedly in news stories. The sex of a subject sometimes is a key element of the story, and it is appropriate to mention it. The sex of the golfer is clearly part of the story when a woman's lawsuit forces an exclusively male club to admit her.

Physical descriptions are another minefield, because traditionally women were described by looks ("blonde, blue-eyed, petite"), but men were not. Reporters should ask themselves whether description adds to the story or is gratuitous, and editors should ask as well. Reporters sometimes complain that questioning such descriptions is political correctness run amok. This isn't a political correctness issue; it's one of fairness and common sense.

It is common to think of sexism as an issue primarily of stereotyping or of demeaning women, and, historically, that has certainly been the case. Sexism can cut both ways, however, and it also requires vigilance to spot sexist references that cut men out of the picture. Consider the following lead, which appeared on a food-page story about new approaches to nutrition:

> Mothers aren't the only ones who can tell us how to eat properly. A computer can, too.

How about fathers and grandfathers? Or grandmothers? In a day when so many families are nontraditional, assumptions embedded in such leads can alienate significant portions of the population. A careful editor will ask: Is the image worth the risk?

That example is a case of what might be called subtle sexism. It's a trap that's easy for a writer to fall into and easier for an editor to read over. Because most farmers are men, it seems natural to use the masculine pronoun in generic references to a member of that group. Or because most nurses are women, it's easy to overlook the use of *she* or *her* in a sentence that is speaking about nurses in general:

> The county agent is asking any farmer who identifies potato blight to call his chemical dealer or the county's extension offices.

> If you think that a child has swallowed a toxic substance, call a nurse at the hospital's emergency hotline number and ask her what you can do.

Such sentences can be recast with plural pronouns or with no pronoun reference without any loss of clarity. The rewriting is the easy part; the harder part is spotting the problem.

AGE

Age is another tricky area. Unusual accomplishments of older people are newsworthy. A runner who finishes her first marathon at age 75 is worth writing about, and age is certainly part of the story. But here, as in the Hillary Clinton example, copy editors must take care that the newspaper does not make the same mistake—to highlight behavior that might be unusual for some members of a class of people but not for a particular person.

> Without consulting her notes, Gray Panthers leader Maggie Kuhn adroitly fielded a dozen questions about the proposal to cut Social Security payments.

In effect, such wording perpetuates stereotypes. An unreflective use of a word such as *elderly* can pose the same problem:

> An elderly Oregon couple trekked 10 miles through the desert to get help when their car broke down east of Prineville around midday.
> James and Karen Smith, both 65, covered the distance in four hours. The Smiths are longtime members of The Obsidians, a hiking club based in Oregon, and they often hike Cascade Mountain trails.

Are the Smiths *elderly?* At what age does one become *elderly?* If someone who has just turned 70 completes a 70-mile bike ride to celebrate it, is that person *elderly?*

Example of bias are also examples of imprecision, as some of the previous examples suggest. They reinforce stereotypes, which invite people to think of individuals solely in terms of one facet of their identity. That is imprecise.

CULTURE AND RELIGION

Precision in reporting about culture, nationality and religion is increasingly important in a fractured and fractious world. *Arab,* for example, is a cultural term; it refers to linguistic ancestry and is associated with people of southwestern Asia and northern Africa, but it often is misused in religious contexts as a synonym for *Muslim.* Many Arabs are followers of Islam, but many are members of other religions.

Words can be popularized imprecisely, and the misuse can become the source of friction. The word *sheik,* according to "100 Questions and Answers About Arab Americans," a handbook published by the Detroit Free Press, is an example of a word whose misuse irritates Arab people:

> "A sheik can be the leader of a family, a village, a tribe or a mosque. Press accounts popularized the term 'oil-rich sheik.' This contributed to the misconception that the people who became wealthy from oil were sheiks and that sheiks had oil money. Neither is true."[1]

Such terms as *cult* and *fundamentalist* also should be used with care. *Cult,* for example, has various meanings, according to "A Guide to Religion Reporting in the Secular Media." Some of those meanings are "value-neutral," and others are not. One is "a religion that is unorthodox or spurious."

> "Some religions that are now considered mainstream, such as the Church of Jesus Christ of Latter-day Saints, began as persecuted 'cults.' Other groups that became synonymous with 'cult,' such as the People's Temple of the Rev. Jim Jones, began as a respected progressive Christian congregation headed by an ordained minister with the Disciples of Christ, a mainline Protestant denomination."[2]

Some Christians now feel that the term *fundamentalist*, which historically referred to a Christian movement that stressed a literal interpretation of the Bible, is now derogatory, according to the guide.[3]

Such words as *cult* and *fundamentalist* can be used in newspaper reporting, but they should be used carefully, when they are appropriate. News organizations have a responsibility—and an opportunity – to retard the spread of imprecision in sensitive areas. Guides such as the two just mentioned are readily available, and if news organizations do not have copies, individual copy editors can get them.

FAD WORDS, OVERUSED WORDS AND WORDS BEST NOT USED

In a monthly newsletter to the staff, Jack Hart, managing editor and former writing coach of The Oregonian, often pointed out the overuse of the latest term *du jour*. He supported his criticism by using the search capabilities of his newspaper's archive system to document how many times a given term had been used in recent months. Terms and turns of phrase such as *the mother of all . . .* and *Not!* can become instant clichés. A simple count of how many times such terms appeared, as Hart would report, makes the point very well. As in headline writing, fad terms can be clever if used very sparingly. But when they appear often, they simply read like a joke you've heard over and over.

Clichés are particularly troublesome, because one person's cliché is often another's clever turn of phrase. Same with metaphor, literary allusion and arcane or highbrow words. New York Times columnist Maureen Dowd is a very good, clever and readable writer, but many of her columns include at least one word that is simply too arcane for breakfast-table reading. In a column that appeared in April 2002, she wrote:

> Three decades after feminism blossomed in a giddy wave of bra-burning, birth-control pills and unisex clothes, the female ideal of having it all is a risible cliché.

Risible means *laughable* or *ludicrous*. To me the word *laughable* fits the context, but either word would have been fine depending on what Dowd intended to say. Using the highly uncommon word *risible* cloaks that intention and may simply appear odd to many readers, including many of the New York intelligentsia who read The New York Times. One danger in using accurate but rarely used words is that people won't understand them. A second is that readers might think the writer is showing off. If you want people to read what you have to say, you don't want them to pause and scratch their heads or drive them to a dictionary.

James Kilpatrick in a May 2002 column makes a similar point: One writes for an audience. "Without a shared vocabulary," Kilpatrick writes, "communication bogs down in mystification and misunderstandings." A writer, as well as an editor, must know the vocabulary of the audience, and a general newspaper audience does not use the word *risible*. In a February 2003 column, Kilpatrick raises the issue again. He mentions examples from newspaper writing, including one that refers to Saddam Hussein as "an epigone" of Joseph Stalin. The word *epigone* means "a second-rate imitator," but how many readers would know that unless they reached for a dictionary? John McIntyre, copy chief of The (Baltimore) Sun, makes the same point about literary allusion and other often bad ideas. A session called "That Crepuscular Light: Descriptive Language and Metaphor" that he has presented several times at American Copy Editors Society annual meetings offers many examples of writers whose reach sometimes exceeds their grasp, including the one who used the term *crepuscular light* in a story.

Wording issues can lead to difficult interactions between editors and writers.

McIntyre, in notes for the session, says:

> "One of an editor's most delicate tasks is dealing with a writer who has fallen in love with a lead, an image or a metaphor that is completely unsuitable. . . . When you are accused of 'draining the life from the story' or 'interfering with

the writer's voice,' you must be prepared to offer clear and compelling support for your objections."

Writers do not use words such as *risible* or literary allusions lightly. They intend to use them. Perhaps they like the sound. Maybe they want other people to like them too. Changing such words is an area of copy editing in which discussion is needed, and sometimes copy editors will lose the argument. Both parties may agree to disagree. But copy editors should make the attempt. When they win, the embarrassment they save will be the reporter's and the newspaper's.

PROBLEMS WITH NUMBERS

Journalists are notoriously math-phobic, a touchy situation in light of the important role numbers play in the news. Several books, such as "Innumeracy" and "A Mathematician Looks at the News" by John Allen Paulos,[4] discuss this problem. Innumeracy, to be blunt, is the inability of highly educated journalists to understand numbers as well as reasonably bright sixth-graders can. The Dow Jones Newspaper Fund's national copy editing test always includes errors involving numbers. Chances are good that most daily newspapers contain at least one math error, and probably more, each day.

Some of the biggest stumbling blocks are the simplest things. Failing to check the count in a list of names is a common mistake. A lead says 16 students from Jefferson High School were National Merit Scholars. The story lists 15 names. Are there only 15 finalists, or did the reporter miss one in compiling the list? In a small town, that's a big deal. In a big town too. One can only answer the question if one asks it. One can only ask it if one counts the names and compares the total to the lead. The first rule of editing numbers is count what you can count. Always.

Another simple mistake is technically not even a "math" mistake, though it involves numbers. Too often a reported number is inconsistent between a story and a graphic or a story and a photo. In a story about the impact of a sales tax, one newspaper said Family X would pay $190 more; the accompanying graphic said $210. How does this happen? It may be a case of a story being updated with new information or a reporter catching a miscalculation and forgetting to pass it on to the graphic artist. It could be a simple transcription error. Here the issue is not math so much as paying attention and catching numerical inconsistencies.

Writers often make simple math mistakes in adding, multiplying and figuring percentages. Sometimes they (or their editors) make a bigger mistake by assuming that somebody else, perhaps the source of the information, did the math correctly. The corollary to the first rule of editing numbers is as follows: Always do the math yourself. Add what you can add, calculate percentages when you can. If you have a sentence such as the following, do the math:

> The United Way of Jefferson County has awarded $23,000 in supplemental funds to three agencies. The additional funds will go to the Boy Scouts ($11,000), the Girl Scouts ($9,000), and the Salvation Army ($4,000).

Does it add up?

If a story says that a battle over preserving a Civil War battlefield is raging 150 years after the war ended, do the math. That date won't occur until the year 2015.

Big numbers sometimes lead to big mistakes. Few people have an intuitive grasp of the difference between billions and hundreds of millions, or even tens of millions. It's much easier to spot problems with hundreds or thousands because it's easier to visualize them and to understand their magnitude. Cars cost thousands of dollars; bikes hundreds. College tuition costs thousands (or tens of thousands); airline tickets cost hundreds, maybe thousands on that vacation of a lifetime or if you miss the advance-purchase deadline.

Numbers of that magnitude are part of everyday life. The difference between hundreds of thousands and millions, or between millions and tens of millions, is not so easily grasped. Most people don't deal in numbers of that magnitude. But many stories do, such as budget stories at the local, state and national level. Legislation comes with price tags that can range from millions to billions (or more). In stories about federal spending, copy editors might do well to recall the quote often attributed to former U.S. Sen. Everett Dirksen about the federal budget: "A billion here, a billion there, and pretty soon it adds up to real money."[5] "Billions" in such stories may be petty cash. On the local government level, billions are probably too much, unless it's for a large city. It takes a pretty big city to have a billion-dollar budget. Big numbers are all over the newspaper. They are corporate earnings and losses, sales and revenue figures, athletes' salaries, the cost of a new federal courthouse or hospital, the dollar value of mega-mergers and many others. Copy editors should develop an educated skepticism about numbers in general, and they can develop a sixth sense about big numbers, an "it doesn't sound right" mentality.

PERCENTAGES

Percentage mistakes seem to have increased a hundredfold. Some are simple math errors, reflecting use of the wrong number as the base.

> Since the 1960s, the Oregon Institute of Technology has continued to grow. With an enrollment of 2,679—almost 30 percent larger than Eastern Oregon's 1,900 students—OIT has played a more and more prominent role in the community.

Remember the corollary to the first rule of editing numbers. If you can do the math yourself, do it. In the previous sentence, you have everything you need. Subtract 1,900 from 2,679 and get 779. Now what? The reporter guessed wrong, dividing 779 by 2,679. That yields .29, or almost 30 percent. But that's not what the sentence is saying. If the issue is how much *larger* OIT is, the base is 1,900, the smaller school's enrollment. Dividing 779 by 1,900 gives .41. The sentence should have read "more than 40 percent larger than Eastern Oregon's 1,900 students." It would also be correct to say that Eastern Oregon's enrollment is almost 30 percent *smaller* than OIT's, but because the story focuses on OIT, that would be the wrong comparison.

The other common mistake is the failure to differentiate between *percentage* and *percentage point*. If your state has a 5 percent income tax, and a legislative coalition has proposed raising it to 6, you should not say that the group is asking for "a 1 percent increase" in the tax. The coalition is proposing a 1 percentage point increase, which translates to a 20 percent increase in dollars. That is a big deal. The Dow Jones test often includes a percentage/percentage point mistake because those mistakes occur frequently. Here are two examples that appeared in newspapers:

> Already threatened with a proposed 0.5 percent utility tax increase, the city's water users face a possible rate increase of 63 percent by 2005.

> American Express announced that its OMNI Card will carry an ad-

> justable rate set monthly at 4 percent above the prime rate. Ameri-
> can Express said this would put the Omni card in line with other
> variable-rate cards.

Common sense goes a long way in catching these errors. In the first example, 0.5 percent has to be 0.5 percentage points. A 0.5 percent increase is
insignificant in the context of most anything, but particularly utility taxes,
which often are in single digits. The other clue is the 63 percent figure. An
increase of 0.5 percent is a much different order of magnitude than 63 percent; it doesn't make sense to speak of them in the same sentence. The
second example makes the same mistake. If a company offered a card
whose rate is only 4 percent above the prime, it would not be in business
very long. It has to be 4 percentage points above the prime. Do the math,
then ask the reporter.

It is also important to know what you don't know about numbers and
where to find out. Editors often deal with stories written about surveys. For
comprehensiveness, poll results often require other numbers, such as the
number of people polled and the margin of error.

Figures often need other figures to put them in context, as longtime
Texas editing professor Martin "Red" Gibson used to say. Gibson offered
the following example in a column:[6]

> Thirty-three percent of Vassar's first female students married pro-
> fessors.

The statement is true, but what question do you need to ask? How many
female students were in the first class? Three. One married a professor. Percentages sometimes require raw numbers for interpretation, because percentages can be misleading when the raw numbers are low.

AVERAGES

The average is a commonly used statistic, and it often can stand on its
own. But it can be misleading. Consider the following: A real estate agency
has 10 salespeople. One primarily sells expensive homes and makes $3,250
a week; nine others make $750 each. Is the average $1,000 a week an appropriate statistic to use? It really describes none of the 10 very well. The
"outlier," the superseller who extends the range, skews the average. It

would be better to report the average of the nine and point out that the 10th makes a great deal more money.

Another statistic that summarizes a set of numbers is the *median*, the point at which half of the cases are below and half above. The median is not used as extensively as the average, but it does appear often in such contexts as income and housing. It is often used to describe housing prices in a community because a small number of houses on the very high end can skew an average significantly. The same is true with incomes.

Students and professionals who think they've avoided math by going into journalism have miscalculated—badly. Math mistakes are job security for copy editors, and good copy editors are expected to catch them

TRADE NAMES

Another precision issue is the reporting of trade names. Owners of trademarks must be vigilant in protecting their property, or else they risk losing exclusive use. For this reason, news organizations might hear from a lawyer when they loosely use the word *Frisbee*, a trade name held by the Wham-O Corp. that is properly used (with an uppercase "F") only to refer to a specific product made by that company. Most people probably recognize Xerox as a trademark, and many realize that it is improper to say someone *xeroxed* a report. But there are others, such as Sheetrock, Magnum and Plexiglas, that appear in everyday speech and seem to be part of the language but still are trademarks. Other terms, such as linoleum and trampoline, once were trademarks and no longer are. Newspapers that care about precision preserve the distinctions that are made in law, using trademark terms when they specifically refer to the products and not when they don't. The AP Stylebook mentions some of the most abused examples; the Trade Names Directory is a more general source. A helpful trademark Web site is the INTA Trademark Checklist (www.inta.org/tmcklst1.htm), developed by the International Trademark Association.

CLARITY

Lack of clarity is indefensible. The point of journalism is to enhance understanding, not to muddy the water. Words or concepts that appear in type should be clear; phrasing and sentence structure should be clear; basic facts should be clear; and context should be clear. Ensuring clarity is one of the most important word-editing functions of copy editors. To perform this task well, though, requires a different strategy than ensuring accuracy does. At the level of clarity, one must approach the story not as a detective but as a typical reader. This approach is one of the most difficult, because copy editors work with other journalists and tend to think as the others do. An editor should strive to read as readers would, not as a journalist might. If readers would scratch their heads at an explanation or description or pause at technical jargon, an editor should raise a flag and seek clarification. If readers would pause, back up a few paragraphs and reread, that's a cue for an editor to analyze what is confusing and take steps to clarify. Here are two versions of a lead:

> SALEM, Ore.—Oregon schools' scholastic improvements are coming despite less operating funds, according to State School Superintendent Norma Paulus.

> SALEM, Ore.—Oregon schools are improving scholastically even though operating funds have declined, said State School Superintendent Norma Paulus.

The original is understandable though somewhat awkward, and clumsiness almost always makes a sentence less clear than it can be. The recast is minor but effective. The following example shows more serious wording issues:

> SALEM, Ore.—A worker helping to renovate the earthquake-damaged rotunda at the Oregon Capitol slipped from a scaffolding near the top of the dome and crashed onto another 90 feet above the floor.
> Robert G. Sims, 51, suffered only bruises in the 6-foot fall, but it took firefighters more than two hours to reach him.
> Getting to Sims was no easy task, said Battalion Chief Bob Davis of the Salem Fire Department.
> "It's got scaffolding floor to ceiling," Davis said. "That makes it difficult for us. There's no free space to maneuver."
> The firefighters used ropes, pulleys and mountain-climbing equipment.
> Sims' fall was broken somewhat when a fellow worker reached out for him.
> Renovation began last month to repair damage caused by an earthquake on March 25, 1993.

Reading the lead once is not enough. Reading it twice doesn't help much either. What exactly happened? How far did the worker actually fall? The second sentence attempts to clarify by mentioning "the 6-foot fall," but the lead is so confusing that the clarification gets lost in the noise. It is possible to puzzle out what happened, but readers who want to solve puzzles turn to the cryptogram. They deserve better in the news columns.

Here's a better way to start:

> SALEM, Ore.—A worker slipped off a scaffold near the top of the Oregon Capitol Rotunda and fell six feet, landing on a second scaffold 90 feet above the floor.
> Robert G. Sims, 51, who was renovating the earthquake-damaged section of the dome, suffered only bruises, but it took firefighters more than two hours to reach him.

The key is to use the word *scaffold* twice in the lead for clarity. Some writers resist using the same word twice in the same sentence. Repetition of a word often is unnecessary because synonyms can be used or because the passage can be crafted without the repetition. In this example, there really is no commonly used synonym for *scaffold*, so the solution is to use the word twice.

Unclarity in leads is a particular problem, one that is difficult to fathom. Because most writers spend a disproportionate time writing the lead, one would expect the lead to be the clearest paragraph in the story. Problems tend to occur because the reporter tries to do too much, perhaps add too much description, background or context, which can twist a straightforward subject–verb–object construction into something that looks like a corn maze at eye level.

Here's an example from an AP story that was published in many papers in February 2002:

> WASHINGTON—Seated in a circle, Democratic House leaders listening intently, former employees of Enron poured out the details of their layoffs, their depleted retirement savings and their bleak financial futures.

To understand the point of the story, it really doesn't matter who was sitting in a circle: the House leaders, the former Enron employees or both groups. But using it draws a reader's attention, and as in daycare centers, not all attention is good attention. Confusion that is not muddying the main point is still confusion, and it may serve to divert a reader's focus from what the story is actually trying to say. Assuming that I have interpreted the lead correctly, an assumption that a copy editor should never make, the following would be better:

> WASHINGTON—As Democratic House leaders listened intently, former employees of Enron poured out the details of their layoffs, their depleted retirement savings and their bleak financial futures.

It loses the descriptive detail but gains clarity. The image of the former employees sitting in a circle can easily be worked into a subsequent paragraph. That is the point one should make when discussing such a lead change with the reporter.

CLUTTER

Journalistic writing should be tight. Unnecessary words can get in the way of meaning. Here are some wordy sentences and tighter sentences that make the same points:

> Middleton ended his talk to the audience with a joke.
>
> Middleton ended with a joke.
>
> The Franklin Award could have gone to either of the two youths.
>
> The Franklin Award could gave gone to either youth.

The following sentence can be reduced to four words without loss of meaning:

> Discussion centered on the topic of wilderness survival.
>
> They discussed wilderness survival.

Sometimes stories are just overwritten:

> Dallas was the leading city in the state of Texas in the number of murders recorded last year, according to FBI information released this morning.
> The information was detailed by the bureau in its Uniform

> Crime Reports, which are released quarterly. Dallas was listed in first place in Texas and fourth in the nation in the number of murders committed, with 346 murdered in the calendar year covered by the FBI report.

The following, which is less than half as long, says everything the original does.

> Dallas led the state in murders, the FBI reported yesterday.
> The bureau's quarterly Uniform Crime Reports also listed the city fourth in the nation, with 346 murders last year.

Copy editors also can tighten up passages with lengthy quotes by keeping the best parts of the quotes and paraphrasing or summarizing the rest (see Chapter 5).

Tight writing doesn't mean telegraphic writing. Spoken and written English is full of redundancy. If that were not true, it would be impossible to write headlines, which often have to convey the essence of a 25-word statement in four or five words. Good copy editors learn to trust their ear, removing unnecessary wording and leaving in words and phrases that might not be crucial for comprehension but that help the flow.

ACTIVE VOICE AND PASSIVE VOICE

Reporting textbooks and English teachers admonish writers to use active voice whenever possible. It's good advice. Passive voice often makes a sentence weak by shifting perspective from the person or institution that takes the action to the person or institution that receives the action. Many sentences cast in passive voice unnecessarily back into the point and may lead readers to pause for a moment to reflect on the meaning. Because passive voice can weaken the thought, it can lead to a mild erosion of clarity. The stronger the sentence, the clearer the sentence.

> Highway 140 from Lakeview to the Nevada border was closed Thursday afternoon because of heavy smoke caused by major fires in Nevada.

> Heavy smoke forced officials to close Highway 140 from Lakeview to the Nevada border Thursday afternoon. The smoke came from major fires in Nevada.

> A bid was made by Thurston Conservation District officials to per-
> suade three nearby communities to join the district.

> The Thurston Conservation District is trying to persuade three
> nearby communities to join the organization.

Some sentences, however, are better stated in passive.

> Police arrested Adam Smith, president of Capitalistic Financial
> Services, at Logan Airport, just before he was to board a plane to
> Europe.

> Adam Smith, president of Capitalistic Financial Services, was ar-
> rested at Logan Airport just before he was to board a plane for Eu-
> rope.

In cases such as this—indeed, in many crime reports—the receiver of the
action is more important than the actor (the police or "authorities"). It is a
rare event when police or other law enforcement officials are not the ar-
resting agents. "Adam Smith . . . was arrested" places the horse before the
cart, where it belongs.

TIPS AND STRATEGIES

• Keep all levels in mind. Copy editors often miss precision errors,
particular math errors, because they focus too closely on other things. This
example from a Dow Jones copy editing test several years ago demonstrates
the pitfall (and probably kept a number of test takers from qualifying for internships):

> A Transnational Airlines jetliner crashed shortly after takeoff in
> Philadelphia last night, injuring 17 and killing seven, including the
> pilot.
> A Federal Aviation Administration spokesman said the pilot,
> whose name was not released suffered an apparent heart attack
> as the plane took off.
> The spokesman said that the pilot had flown more than the
> FAA maximum of 1,000 hours a month. Obviously, that could have

been a factor," he said. "But we are just beginning our investigation and we won't have any definate answers for some time."[7]

This short exercise has plenty of problems, including several punctuation mistakes and a spelling error (*definite*, not *definate*). Beyond those, it would make more sense to put the deaths before the injuries in the lead, and it is impossible to suffer an "apparent" heart attack. A person might apparently suffer a heart attack. But most students (and most test takers, no doubt) miss the math problem because they are focusing intently on the leaves and ignoring the trees. The FAA "maximum" of 1,000 hours a month is the problem. Nobody can fly 1,000 hours in a month. Why not? If you do the math, you'll see.

• Once again, look out for the two-error problem. If you catch a glaring problem in taste or sensitivity, don't forget to watch out for the grammar, spelling or style mistake in the same sentence.

• Watch your language. Taste often is in the eye of the beholder, but because newspapers serve many different types of reader, copy editors should be careful about gratuitous obscenities. Because of generational differences and changing cultural norms, a word that makes one person cringe doesn't even raise another's eyebrow. Many reporters and copy editors are young adults who think nothing of soft-core obscenities, which they have heard in songs and on TV sitcoms for years. People have a tendency to write and edit for people like themselves. Newspaper readers, however, are much older on average than the staff members writing and editing the paper. A casual use of a word such as "damn," which is relatively innocuous to a 24-year-old, might offend many 54- or 64-year-olds.

Ask yourself how your parents or grandparents would react to the word. Ask yourself if the word is necessary or gratuitous.

News organizations often have written policies about the use of obscenities. In general, the more crude an obscenity, the higher the editor who must approve it. One egregious breach of policy at a metropolitan newspaper caused the managing editor to tell the metropolitan editor: "I may be a bullshit editor, but you're just a goddamn editor."

• Keep learning. An excellent place to learn about precision and language issues is the syndicated column written weekly by James Kilpatrick. Every copy editor should consider the column required reading. Many copy editors become students of language, and they can act as teachers too, helping colleagues understand both the history and the current connotations of words.

Other ways to improve in the area of precision are to take it from experts. A book that can help with writing clarity is "On Writing Well" by William Zinsser.[8] A good reference on issues of sexism in writing is "The Handbook of Nonsexist Writing" by Casey Miller and Kate Swift.[9] Two books that explain how to report polls are "The Newsroom Guide to Polls and Surveys" by David Weaver and "The New Precision Journalism" by Philip Meyer.[10]

A couple of clearinghouse web sites aimed at editors and reporters can help in the search. One is the resource page "Words on Words" on the American Copy Editors Society Web site (http://www.copydesk.org/words). This page has links to many tip sheets on clarity, wording, number problems and other aspects of the copy editor's craft. The Poynter Web site (http://www.poynter.org) also is an excellent resource.

5

Logic and Form

To edit for logic and form, copy editors needs to shift their focus from the trees back out to the forest. Here one encounters such issues as what background is necessary and when does the reader need it? Does the story follow? Is it internally consistent? Does it make sense? Does the bottom support the lead; do facts deep in the story contradict generalizations made up high? Does it deliver less (or more) than it promises in the lead?

Is the structure appropriate? Does the delayed lead work, or is it gratuitous? Would a straight, inverted-pyramid treatment serve readers better? Would a more creative lead work better than a straight lead? Does that dramatic tale distilled into the lead anecdote offer the right window into the story, or is it an extreme case chosen for shock value? If the latter, might it be misleading? Is the story written for insiders or for the general public?

The degree of attention that copy editors pay to issues at this level is one characteristic that sets very-well-edited papers apart from the rest. It is an area that often gets short shrift, though, for a variety of reasons. Many copy editors become mired in minutiae, or the unwritten rules of newsroom culture might discourage copy editors from raising questions at this level, or deadline pressures are too great to allow copy editors to spend time looking for bigger problems. Broader questions should be addressed before a story reaches the copy desk, but many problems with logic, organization, consistency and thoroughness still slide through originating desks, shoot through the copy desk and appear in print. Copy editors who treat this level as part of their responsibility will be greater assets to their publications and to the readers.

BACKGROUND

What does the reader need to know, and when does the reader need to know it? How much background is enough? Where does the background need to be placed? Formulas do not work well here. Questions must be answered on a case-by-case basis. On the Web, news organizations can link to extensive background information if they choose to do so. Print has no such luxury. There is not enough space to explain everything, and reporters and editors need to make decisions about what readers need to know to understand stories.

What background is essential depends to a degree on the readership and the section where the story will appear. But assuming too much reader knowledge can be a trap; it is unwise to assume that everyone in a community knows enough about what went on *before* to understand what's going on *now*. Many newcomers look first to a local newspaper for information about the community. They might not know, for example, that Jane Shippen was the mayor for 20 years until she retired in 1987 or that the town where they now live once was a stop on the Underground Railroad or once served as the state capital.

The readership of a magazine about aviation will know far more about the basics of piloting an aircraft than your mother, father, brother or neighbor likely would. So an article about the safety of ultralight aircraft would not require the same level of background in a specialty publication as it would in one that reaches a wider audience. Newspaper departments, such as a business staff or an education team, often develop great expertise in their areas, and they sometimes forget that potential readers do not have the same store of background knowledge that their regular readers might have. Departmental reporters who write for various subaudiences of "initiates" run a risk of marginalizing themselves to the general reading public. "Inside baseball," whether on the sports pages, the business pages or the food section, invites some readers to simply turn to the next, more inviting, section.

A related danger occurs when reporters become too close to a subject and assume that readers know it as well as they do. Reporters who have covered a beat for years—the environment, the public school system, the

Statehouse, etc.—often tend to assume that their readers are as familiar with the subject as they are. Their stories may tend to take on an "insider" cast. Copy editors who think of themselves as surrogates for readers can help solve the problem by raising the same questions readers would.

Many problems with the placement of background are really logic problems. To understand B, you need to know A, but A appears too far down into the story. Most are easy to solve. Here's an example from a story that ran in a college newspaper:

> Most English-speaking people don't realize they use Arabic on a regular basis.
> Chemistry students use the word *alkaline* when referring to a chemical with a pH greater than 7. Alcohol and algebra were developed by Arabic people.
> Beginning winter term, a three-credit class in beginning standard Arabic will be offered by the linguistics department, taught by a native speaker. Abed Khooli, a physics graduate teaching fellow from the West Bank, is planning the class. . . .

The story, which uses a short feature-style lead to top a routine news story about a new language-course offering, continues for five paragraphs before answering the question implicit in the lead: How exactly do English-speaking people use Arabic? If it is important enough to hook the reader in a lead, it is important enough to explain—quickly. Here's the answer:

> English has borrowed several Arabic terms over the centuries, many of them beginning with the prefix *al-*, which is equivalent to the word *the*.

That sentence should have appeared immediately after the second paragraph.

Here's an example from a Washington state newspaper:

> The state Department of Licensing will try again to find someone to study what should be done now that the LAMP computer project has been terminated.
> Department of Licensing officials announced Friday that they will again request proposals on a $939,400 study to find out what can be salvaged from the debris of the project and how the Legislature and Gov. Gary Locke's administration should proceed.

> The department thought it had a successful bidder earlier this month. . . .

The story was 12 paragraphs long. The following was the 11th:

> LAMP stands for Licensing Application Migration Project and was designed to combine licenses for drivers, vehicles and vessels into one computer system.

That paragraph would be helpful much higher in the story. A reporter might disagree, pointing out that this is the 15th story written on the LAMP problem in the last year. A copy editor should point out that even so, some readers will not know the background and that they will not have a clear understanding of the issue until they hit that second-to-last paragraph. A reporter who covers a government agency for a lengthy period becomes as knowledgeable about the workings of the department as staff members are. It's easy to bury the sentence of background or to omit it altogether. Editors who read with an independent eye can spot these problems and solve them quickly.

Here's an example from the same paper of placing relevant background right where it belongs:

> Olympia is considering ways to give developers breathing room to pay sometimes heavy impact fees.
> The fees, which are controversial with builders, must be paid when a building permit is issued. They can amount to several thousand dollars on a housing project.
> The Community Planning and Development Department has proposed a system that would allow payments to be deferred as long as 18 months. . . .

Developers understand impact fees, but many readers might not be familiar with the concept. The reporter who crafted that second paragraph, or perhaps the editor who moved it higher in the story, thought of those readers. Some writers might balk at placing a background paragraph immediately after the lead, arguing that it might get in the way of new information. It certainly is not necessary to place background so high all of the time. But in a case such as this one, a reader needs to understand impact fees in order to make sense of the story, and the background, rather than getting in the way, enhances comprehension.

A similar problem often occurs in specialized coverage, say of sports or business. Reporters assume that their readers understand key terms. A financial reporter tosses around such terms as *derivatives* and *rollovers*. A sportswriter casually mentions the *reserve clause* in a baseball story or *doping* in a bicycle racing report. Regular readers of the section might understand the terms; many others won't. There's no better way to keep readership of a specialized section stagnant than writing as if the readers were members of the same priesthood as the sources (and the reporters).

How much background is too much? A newspaper can assume that readers have some background knowledge of an issue or a news event, but it's a tricky line. It varies from story to story and community to community, and it can change on an ongoing story. An ongoing story about a controversy over a proposed expressway that would cut through sensitive wetlands does not need to include all of the relevant background about route and which species are threatened each time the story is updated. The fifth-day story on a forest fire might not need to explain some of the same terms that previous stories clarified. Common sense helps.

In coverage of forest fires in the summer of 2002, a community named Show Low appeared prominently in national news reports over a period of more than a week. How many people wondered why the community had such a strange name? Several days into the story, AP reports began mentioning that the community was named after a play in a card game. In the big picture, it was much more important to report the fire's progress, the number of people evacuated, the number of homes burned, the acreage involved, the cost of firefighting, and so on. But dropping that little bit of background about Show Low into the story helped too. It took only a few words, but it answered a question that probably caused many readers to pause momentarily, asking themselves if the name was just wrong, or simply wondering why that name. The best advice I've heard on the issue of background came from an AP writing coach, who said writers and editors should err on the side of too much. "If a reader already knows the background, she'll skip it," the coach said during a regional workshop. "If a reader doesn't know the background, he'll thank you for it."

CONSISTENCY

Consistency is both a micro and a macro issue in editing. At the micro level, style, spelling, names and numbers can be inconsistent. Those problems are relatively easy to notice and fix. At the story level, inconsistency is more difficult to catch. The key skills are memory and logic. A copy editor who can recall assertions and generalizations made at the top of a story, even a very long story, is in a better position to spot problems in the middle or at the bottom, or even between today's story and the one that ran last week on the same subject. A good memory makes copy editing more efficient, but memory can be augmented by simple approaches, such as taking notes while copy editing and checking later. An editor can jot down areas that need to be confirmed and assertions that need to be supported lower in the story. Logic helps a copy editor detect flaws in argument, for example, when a source's statement contradicts a generalization made earlier or perhaps another source's comments. News stories are not usually constructed as arguments, the way essays or opinion pieces are. But it is possible to look at them in such terms: Does B follow A? Does B contradict A? If it does, is the contradiction explained or at least acknowledged?

One of the chief areas of inconsistency at the story level is a discrepancy between a generalization and supporting information or between an assertion and the facts that back it up. An example might be a strong statement made in a quote that is left without corroborating evidence, or worse, that is contradicted by what comes later without any explanation of the contradiction. It can be a broad statement in the *nut graf*—the short section in many feature stories that summarizes the focus—that is contradicted or qualified by information later in the story. A retrospective story about a major storm says at the top, "It was the most expensive hurricane in history." Later, you find out that the storm was the most expensive in U.S. history, and then only if you ignore the effect of inflation. A story says a representative is the "only" official to have been expelled from the legislature in the state's history when he does not have that dubious distinction—a state senator was removed from office 50 years earlier. Journalists tend to focus on the present and sometimes ignore history. Generalizations that invite historical comparison can be questioned and checked. Be extra careful that superlatives are not exaggerations. Things that are described as *biggest, fastest, longest, widest, deadliest,* and so on, all can be checked. It's surprising how often they aren't true and aren't checked.

Inconsistency can appear between promise and delivery. Such problems often show up between the lead and the body, or between the *establishing section*, where a summary statement is presented, and the *body*, where little or no detail supports the statement. The nut graf says researchers are only a few years away from human cloning; scientists are quoted 30 inches lower saying that it could happen in a few years but likely will take much longer.

A third area of inconsistency can occur between tone and topic. An example might be an inappropriately flip or clever treatment of a serious subject, or even a lone comment in a very long piece. A story marking the hundred-year anniversary of the invention of the escalator includes a throwaway line near the top that says escalators never make the news until they "squish" someone. It's fair to ask whether that flip comment about a less-than-humorous occurrence is consistent with the rest of the story. It is also fair to ask whether it is in good taste.

NEWS JUDGMENT AND EDITING

Another way to look at much of what copy editors do at this level is through the lens of news judgment. The term *news judgment* is typically understood as a set of principles applied to coverage by assigning editors and news editors, not necessarily copy editors. It refers to decisions made about what gets covered, how extensively it gets covered and where it is placed in the paper. Will it be a long story that begins on Page One, or a brief on 6-B?

Some news judgments will be near-universal. The Sept. 11 attack on the World Trade Center and its aftermath dominated front pages everywhere in the country. But news judgment differs, depending on the size of the paper, its mission and its readership. The choices made by the Press-Enterprise, a small daily in Bloomsburg, Pa., and The New York Times will be different because they serve different readerships. In Bloomsburg and other small towns, the emphasis will be on local news, local sports and local features. Stories involving the state university in Bloomsburg will get strong play, because the university is the dominant institution in the small community. Major national and international news will be covered through wire service and syndicated copy. The New York Times also will cover its region, including its higher education institutions when they are newsworthy, but it will play national and international news more prominently, and most of those stories will be written by Times staff members and correspondents.

Copy editors sometimes share this level of news decision-making. If they act as department editors or wire editors, they make decisions on coverage and play. If they don't, they still can act as a check by raising questions. Copy editors can ask why a medical breakthrough that might affect millions of people or a story about a toxic waste plume underneath a suburban elementary school is buried on Page 17-A or 4-B, while a fluff piece on a stuffed animal craze is anchoring the bottom of Page One. Or why there is no locator map to accompany the story about a wildfire that is threatening several communities in the state. Or they can ask why in a three-way race, there are only two head shots and the one that's missing is of the black candidate. There could be a reason: the candidate's photo is not in the paper's archives, and it's too late to go out and shoot one. But readers will still wonder why the candidate's picture is missing, and some will accuse the paper of racism if all three photos aren't published. Copy editors can look at news judgment as a reader might and call attention to potentially embarrassing problems.

Another aspect of news judgment is more directly in the copy editor's court. Copy editors should exercise news judgment within stories, when they edit stories. News judgment includes weighing whether a story is fair, appropriate in length, focused and balanced. Critical thinking is the key, and copy editors apply it in a variety of contexts, from the word level to the story level. For example, a copy editor should ask: Is the lead appropriate? Does it crystallize the essence of the news immediately? If it doesn't, is a softer or more indirect approach justified, or does it seem to have no real purpose? If the lead is an anecdote, is it an appropriate anecdote for the story, or is it hyped? Is the lead in good taste, or is it a throwaway designed to attract attention but has nothing to do with the story? These questions and others like them are primarily questions for reporters and assigning editors to discuss, but copy editors should also exercise their own judgment and give them another, independent, look. Some of the worst problems with leads can be addressed if they do. For example, here is a wire service lead:

> SAN FRANCISCO—The city that has opened its arms to same-sex couples, AIDS patients and medical marijuana users isn't doing the same thing for fuzzy ferrets—at least not legally.

A copy editor exercising news judgment will ask, What do same-sex couples, AIDS patients and medical marijuana users have to do with ferrets? The answer clearly is "nothing." The lead was an offbeat idea, a throwaway that didn't work, and it is the copy editor's responsibility to point it out.

If the focus of the story is about a controversy or a dispute, does the structure of the story attempt to provide balance? Does it, for example, allow one side to have its say for the bulk of the story and diminish the importance of opposing voices by cursory coverage of their views or by relegating their comments to the end of the story? If the story is about a proposal to close a school because of changing demographics in a school district, does the story overemphasize heart-wrenching comments from parents about the loss to the community and underemphasize comments from school board officials that explain the school's costly maintenance problems and the economics of the decision? Anecdotes give life to a story, but too many anecdotes or too many one-sided anecdotes and comments can create an impression in readers' minds that is difficult to counter. Copy editors who watch for such problems are exercising news judgment.

FORM OF THE STORY

Reporting texts discuss stories from the perspective of the writer. What type of lead to use? What overall structure works best? How should the story end? Copy editors can ask the same questions, but they should try to put themselves in the reader's place. Do the lead, structure and ending make sense, given the focus and the information gathered? Does the story read? Does it flow?

A reporter, often in consultation with the assigning editor, chooses a form for a story. It might be a traditional inverted pyramid, an anecdotal lead/feature approach, or an "hourglass" in which the top begins with a summary lead and then shifts to a chronology. The copy editor's role is to look at the story with an independent eye and ask, "Does the form work? Is it appropriate to the material?" The idea is not to encroach on the writer's turf but to provide a service more like one of the "checks and balances" found in the governmental system.

Questions copy editors will ask themselves while reading for form vary depending on the type of story. Here are some issues to keep in mind:

NEWS STORIES

For news stories, should the lead be "hard" or "soft"? Should the lead focus on the main point of the story, as a traditional summary lead does, or can it be delayed, following an anecdote or a contrast?

If it's a summary lead, is the most important information there? Does the lead try to convey too much information? Does it get to the point quickly, or does it delay the reader with a long, contextual introductory phrase or clause that could easily be saved for the second or third sentence? Several of the largest newspapers in the country write leads that are 50 percent context and 50 percent new information. Is that the right percentage? Sometimes that approach is appropriate; many, many times it isn't.

The following lead places the news second and the context first:

> Despite the deepest diplomatic rift in decades with some major European allies, a parade of top Bush administration officials closed ranks Thursday and demanded in closely parallel speeches and statements that Saddam Hussein disarm Iraq.

A reporter might argue that the context is important and belongs first. A copy editor certainly has the right to raise a question about it. Here's the lead on a sidebar story about the Democratic reaction the day after President Bush gave his 2003 State of the Union speech:

> Spurred by polls showing President Bush's popularity slipping, Democrats on Tuesday challenged his assessment of the state of the union with a boldness and bite that was unthinkable when he last addressed a joint session of Congress one year ago.

A copy editor might reasonably ask whether the context in this case is more important than the gist of the story—that the Democrats sharply challenged Bush. A reporter might say that the "why" of the Democrats' action is very important and makes their behavior more understandable. Fair enough, but a copy editor might also point out that the structure of the lead raises a second question: Is the lead supported? The story said very little about polls and the president's popularity. One sentence deep in the story was about all. A copy editor should ask whether that is enough. A 20-inch story should provide some details to back up the strong suggestion in the lead that the Democrats' boldness had something to do with public opinion polls.

Here's an example from an advance story on a speech. It used a "delayed" lead:

> During his 81-year life, John Dobson has carried many titles:
> astronomer, cosmologist, inventor, theologian.
> Monday night, the internationally known speaker will answer
> the public's questions about the stars. . . .

The story, which was about 10 column inches long, talked about Dobson's experience as an astronomer and cosmologist. It said nothing more about his roles as inventor and theologian. Those two careers are unusual for an astronomer, and if they were interesting enough to place in the lead, they are interesting enough to explain in the story.

Does the lead (say of a city council story) really need to summarize several pieces of legislation introduced at the meeting, or would the story benefit from focusing on the most important action, mentioning the others briefly high in the story, and providing details on them later. Beware of a "false democracy" of ideas. Often stories are more understandable if a reporter makes a firm decision that X is more important than Y or Z. Reporting, like editing, is decision making.

Is the summary lead followed by important supporting information, or does it wander off into less important detail? If there are several secondary points beyond the focus in the lead, are they mentioned early enough, say in a summarization paragraph near the top? The classic example is a council meeting at which several major actions were taken.

Does a human voice appear in the story soon enough? If a principal source is not quoted by the third, fourth, or fifth paragraphs, why not? There might be a good reason, but it could be worth a question. What's not a good idea is to bring up a quote from the bottom without consulting with the reporter. A reporter might have intentionally placed that quote lower in the story. Quotes, as reporting textbooks point out, can be used very effectively to provide key information, to reflect deeply held feelings and to break up the monotony of long expository sections. But strong, one-sided quotes early in a story also can color a reader's perception of the entire story.

Alternatively, a copy editor might ask whether that quote in the third paragraph is too pedestrian or whether it is out of synch with the story. If the quote doesn't serve a purpose or solve a problem, should it be removed or replaced? Poorly chosen quotes can harm a story, slow it down or even make it confusing.

Does the story make sense, is there enough background, and is that background placed where it will do the most good but not get in the way of new information?

Does it follow the classic inverted-pyramid form, that is, could it be cut from the bottom if necessary? Is a fact introduced at the bottom too important to stay down so low? What if that fact were trimmed for space?

FEATURE STORIES

Is the lead inviting—and appropriate?

If the lead is an anecdote, does the anecdote work? Does it lead smoothly into the story? Is it striking but off the point? Does it mislead? Is it clear?

Take a suggestion offered by Roy Peter Clark and Don Fry in "Coaching Writers": show the anecdotal lead to someone who doesn't know what the story is about and ask that person to tell you what he or she thinks the story will be about.[1] If the answer is way off the mark, the anecdote probably isn't the best choice.

Does the lead flow clearly into a section that explains what the story will cover (known variously as a "nut graf" or "establishing section"?) Is there enough information, evidence or detail to support the generalizations in the nut graf?

Are there interesting quotes and inviting anecdotes throughout? Is description used well, or is it gratuitous? Does the story move logically and smoothly from paragraph to paragraph, or does it seem unfocused or choppy?

Does the ending work? If it's a quote, is it a good one? Does it tie back to the lead, provide a contrast, or an unexpected twist?

TREND STORIES

Trend stories are the staple of weekend papers. They are among the most interesting for reporters to write and readers to read. They explain what is happening in politics, culture, society, business or the arts in a way that print can and broadcast typically can't. Examples are:

The relaxation of standards for language in sitcoms.
The shift from football to soccer as an organized sport for children.

The problems retirees face when the stock market plummets.
The tattoo trend.
The controversy over human cloning.

Sunday and Monday morning papers are full of these stories. On those days, editors have less breaking news of politics, government and business to choose from, and there is more space, allowing for longer treatment of issues and themes.

Trend stories and longer explanatory and analytical pieces pose problems that, while like those one might find in daily breaking stories, are somewhat different because of the scope of the stories.

Copy editors should ask:

Do the examples support the trend? Are there enough examples to back up the general statements made at the top in the nut graf? One or two instances of the trend are probably not enough. Are experts (researchers, scientists, government officials, citizens who should know) quoted? Is there statistical support for generalizations that demand it? Who has studied the phenomenon? Does the information come from a reputable source, such as a rigorous scientific survey, or is it fluff, say a self-selected Web site poll that users can respond to over and over? If the story depends heavily on information from polls or surveys, does the story provide enough information about the survey, such as who paid for the survey, the size of the sample, the margin of error and other criteria that help readers determine whether a survey is solid?[2]

Another way to phrase the key issue in trend stories is: Does the story deliver on the promise made at the top?

Here is a summary paragraph from a trend story that appeared in the New York Times in early 2002:

> The sagging economy has created a bonanza of applicants for the nation's schools of business, law, journalism, education and many other graduate programs as laid-off workers and college seniors are deciding to wait out the recession by honing their skills.

The lead makes a blanket assertion about a trend, and the story offers a number of examples of business and law schools that reflect the trend. It offers no evidence to support the assertion that education and journalism schools were facing the same growth in applications. Common sense suggests that journalism and education schools would face the same forces.

But that isn't enough. Indeed, the story pointed out that medical schools were not seeing such growth in applications and explained why.

News organizations should not ask readers to trust that the reporters did enough research to make unsupported assertions. If the story does not have supporting information, such as comments from journalism school or education school deans or statistics on applications, it is inadequate, and copy editors should raise a flag. Often the reporter has done the work and failed to include the information because of an oversight or because of limited space. Regardless, promises made in the lead must be met, and some of the information needs to be in the body of the story to support the assertion in the lead. Other times, the reporter or assigning editor just went too far, generalizing beyond the reporting done. Then either additional reporting needs to be done or the reference that is unsupported removed. Copy editors need to ask, "Why do you say that?" If the answer is "I'm not sure," changes are necessary.

STORY FLOW AND QUOTES

News reports and feature stories, the bread and butter of daily journalism, are peculiar forms of expository writing. One of their hallmarks is the liberal use of quoted material from sources. A writer's challenge is to construct a story, say a news story, so that the quotes follow expository paragraphs logically and lead logically into what follows. Copy editors can help writers meet that challenge.

News and feature stories often exhibit a structural logic, such as exposition, description, quote or anecdote, exposition. These patterns often are repeated throughout a story. Flow has a lot to do with logic. Paragraph C follows B, which follows A logically, and forced transitions are unnecessary.

Flow can break down when the type of writing shifts, and one of the most likely places is before or after quoted material. Quotes should be set up smoothly. The best quote is one that flows out of the sentence before it, and when a story is structured well, transitional devices are largely unnecessary. The quote follows without transitional words or phrases because the sentence that sets it up provides the context, thus the transition, for the quote.

One problem with students and inexperienced reporters is the tendency to set up quotes redundantly. The sentence leading to the quote repeats the wording or the substance of the quote. That interrupts the flow.

The writer's instinct is correct; it's to provide transition, but it's often a forced, or even an unnecessary, transition. A better way is to structure the passage so that the quote flows naturally from the paragraph that precedes it. Often, the solution is to simply remove the transitional setup paragraph.

The top of a story about an air show demonstrates this problem:

> As Cliff Kallenbach watched the F-15s, F-18s—and even a World War II P-51 Mustang—roar overhead, his thoughts returned to his youth and the days he wanted to be a jet pilot.
> Fluffy clouds graced the blue skies above Kingsley Field, and the air between Kallenbach and the squads of departing F-16s melted and shimmered with the heat of burned jet fuel.
> Ever since he was a kid, Kallenbach loved flying.
> "I've always had a love affair with airplanes," he said. . . .

Many, if not most, general assignment reporters have been assigned to cover an air show sometime in their careers. This reporter's approach was a good one: focusing on what it meant to a resident of the community. A copy editor could have helped the story by making a simple suggestion: lose the third paragraph. From the lead, a reader knows Kallenbach was interested in aviation since he was young. The quote "I've always had a love affair with airplanes" is a good one, but its impact is reduced because the short third paragraph, written as a transition, says the same thing. The second paragraph sets up the quote quite well; there's no need to force a transition.

Another problem with quotes is wordiness or triteness, both of which can interrupt the flow of a story. Newspapers, in general, do not allow rewording of quotes for clarity or comprehensiveness. Some allow minor rewording to fix blatant grammar or usage mistakes, but others do not. AP style prohibits even that level of editing of quotes. The rule newspapers tend to follow is that if a quote must be changed because it is unclear, it no longer appears as a quote. It must become a paraphrase, an attributed statement that clarifies the original quoted material, preserving the meaning and context.

Here's an example from a feature story about people who enjoy train travel:

> "I like the dining cars. They serve good meals," said Bonnie Myers, who wasn't packing along snacks. "I like to travel on the

> train. It's relaxing to me. I enjoy catching up on reading, seeing the scenery."

Here's a version that paraphrases part of the quote and trims a bit:

> "I like the dining cars. They serve good meals," said Bonnie Myers, who wasn't packing snacks. Meyers said she finds train travel relaxing. "I enjoy catching up on reading, seeing the scenery," she said.

One could argue that material left as a quote is not as bright or sharply focused as one would like quotes to be. Often, copy editors have little choice. They have to work with what they're given.

TRIMMING STORIES

Trimming stories will be part of the job description for newspaper editors until space and time have been conquered. Any medium that has a fixed amount of space and tight deadlines will occasionally need to have copy cut for space. Better planning and careful design can reduce the need for trims but not eliminate it. At newspapers, things change, and editors must know how to accommodate change. New stories appear. Planned stories die or are held. Stories come in too long or too short. Photos need to be played larger than expected. The list goes on. Copy editors, who often do the trims, typically do so for one of two reasons:

- To make a story fit. Most trims fall under this category, because newspaper space is limited and there always is another story that should make the paper.
- For cause. A story is wordy, overwritten or includes unnecessary detail, and trimming makes it more manageable.

Trimming stories, especially news stories, once was easy. Almost all news stories were written as inverted pyramids. The most important information was in the lead, and the least important was at the bottom. The theory was that a reader could stop at any point in the story and still get the most important information. In practice, things were never that simple, but editors could trim quickly from the bottom in the composing room. For the bulk of the 20th century, stories were typeset in hot lead ("hot type"), and editors could have compositors trim paragraphs at the end quickly. When technology shifted to photocomposition ("cold type"), the same kind of trimming could be done with Xacto knives. And most often those trims were fine.

Computer editing and typesetting technology have made it much easier for editors to trim for length within stories, and the efficiencies that accompanied the ability to trim from the bottom loom less large. Today, as more reporters are experimenting with different structures, borrowing from magazine-style feature forms and creating new ones, simple trimming from the bottom is often unwise or even impossible. Trimming now requires greater news judgment.

Nobody likes to trim stories, but a few strategies can make the job less onerous and help copy editors preserve a well-written story.

Don't start by trimming quotes. It may seem more expedient to do so—it's certainly easier to preserve continuity by cutting quotes. But trimming quotes often is a false efficiency. If a quote is well chosen, it belongs in the story. It provides a human voice, perhaps adds emotion, even drama, to otherwise dry prose. Find another way.

Though it might be unwise to cut entire quotes, it often is possible to tighten up quotes by preserving the best parts of a source's comment as quoted material and paraphrasing the rest. The following is a passage from a feature story about a poker player:

> The other aspects of the game are not so uncomplicated.
> "Learning to read your opponents is very important. Poker is one if the most interesting games in the world because it's a people game, and it changes people. It brings out the best and worst in them. It's the gambling element that makes it so exciting," he observed.
> The game draws all types.

That quote is a mouthful, and the sentence setting it up is awkward. Here's another version:

> He said the other aspects of the game are more complicated, such as learning to read your opponents.
> "Poker is one if the most interesting games in the world because it's a people game, and it changes people. It brings out the best and worst in them," he said.
> The game draws all types.

The recast version paraphrases the beginning of the poker player's quote and uses it to create a more graceful lead-in. The quote itself is shorter, but the best part is saved. The last sentence in the quote is cut because it adds little and does not lead into the next paragraph. Such techniques can be used if trims are needed, but they also can be used simply to help the flow. A section trimmed this way often reads much better than the original. A copy editor must take care to preserve the context of the original quoted material as well as important qualifying information.

After trimming stories, reread them, paying particular attention to first and second name references. It's easy to lose a first reference in a trim. Pay close attention to enumerations—if the original story reported that the city council took *three* actions and detailed them in later paragraphs, make sure you don't cut the third action.

A March 2002 story about a National Eye Institute study illustrates the problem. The study, which moved on the AP wire, pointed out that the aging of the baby boom generation could lead to a dramatic increase in the number of Americans suffering from serious eye diseases in the next few decades. After five paragraphs summarizing the study and providing comments from medical and government officials, the following sentence appeared:

The study listed four primary threats:

The rest of the story introduced and explained each of the four threats— diabetic retinopathy, macular degeneration, cataracts and glaucoma—in two- or three-paragraph sections. Trimming such a story from the end, as one newspaper did, eliminated one of the primary threats: glaucoma. The structure of the story—listing and detailing the threats one after another—made it impossible to cut from the bottom. But a hurried trim to make the story fit meant that readers lost crucial information. A bad trim in this case created an inconsistency problem: The top mentions four threats, but the story talks about three. If a trim is needed, a better approach is to list all four threats in the introductory sentence, then internally trim details to preserve the most important information about each.

SUGGESTIONS FOR TRIMS

• Make sure to preserve the logic, the thread and the flow. For example, in a science story that explains a biological, physical or mechanical process, be careful about making internal trims. Hastily cut sentences or paragraphs might contain crucial information that explains a step in the process or helps make the entire process understandable.

- Make sure that you don't lose important qualification or detail that supports the top of the story.
- Make sure to not trim too much of a rebuttal or an opposing view. Sometimes this happens when the opposing view is in quoted material and an editor makes a too-hasty trim of the quote.
- Reorganize if necessary. Sometimes trimming requires a bit of shuffling or summarization to preserve the flow. If so, copy editors need to make sure that they don't introduce errors into the story. Here are a few typical pitfalls:

1. The first reference becomes a second reference. A source's second name appears alone first, then the full name later. The opposite problem occurs too—a story winds up with two first references.
2. A pronoun reference loses the antecedent. References to phantom *he's* or *she's* or to the wrong *him* or *her* are left in the trimmed version.
3. Qualification is lost or becomes ineffective. A sentence or phrase that qualifies an assertion or a fact winds up trimmed or someplace else in the story and loses its impact.

Trimming can be the source of bitter conflict between reporters and editors. In a perfect world, reporters would be able to trim their own stories. Most often, that strategy isn't available; the reporter has left the office for the day, or the press of deadline makes such collaboration impossible. A bad trim makes the reporter, not the copy editor, look incompetent, and reporters never forget a bad trim. Copy editors should try to put themselves in the reporter's shoes. Would they like the trim? An elusive, but often attainable, goal in trimming is to do such a good job that the reporter won't even notice what's missing.

LONGER STORIES

The issues are the same in editing long stories as they are in short ones, with a few caveats. Consistency is a more serious concern. The longer and the more complicated the story, the more opportunities for inconsistency and contradiction. Long stories should be read well before deadline if possible.

Structure and organization are more important. Research consistently shows that many readers do not read very long stories. (It also shows that they do not like to follow continuations of stories on inside pages.) Avoidance of lengthy stories is not surprising, given that the average time a reader spends with a daily newspaper is about 20 minutes. To be read, long stories must capture reader interest and hold it. An inappropriate structure such as a very long inverted-pyramid treatment or a confusing sequence of information in a long story may invite readers to give up.

At the detail level, identification of subjects in the story can be a problem. In very long stories, a subject who appears toward the top of a story might not appear again for many column inches. It's easy for a reader to forget who the person is and why he or she is in the story. Consequently, it's often a good idea to restate the identification to jog a reader's memory. In a lengthy story about new fuels for cars, a lawmaker who first introduced legislation promoting electric cars in California, can be re-identified late in the story as "Smith, the senator who wrote the electric-car legislation in California. . . ."

A lot of myths exist about long stories and newspapers. Students thinking of journalism careers often shy away from newspapers because they feel that magazines and books offer better opportunities to cover topics in depth. That view is both true and untrue. Books certainly offer the best opportunities for depth, but few writers start out producing book-length work, and few editors start out editing books. Many successful writers of nonfiction books developed their reporting and writing skills working for newspapers, magazines or both.

The "typical" magazine article is probably longer than the "typical" newspaper story, but there are many examples in both media that do not fit the mold. One trend in magazines these days, especially in many niche publications, is toward more and shorter pieces. Newspapers traditionally run many short articles, of 300 to 1,000 words in length, but larger newspapers regularly publish much longer, magazine-length or longer, pieces of 2,500 to 4,000 words. Some even run book-length series periodically on topics of major importance. Many of the skills one learns and uses in newspaper editing are the same skills one uses in editing for magazines, books and the Web.

TIPS AND STRATEGIES

• When reading for organization, ask yourself whether any questions are unanswered. Are any answered much later? Then ask yourself why a question is not answered sooner. A well-constructed news story answers readers' questions before they get a chance to ask them.

• Stay cool. Some of the questions that you might ask while editing at this level can be contentious. Try to put yourself in the writer's place before you raise the questions. This shift of perception should not be difficult. Most editors were writers (and many still are). As a writer, how would you have responded to those questions?

• Read a story as many times as you have time for. In a perfect world, an editor could read copy as many times as needed, perhaps even once for each level discussed in this book. In practice, there never is enough time. If you have time for two reads, I'd suggest a first read for focus, organization, support for the lead, balance and fairness. The second read is for detail, mechanics, accuracy and precision. This approach reverses the structure of the text, but that's because when learning to edit, it is easier to move from the micro- to the macro-level. When actually editing, it's probably better to move in the other direction. That way, you'll notice bigger problems, problems that often require discussion or additional work, before you focus on smaller ones, which are often easier to address. Of course, if you notice a typo or a misspelling in that first read, don't ignore it.

If you have time for three reads, make the third read a catchall. Double-check to see that you haven't introduced any errors, such as typos, into the story during the editing. Edit yourself. Try to look at it again with fresh eyes, as a reader would. If you have time for only a single read, you'll need to keep shifting your focus from the broad to the narrow. This approach is the most difficult and unfortunately tends to be used close to deadline on late-breaking stories, where a more careful read is needed. Copy editors should be capable of shifting from two or three reads to one, because sometimes that's all they get. Sports copy editors often find themselves in this situation, having only minutes before deadline to read game coverage.

Some copy editors find that reading a story sentence by sentence backward is an effective way to find problems. It forces you to look at the sentence on its own. It can help you catch mistakes, particularly grammatical or usage mistakes, that you might have failed to notice while reading from beginning to end. If you grasp the meaning, sometimes you can miss the details.

• Learn from experts. Some newspapers are known for well-structured stories. The Wall Street Journal is one; its front-page feature stories are a model of good structure. The Christian Science Monitor is another. A couple of books that may help are "On Writing Well" by William Zinsser, and "Beyond the Inverted Pyramid" by George Kennedy, Daryl Moen and Don Ranly.[3] Many Web sites offer tips and approaches to writing and editing. One of the best newspaper training sites is "The Power of Words" (http://www.projo.com/words), developed by The Providence Journal. It includes an excellent archive of tips about reporting and writing as well as other newsroom issues. Another very good training site developed by a newspaper is "The Freep Academy" page (http://www.freep.com/jobspage/academy/index.htm). The Detroit Free Press site includes many pages of suggestions and tips on writing, editing, story structure and copy editing. The Poynter Institute Web site Poynter Online (http://www.poynter.org) includes many resources on writing and editing.

Ask the tough questions. The most difficult questions to raise are the big ones: Should the story be held? Should it be killed? Occasionally, those are the only sensible questions to ask when editing at the macro-level. Sometimes there are just too many holes to fill before deadline. Sometimes the story is unfair or in poor taste. Sometimes there isn't much of a story. Copy editors should not necessarily have the authority to hold or kill stories, but they should be allowed to raise those questions, and other editors should listen. Chapter 7 deals with such issues—and with the controversies that accompany them—in greater depth.

6

Fairness and Legality

A story from a suburban reporter reaches the copy desk. The subject is a developer's plan to build several houses on a small tract of land adjacent to a Superfund site. The story quotes township officials, a water-quality expert and neighbors. The township officials express concern; they don't think the houses should be built, but they don't believe they have the power to block the development. The water expert says there is a good chance that pollutants from the toxic site could migrate through the water table to the proposed development. The neighbors are angry; they say the developer doesn't care about people, just about making money.

The copy editor reads the story beginning to end and sees no comment from the developer. He asks the regional editor why, pointing out that the story seems to be making a broad accusation that the developer is acting unethically. The regional editor says that the reporter left a message at the developer's office and that no one had responded.

The copy editor is unsatisfied. He thinks the story is unfair and potentially libelous, and he doesn't feel that it should run without comment from the developer. The regional desk disagrees, saying that the reporter made the attempt and that the desk needs the story to fill its section. The copy editor decides to ask the regional editor's supervisor to look at the story. The supervisor agrees that comment is needed, and the story is held. The regional editor is annoyed, but he grudgingly agrees to find another story to fill the hole.

The next day, a different story about the proposed development moves to the copy desk. The developer is quoted at some length. He says that he did not realize his project was next to a Superfund site and that he was reconsidering his plan to build.

Would the story published without the developer's comment have been libelous? That's difficult to say. The story could have been seen by potential homebuyers and members of the construction community as defamatory—it could have injured the developer's reputation and hurt his business. Libel issues are complicated, and definitions vary from state to state. Would the story have been unfair? Absolutely. In this case, an appeal to fairness by the copy editor led to a revised story, one that did not lead to a complaint about biased reporting or a libel suit.

The title of this chapter reflects two areas of great concern to copy editors and other journalists, and the order in which they appear is intentional. One of the tasks of copy editors is to help ensure that copy is free from libel and does not invade anyone's privacy. But copy editors are not lawyers, and it is unrealistic to expect that besides being professional wordsmiths they will also be libel and privacy experts. Even many lawyers don't understand these issues very well. Indeed, such cases tend to be handled by those who have spent many years developing the expertise.

It is important for all copy editors to have a general knowledge of libel and its elements. In general terms, libel is damage to a person's reputation. Don Pember, in "Mass Media Law" writes, "In simple terms, libel is the publication or broadcast of a statement that injures someone's reputation, that lowers that person's esteem in the community."[1] The AP definition is more succinct: "At its most basic, libel means injury to reputation."[2] The First Amendment Handbook, a publication of the Reporters Committee for Freedom of the Press, says, "Libel occurs when a false and defamatory statement about an identifiable person is published to a third party, causing injury to the subject's reputation."[3] These definitions seem fairly straightforward, but libel issues become more complicated quickly, as the terms used are in flux and differ to some degree by state.

Copy editors should be aware of the standards under which libel can be established, and they should be familiar with libel defenses, such as truth and opinion. In general, plaintiffs in a libel case must prove that the information published is false, and pure opinion cannot be libelous. However, these and other privileges have been qualified and reinterpreted by courts or by legislatures. For example, according to Pember, a public person generally has to prove a statement is false in order to successfully sue the mass media, but a private person does not necessarily have to do so.[4] The context is important, that is, whether the story concerns a matter of public interest. The media organization might have to prove a statement is true, which sometimes is difficult, and statements of opinion that are factual enough that they can be proven true or false can still be actionable.

Copy editors should have an understanding of the development of key definitions that figure in libel cases, such as the distinctions between public officials and figures and private persons that were articulated in the famous New York Times v. Sullivan case and its successors. They should know that the criteria applied in libel cases differ depending on those distinctions. For example, the Times v. Sullivan case established an "actual malice" standard, defined as knowledge of a statement's falsity at the time of publication or reckless disregard for the truth, as the standard for public officials. The standard for citizens who are not public people is lower, generally negligence.[5] Copy editors should be aware of the concept of privileged sources and contexts. For example, a fair and accurate report of a statement made by a legislator in a speech on the Statehouse floor is safe to publish, even if it includes defamatory material. An accusation that a neighbor makes about a suspect in a crime isn't.

It is also important for copy editors to have a basic understanding of privacy law, another ever-changing body of doctrine and case law. Editing and reporting textbooks and classes can provide a taste of this body of knowledge, but they are no substitute for a class dedicated to media law issues.

In practice, however, fine distinctions and criteria established in legislation and case law do not figure significantly in day-to-day editing. Editors and reporters worry a great deal about whether stories are safe to publish, but they do not sit around discussing whether a source is a "public figure" or a "limited public figure" when they make decisions about whether to use a comment from that source. On sensitive stories, an editor can consult with a lawyer, who might point out such distinctions. But for most stories, editors at all levels follow what might be called "everyday criteria." They tend to ask whether information is accurate, whether the paper could prove that it is accurate, whether the information is fair, whether the person making an accusation is an appropriate source, whether a story tramples on a person's privacy, and so on. They need to watch for fairness and balance and remain vigilant about preserving the presumption of innocence and other basic rights of the accused. Fairness is at the core of those criteria.

A concern for fairness offers a copy editor more practical guidance than an examination of case law. A lawyer might analyze whether the newspaper can safely say something about Mr. Jones, who is a "limited public figure," that it can't safely say about Mr. Smith, who is not. A copy editor can ask whether it is fair to make the statement about either man.

Fairness itself does figure in libel. For example, the press has a qualified privilege in the reporting of news about crime and those arrested if the report is a fair and accurate account. The AP Stylebook states, "A fair and accurate report of a public proceeding cannot provide grounds for a libel suit."[6] The requirement that news reports be fair is also an ethical one. In everyday editing, copy editors who think of fairness and legality as two sides of the same coin will be acting ethically and will help ensure that coverage avoids libel.

What does fairness in coverage mean? Here are a few practical guidelines:

• A story accurately and completely conveys various sides of a dispute, an issue or a police matter. It means that the newspaper does not appear to be taking sides or is actually taking sides.

• Crime reports of arrests and court actions preserve the presumption of innocence. That fundamental principle can easily be undermined by unfair pretrial coverage. Is it fair, for example, to report a neighbor's comments that lead readers to infer a person's guilt? It also means that stories about civil disputes don't appear to take sides. They maintain balance. The ethics code of the Society of Professional Journalists urges journalists to "be judicious about naming criminal suspects before the formal filing of charges." It also says journalists should "balance a criminal suspect's fair trial rights with the public's right to be informed."[7]

• Loaded words such as *crook* and *cheat* are used rarely, if ever. Verbs of attribution are neutral—for example, to say a person *claims* to be innocent suggests doubt. To say he *contended* or *said* he was innocent is more neutral.

• People's words and their photos are not used out of context. They should not be used as examples in unrelated stories simply for the sake of expedience. They definitely should not be used, as The First Amendment Handbook points out, "when reporting on an activity that might be considered questionable."[8]

How do copy editors approach fairness and libel issues in stories?

Much as in editing for content, when copy editors read for fairness and legality, they focus at several levels: from the single word through the entire story.

THE WORD

Some words are simply trouble in themselves.

Crook, cheat, liar, incompetent and similar "loaded" words are highly judgmental and defamatory. They are considered damaging to a person's reputation on their face. Such words could provide ammunition for a libel suit if it can be shown that they are false or if it cannot be proven that they are true. As a practical matter, it is very difficult to prove that such words are true. News organizations do not prohibit the use of such words, but they do need to be very careful about publishing them. They might use them on rare occasions when circumstances warrant it. Editors and reporters should discuss whether such words are appropriate in a story, and copy editors often should be a part of the discussion. They should pay particular attention to the nature of the source of the words and the context of their use. A legislator speaking during a committee meeting might call a corporate executive a cheat or a liar, and a newspaper that provides a fair and accurate account of the proceeding could print it safely. If a rival executive calls the person a cheat or a liar in a news conference or in an interview and a newspaper publishes the accusation, even in quoted material, it is on much shakier legal ground.

From a fairness standpoint, both accusations can be questioned. A newspaper might decide not to print the legislator's accusation or to do additional reporting to determine whether the accusation is justified before printing it. The paper might wait until it can get the target of the accusation to comment on it. It might print the accusation and follow it with information gathered from other sources that calls the accusation into question. News organizations have learned a few lessons over the years. Their coverage practices have been abused by shrewd legislators, such as U.S. Sen. Joseph McCarthy, who in Senate Committee proceedings during the Cold War accused many people of having Communist leanings. He did so knowing that newspapers would print the accusations, because they were made by a privileged source, and that news organizations often would not have time to contact the targets before deadline.[9]

Words that are not normally loaded may appear loaded in context. Verbs of attribution, for example, can create an appearance of bias.

Admitted is a perfectly legitimate word in some contexts, but in others, it can connote more than it should.

> The legislator admitted that the trade association paid for his trip to Jamaica.

In the previous sentence, *admitted* might suggest that the legislator would rather not have commented on it. It can also connote guilt or behavior that is less than honest. The three examples below are more neutral:

> The legislator acknowledged that . . .

> The legislator confirmed that . . .

> The legislator said that . . .

SEEMINGLY INNOCUOUS WORDS

Libel lawyers hate the word *but*. Consider the following passage:

> City Manager Joe Martin denied allegations made during last night's City Council meeting that he had taken $20,000 of Parking Authority money to repay gambling debts.
> "I never took a cent," Martin said. "It's true I have had a gambling problem, but I am working on paying my debts. There has to be a good explanation for the discrepancy."
> But $20,000 is missing from the city's parking fund, which is under the city manager's direction.

The last paragraph is a problem. The statement is true, but the wording invites readers to conclude that the city manager is being less than honest about the missing money. The word *but* is used primarily as a transitional device to the short background paragraph. An injudicious use of that word can raise doubts about innocence or suggest guilt. That isn't fair. A better way to word that final sentence is to drop the *but*, to cite a source for the information and to place the final piece of background information in better context:

An audit released last week reported that $20,000 is missing from the city's parking fund and is unaccounted for. The fund is one of several city accounts under the direction of the city manager.

Most libel issues that face copy editors involve crime news, one of the staples of daily newspaper coverage for the better part of two centuries. Copy editors should pay particular attention to sentence structure and wording in reports of arrests and charges. Two criteria are important: telling the story clearly and preserving the presumption of innocence of the accused. The criteria serve both readers and suspects. Here's a story that needs editing:

Dillon R. McLeen, 28, of Eugene, and a 15-year-old juvenile escapee were arrested after they burglarized a Eugene home, beat a woman, tied up her son and led police on a 70-mile high-speed chase to Roseburg in the woman's stolen car before smashing it into a building.

McLeen of the 300 block of Amazon Boulevard, was charged with assault, burglary and car theft and was held in the Douglas County Jail. A 15-year-old boy, who had escaped from a juvenile facility in Lane County, was being held in the Douglas County Juvenile Detention Center, police said. The youth's name was not released.

According to a Eugene police spokesman, the duo entered the home at 1:45 a.m. Sunday and beat the woman, 46, after tying up her 14-year-old son. They took an undetermined amount of cash and property and fled in the woman's car. The woman then called police, who spotted the suspects nearby.

Several police departments, including the Oregon State Police, took part in the chase on Interstate 5. In Roseburg, the car smashed into a storage building, and the pair were arrested after a brief foot chase.

Police did not release the names of the woman or her son.

There are several problems with this story. The lead, in effect, convicts McLeen, the suspect. It says in so many words that he and the unnamed teenager committed several crimes. It might appear that this is an open-and-shut case, but that doesn't matter. People are innocent until proven guilty, and the wording of stories should preserve that presumption as much as possible. Worse, the lead is unattributed. The newspaper, in effect, is making the statements about the crime and who did it. That is a potential libel problem. Information about criminal arrests or charges should be attributed to the source, for example, the police or the district attorney's office. A third problem with the lead is that it contains too much information: it tries to tell the whole story in one sentence. Here's a safer, more readable version:

> Two intruders beat a Eugene woman, tied up her son and then led state police on a high speed chase to Roseburg, a Eugene police spokesman said. The car crashed into a storage building in Roseburg, and Roseburg police arrested a man and a boy after a brief foot chase.
>
> Dillon J. McLeen, 28, of the 300 block of Amazon Boulevard, was charged with assault, burglary and car theft and was held in the Douglas County Jail. A 15-year-old boy was being held in the Douglas County Juvenile Detention Center, Eugene police said. They would not release the name of the youth, who they said had escaped from a juvenile facility in Lane County.
>
> Eugene police gave the following account of the incident: A man and a teenage boy broke into a home in the Ferry Street Bridge area at 1:45 a.m. Sunday. They beat the woman, 46, after tying up her 14-year-old son. The intruders then took cash and property and fled in the woman's car. The woman then called police, who spotted the car nearby.
>
> State police and several local jurisdictions took part in the chase on Interstate 5. The car smashed into a storage building in Roseburg, and police said McLeen and the teenager were arrested after a brief foot chase.
>
> Police did not release the names of the woman or her son.

The rewritten version tells the story in the lead, moving unnecessary details down. The lead is attributed to the police department that provided the information. The arrested man is named in the second paragraph, and his address is given to clarify the identification. It is possible that there are two Dillon McLeens in Eugene; using the address makes it highly unlikely that readers would mistake the one who had nothing to do with the crime for the one who was arrested. The lead-in phrase *Police gave the following account* can help improve readability. It can be overused, however, and some publications still attribute specific allegations of criminality within the section that follows. The edited version removes the jargony loaded word *duo*, and it clarifies police jurisdictions. The wording throughout attempts to provide some semantic distance between McLeen, the man accused by name, and the crimes, though it makes clear that McLeen is the person arrested, as it must.

The goal is to make sure the story reads clearly and safely. Another concern in crime stories is to make sure that anecdotal leads do not inadvertently convict a person who has not yet been proven guilty. Saying that attribution gets in the way of clear writing is not a defense.

In high-profile cases, when the person charged with the crime was observed by many people during the crime, many news organizations will not treat the accused the same way they do in routine crime stories. For example, in the tragic 1998 shootings at Thurston High School in Springfield, Ore., there was no doubt that the person pulling the trigger was Kip Kinkel. Many students saw Kinkel open fire and shoot people. What was in doubt was the disposition of the case—whether there would be an insanity plea, and so on. In those cases, some news organizations will be less concerned about creating a semantic distance between the accused and the crime.

CONSIDER THE SOURCE

A reporter's natural inclination is to tell as much of the story as possible. One of the editor's most important jobs is to step away from the story and ask (1) whether there's enough to go on, and (2) whether it's fair. Those two questions are related. Make sure you don't let a good story (or a quote or juicy information) get in the way of fairness and common sense.

One of the rights that all people deserve is the right to not be convicted in the media by quotes from neighbors and acquaintances. As sure as the sun sets in the West, newspaper and television reporters descend on the neighbors when someone is accused of a particularly heinous crime. Neighbors are not privileged sources. For a neighbor to say, "Yeah, I always knew that idiot would pick up a gun some day and start taking potshots," could lead to a libel action if it turns out that the accused is innocent. Moreover, it is unfair. Neighbors might know the person, but they are not privy to information police investigators and prosecutors have about the crime. Pember points out that one of the most common misconceptions is that a publication cannot be sued if it accurately quotes a person making a defamatory statement that turns out to be false.[10]

One newspaper published an account of a double shooting after a beer party in the woods that liberally quoted teenagers who had been at the party. Several of those at the party told a reporter that a teenager known as a troublemaker had argued with the shooting victims during the party. The reporter included those comments and others like them in the story and used the first name of the "troublemaker." A couple of days later the newspaper ran a story pointing out that a boy from the area with that first name was not a suspect and had not even been at the party. In the first place, the newspaper was on shaky ground publishing accusatory comments from participants at a beer party. They are not privileged sources, and they might not be the most trustworthy sources. And to refer to the person by his first name was doubly dangerous, because an innocent person could contend that he had been identified and his reputation damaged by the report. Moreover, it simply isn't fair to report such allegations. An ear tuned to fairness would have raised a flag about the quotes.

The AP Stylebook's section on media law points out that who is considered a privileged source can be problematic:

> "Statements made outside the court by police or a prosecutor or an attorney may or may not qualify as privileged, depending on what state you are in and on the circumstances in which the statements are made."[11]

ALLEGEDLY

The word *allegedly*, which often appears in wire service copy and in television news reports, is a crutch that doesn't hold much weight. It is used as a quick way to preserve a semblance of the presumption of innocence. There is disagreement about whether it makes a sentence safer at all.

Theodore M. Bernstein, in "The Careful Writer," says that the common use of the term, as in *alleged thief* or *alleged robber*, is technically a misuse because you can allege a crime but not a person. But he also says that "the journalistic need for such a protective qualifier to avoid seeming to impute guilt is so common and so compelling that if this use of 'alleged' did not exist, it would be necessary to invent it."[12] Pember, from a media law perspective, has a different take:

> "Imputations of criminal behavior are responsible for a great many libel suits. Saying someone has done something illegal—from jaywalking to murder—is libelous. The use of the word alleged in these cases is often of little help."[13]

A good approach is the one followed by carefully edited papers, which use the word *allegedly* rarely, if ever. They prefer, instead, to recast the sentence to include the person or group making the allegation. That way, you can also be sure that the source is an appropriate one, that is, one who is in a position to make an allegation in a context that a newspaper can safely report. Moreover, it is fairer to the suspect to say who is alleging what than it is to simply say *the alleged killer*. The following sentence can be improved,

> Smith's alleged killer is in custody in the Jefferson County Jail.

The following rewrites are much better:

> The man police accused of killing Smith is in custody in the Jefferson County Jail.
>
> The man police suspected of killing Smith is in custody in the Jefferson County Jail.

Or, if the man has been arraigned and charged, the sentence could read:

> The man charged in Smith's slaying is in custody in the Jefferson County Jail.

HEADLINES AND LIBEL

Besides watching reporters' wording in stories, copy editors must watch their own wording in headlines. An erroneous headline can be actionable in a libel suit even if the story is correct. Pember cites the example of a Mississippi newspaper that published a headline reading "Three Plead Guilty to Cattle Theft" for a story about three men who had pleaded guilty to a different crime: transporting cattle that had not been tested for disease. The story was accurate, but the headline was wrong. The newspaper lost the case.[14]

Word choice is a big issue in headline writing for crime stories. Headlines are very short, and qualification and nuance are often difficult, if not impossible (see Chapter 9). Still, it is a copy editor's responsibility to preserve the presumption of innocence, even if it means writing a headline that is less elegant. One way is to use prepositions that do not invite a conclusion of guilt.

Mayor arrested for theft of funds

Mayor arrested in fund-theft case

The word *in* used in the second headline appears to be *headlinese*— jargon used only in headlines—but it serves a purpose. It provides a bit of semantic distance between the mayor and the crime. The first headline, though it might not be actionable in a libel proceeding, is not as fair as the second. Read literally, the first headline says the mayor took the money. The culprit is the word *for*. One could argue that readers know that an arrest does not mean a person is guilty under the U.S. system of justice. But many well-edited papers avoid such usage. They realize that the headline has to convey the information that the mayor was arrested and provide some idea why, but they bend over backward to not suggest guilt.

Often, a combination of a headline and a summary paragraph, or "deck," make it possible to convey the news of an arrest and some of the details.

Adelphia cable founder, sons arrested
The former CEO and other
executives are charged
with stealing assets.

PRIVACY ISSUES

Several areas of privacy law are particularly troublesome for reporters and editors. Two problem areas are the reporting of private facts about a person that a reasonable person would consider offensive and the reporting of embarrassing information from the past that has no bearing on the present. The best strategy here is to carefully consider whether such information is newsworthy.

Perhaps a bigger problem is publication of information or photos that place a person in a "false light." For reasons of expediency, newspapers sometimes republish file photos to illustrate current stories. A busy photo editor might grab a file shot of a person arguing with another on a city street to illustrate a story about a law to restrict aggressive panhandling. If the person is identifiable and the incident pictured had nothing to do with panhandling, the newspaper could be in trouble. In his media law text, Pember has a solution:

> "A simple precaution will protect publishers and broadcasters against many false light suits. Refrain from using unrelated photos to illustrate stories and articles." [15]

Copy editors, realizing that the temptation to use such photos is great, should always ask themselves whether a file photo is appropriate, and, if the answer is no, argue vigorously to have the photo replaced. Beyond the legal issues, it's a simple matter of fairness. A person's photo should not be used where it doesn't belong.

TIPS AND STRATEGIES

• Don't be afraid to ask. If you think a statement is potentially libelous but are unsure, ask someone who knows more about the subject. As a practical matter, copy editors usually check with a supervisor, say a copy chief or a newsroom executive. Higher-ranking editors should have a better idea whether the paper can use the statement safely. If not, a supervisor should know whom to ask.

To serve their readers—and their newspapers—best, copy editors should be assertive, if not aggressive, about raising fairness and libel concerns. Raising tough questions can ruffle feathers, but sometimes it's necessary.

Helpful resources are available. The AP Stylebook has a short, useful section on libel and privacy: the Briefing on Media Law. The First Amendment Handbook, which is available online (http://www.rcfp.org/handbook/viewpage.cgi), is a good resource. Some bar associations publish guides for the news media. The Student Press Law Center (http://www.splc.org) is a great resource for student publications.

• Check for comment. It is important from both a fairness and a libel standpoint for reporters to have made genuine efforts to contact the other side for comment. Comment should be sought aggressively, not superficially. The Code of Ethics of the Society of Professional Journalists says journalists should "diligently seek out subjects of news stories to give them the opportunity to respond to allegations of wrongdoing."[16] Substantial reporting of one side of a dispute and nothing from the other is unfair. If the second party declines to comment, stories should say so clearly. Seeking comment from defendants and parties in civil proceedings is often a futile undertaking in crime and court stories because many accused people refuse to talk with the media, often on the advice of their attorneys. But that shouldn't stop journalists from making a sincere attempt.

• Make sure the story structure is fair. For example, consider a story about homeowners suing a developer over flooding problems. They contend that their homes were built on land that was improperly graded and that the developer was at fault. The story is full of anecdotes about people who are victims—who have water in their basements, who face expensive cleanup costs, whose family heirlooms were ruined by water. Anecdotes make stories interesting. In this case, most readers can empathize with the homeowners. But a careful copy editor should ask whether the volume of anecdotes is excessive, whether it might create an impression that is unfair. Many conditions besides shoddy development work could lead to flooding. It could be a case of excessive rainfall. And in a case such as this, there probably is no way to provide anecdotes from the developer's perspective that would tell a different story. Researchers have found that people remember anecdotes and examples better than they remember facts and that the impressions they take from anecdotes can significantly influence their view of a story. Stories should not appear to be taking sides, either by failing to provide one side or by their structure.

• If you think a story might be problematic, try this thought experiment: assume the story is about a friend or relative. Now do you think it's fair?

• If you are a student, take a media law class even if one is not required in your program. The subjects are important enough to warrant treatment beyond the cursory introduction students get in other journalism classes. Some top editors ask whether job applicants have taken such a class and are reluctant to hire anyone who hasn't.

Fairness and legality are among the most difficult issues that copy editors face. Libel and privacy laws themselves change as new cases appear and are adjudicated, and they vary from state to state. The Internet has opened another entire area of legal concern, one that seems to change from day to day. Copy editors who work in print and online do not need to become legal experts, but they do need to realize that they have to be lifelong learners in these important areas.

7

Working with People

Q. How do you keep a $50 bill from a reporter?
A. Hide it in the stylebook.

Q. How many copy editors does it take to change a light bulb?
A. Two—one to put it in, one to take it out, one to put it in, one to
   . . .

These are two of many jokes that play on the relationship between copy editors and reporters. They are based on stereotypes: the reporter who never checks the stylebook and the arbitrary and often inscrutable copy editor. Reporters and copy editors alike laugh at these, but like many jokes based on stereotypes there's a germ of truth beneath them. Too many reporters pay insufficient attention to the stylebook, assuming that it's the copy editor's job to fix anything a reporter fails to look up. That carelessness wastes time copy editors could spend on more important matters. Too many copy editors seem to edit in a byzantine and arbitrary manner, one deleting a word or phrase, another asking that it be restored. That "in-and-out" type of editing wastes reporters' time, keeping them from important things. The jokes, and others like them, reflect real tensions between editors and reporters, both of whom are on the same team but who sometimes seem to play by different sets of rules.

All people in a news organization work for the same publication, but different jobs have different requirements and different rhythms. News professionals who work in different departments also have somewhat dif-

110

ferent values. For example, photographers and designers believe they should emphasize visual considerations, while reporters favor the verbal. Reporters and photographers alike consider themselves storytellers, but photographers focus more on image aesthetics and reporters on writing aesthetics. This is as it should be, but the differences in focus can create problems. Photographers, for example, want to use larger pictures because they are more compelling than smaller ones. Reporters want to write longer stories because they are more compelling than shorter ones. Those conflicting values often clash in battles over limited news space. Reporters balk at trimming stories so that photos can be displayed well. Photographers stew when desk editors blithely crop an already well-cropped photo so that an extra inch or two of type can be squeezed in.

Designers sometimes use type for visual effect, playing with size and shape and tone on section fronts and in elaborately designed story packages. Copy editors value words, placing much greater emphasis on what a headline says than on how it looks. Those values can clash over headlines that designers specify because of the way they look but that copy editors feel are inadequate to tell the story.

Copy editors are taught to represent readers by challenging writing that is adjective- or adverb-laden, self-indulgent or seemingly written for an audience of insiders. Reporters counter that copy editors sometimes act like automatons or "style Nazis" and would, as one city editor was fond of saying, "drain the color from the autumn leaves."

Discussions and debates over conflicting values can be productive. Copy editors often find themselves in the middle of these battles, and it helps to understand why different values can lead to tensions. Hearing what a photographer or designer thinks can be consciousness-raising for a copy editor, and vice versa. The discussions and debates can be destructive, though, if they descend into personality clashes.

The underlying issue is that editing is not just about working with words and images. It is also about working with people. In most textbooks, including this one, the volume of words explaining the technical aspects of editing suggests that editing is mainly wordsmithing. Copy editing is that— but it is more.

Beyond issues of word editing and style mechanics, accuracy, sentence structure, organization, flow, libel and fairness is another realm: that of interaction with people, of dialogue, of negotiation, of criticism and of collegiality. Many copy editors begin their professional careers with little understanding that word-editing ability will take them only so far. And many inexperienced editors find that wordsmithing is much easier than "people-smithing." Both sets of skills are crucial not only in themselves but also because of the way one can depend on the other. How well you succeed in working with words often depends on how well you can work with the people who wrote those words. If an editor and a reporter have a good professional relationship, if the editor can gain a reporter's trust, the reporter's natural resistance to having his or her words changed often melts away. If the reporter and the editor see themselves as adversaries, if they fight over every comma or adjective, the lack of trust and communication will serve nobody, including readers.

Ask a room full of copy editors how they wish reporters would treat them, and the two words that always come up are "respect" and "trust." Ask a roomful of reporters "How would you like copy editors to treat you?" and they will say the same thing.

A copy editor might use slightly or even substantially different strategies for interacting with staff members in different departments, but the basis of all of these relationships is similar: respect. And respect is based on mutual understanding and trust. Mutual understanding implies an awareness of the problems and pressures the other faces. Trust needs to be earned.

Of course, a copy editor must also be a good wordsmith to engender trust: no reporters want sloppy or unskilled copy editors handling their stories or slapping hurried headlines on them. The surest way to erode trust—or to prevent it from developing in the first place—is to introduce errors into a story, to take a well-written sentence and make it less readable or to write a headline that misses the point or is inaccurate. But trust is based on more than technical ability. Reporters must understand that editors really do want to help them tell their stories better and that an editor asks questions and criticizes a story in an effort to improve it. The best, most successful editors understand the secrets of getting along with others as well as they understand subject–verb agreement and the proper use of commas. Moreover, a failure to understand how to work with others on the staff can become a barrier to advancement, both within an organization or at another, even for those highly skilled at the word side of editing.

TENSIONS

Tensions between different newsroom departments typically stem from one of two causes: poor people/personnel management skills or inadequate understanding of newsroom process. Many problems that appear to be people problems are really process issues that manifest themselves as personal conflict. They typically center on deadline issues, particularly missed deadlines, and they stem from an inadequate understanding of how a news organization's copy flow must work if the paper is to be printed on time.

Many reporters, assigning editors, news editors, artists and designers fail to realize that the operation hangs together like a spider web. If someone tugs on one corner, the whole structure reacts, some parts more violently than others. Typically, the copy desk feels the vibrations most strongly. If a reporter takes too long to write a story, if the city editor hangs onto a story for hours when it needs only a minor insert, the copy desk winds up paying for it. If the designer takes too long creating headline specifications, copy editors will not have enough time to do a good job on any headline. Many in the newsroom who haven't spent time on the copy desk fail to realize that copy editors are the cleanup crew—they have to solve problems created by others.

The same tensions can occur within the copy desk itself. A copy editor who spends a great deal of time on one story can improve it, but in a deadline-based environment excessive time spent by one copy editor will have to be made up by others. The rest of the desk will have to work more quickly, and usually less carefully, to handle the work that the first editor couldn't finish, and other stories might suffer from a lack of attention. At times, the extra time might be wisely spent on a story that is full of problems. But sometimes it isn't, and then it breeds resentment.

Most stories could be improved if time were not an issue. Stories always can be constructed in different ways, and it is silly to think that writers necessarily come up with the best version all of the time. Politics has been called "the art of the possible," but it's also true about journalism. Sometimes a copy editor just needs to say good enough is good enough and let it go. At The New York Times, where copy editors often work on only a few stories a night, it might be possible to cross all of the t's and dot all of the i's, to fill in every minor hole and to rewrite every passage that is cumbersome. At most other newspapers, the volume of stories read by each editor is greater, often much greater, and copy editors must make choices about what needs to be addressed and what doesn't. The hour spent rewriting a poorly organized story is an hour lost to many other important tasks. Editors who face tight deadlines must learn to parcel out their time in ways that create the best overall product. Magazine and book publishers have the luxury of longer production cycles and often can insist on a level of editing that is an impossible dream at daily news organizations.

Copy editors likewise often fail to understand the pressures reporters face. They might not realize how difficult it can be to confirm a relatively insignificant fact that they think should be in the story for completeness. They understand, but they often fail to appreciate, that a story already has been through at least one edit before it reaches the copy desk and that a reporter who hears the same questions and has to give the same answers can get irritated. Understandably. Copy editors should not shy away from asking questions. They should, however, try to understand the process from the perspective of the reporter and exhibit a little empathy. It might be as simple as prefacing a question with, "Somebody else might have asked you this question already. . . ."

They also fail to realize that errors introduced into stories by copy editors who make assumptions or fail to discuss changes with reporters reflect badly on reporters.

THE COPY EDITOR–REPORTER RELATIONSHIP

A copy editor's day typically involves many interactions with other departments. The most important of these is working with reporters. Oddly enough, some publications actually discourage this interaction, preferring instead that copy editors follow the chain of command. Some practically require a writ of habeas corpus before a copy editor is allowed to speak with a reporter about any story. Some newspapers insist that copy editors talk with assigning editors, who in turn talk with the reporters. Why they behave this way is puzzling. The benefits of direct discussion between reporters and copy editors far outweigh the potential drawbacks.

The positives include efficiency—it simply is faster to talk to the reporter than to work through a middleman. On many points, the assigning editor would have to check with the reporter anyway. Another benefit is that regular interaction between copy editors and reporters can encourage dialogue, break down departmental walls, build relationships and ultimately build trust. Technological change and the shifting of back-shop tasks onto copy editors have made it more difficult for them to take the time to interact with reporters—and it does take time. But it's time well spent.

One potential downside of direct discussion between copy editors and reporters is the possibility that they might negotiate a change that the assigning editor disagrees with. This concern is real; the assigning editor, the city editor, for example, has a very important role in the overall process, ensuring that a story is complete, fair, well focused and well organized. Often a copy editor might not be aware of a concern the city editor has about a fact or a source. But there are ways to keep the assigning editor in the loop; the simplest is to mention any substantive changes. Another possible downside is conflict. Some reporters and copy editors don't play well together, and some newspapers have adopted practices that make conflict more likely. The solution here is to pay attention to people skills. As Dick Moss, copy chief of the Rochester (N.Y.) Democrat and Chronicle, puts it:

> "I've seen too many situations in which the metro–copy desk tension eroded efforts to produce a quality product. You'll achieve more by working together and explaining your side of the issue in a calm, professional manner—even if the opposite party doesn't. If you don't get your way today, there likely will be another chance to argue tomorrow."[1]

Antagonistic interactions will still happen between copy editors and reporters. At most newspapers, such stories are told, retold and embellished to the point that they become more urban legend than truth. Often the facts appear very different depending on whether it's a reporter or a copy editor doing the telling. Here is one from a very large metropolitan newspaper, told from a copy editor's point of view: One copy editor who had a reputation for irascibility and a penchant for the dramatic changed the term "campaign literature" in a politics story to "campaign stuff." When challenged by the reporter, he replied, "Literature does not arrive in the mailbox addressed 'to occupant.' " The reporter slinked away from the desk muttering to himself.

It's a great war story but perhaps not the best way to raise an objection. And the copy editor could have chosen a better word than *stuff*. Work would be an uninteresting place without such legends. Occasional conflict is harmless, and some conflicts might even generate some light as well as heat. But the danger is letting it get out of hand, which it easily can. Ill will between reporters and copy editors is so common and so potentially disruptive that the American Copy Editors Society presents an educational session at its convention nearly every year titled "What Jerk Wrote This?"[2] to explore the sources of conflict and offer suggestions. One year, the session took the form of the Jerry Springer Show, with copy editors playing the roles of aggrieved and outraged copy editors and reporters. Reaction from the audience suggested that the skits hit close to home.

The problem also extends to assigning desk–reporter interactions. An irreverent, unbylined "Heavyweight Editing in 10 Easy Stomps" that was first posted on a New York Times bulletin board and has found its way into other newsrooms suggests that reporters often clash, with good reason, with their assigning editors. Steps 2 and 3 give some of the flavor:

2. Move reporter's second graf down to the bottom where it can be bitten off in the composing room.
3. Fashion a new second graf from material deep down in the story, preferably with a mysterious second reference to someone not introduced yet.

The best overall approach, as Moss suggests, is to treat people well. Copy editors should try to understand the other person's needs and be willing to negotiate. But sometimes copy editors must take a stand and stick to it. By defending their actions, copy editors can show that they respect their own craft.

John McIntyre, president of the American Copy Editors Society, is one of the most philosophical and most persuasive defenders of the role of copy editors in daily newspapers. In the following excerpt, which he wrote as part of an online discussion about a blowup over a copy editor's elimination of a questionable phrase, he challenged the ACES membership to look at the issue more broadly. A thoughtful discussion of the role of copy editors, McIntyre said, should include the following issues:

"(1) A rueful admission that the besetting sin of copy editors is to get carried away over points of minute importance and to attempt to enforce The Rules in a mechanical and inflexible manner. . . . We shouldn't be too thin-skinned to admit this.

(2) A rebuttal to the attitude that copy editors are merely 'grammarians, spellarians and political correctarians.' Our writ properly extends to questioning all elements of an article, including substance, focus, organization, tone and prose style. We are paid to raise questions, and the editors and writers who ignore those questions are like patients who check out of the hospital against medical advice.

(3) A reminder that writers need editors. I've been listening for more than 20 years to blather and bluster to the effect that if papers would just eliminate the copy desk, we would see an efflorescence of literary creativity unmatched since the England of the first Elizabeth. We know better. We know that writers are not necessarily the best judges of their own work and

have a perverse tendency to cling to their least impressive effects. We know that editors are there to save them from making asses of themselves in public. (And we know that for every reporter who has a complaint about some damnfool thing the copy desk has done, the copy editors have a private anthology of the most ludicrous sentences that have come across the desk.)

(4) A challenge to editors—assigning editors and supervising editors—to acknowledge that their copy desks are a repository of knowledge and skill with the language. If they permit their writers to dismiss the copy desk as a bunch of drones, if they foster a culture of ignoring or discounting their copy editors, then they have established a ceiling, and a low one at that, above which the quality of their publications will not rise."[3]

How can copy editors help create an environment of trust and respect? There are many individual strategies for working with reporters, and there are some institutional ones as well. The following section contains 10 helpful suggestions, strategies used by some of the best copy editors.

10 STEPS TO EDITING WITH RESPECT

1. Have a good reason to make any change in copy. And be prepared to articulate the reason. There are plenty of good reasons to change copy, including inaccuracy, incompleteness, unclarity, poor grammar, poor taste, unfairness, and so on. But one of the worst reasons is "I don't like it." Much bad blood between editors and reporters arises because an editor changes wording because the editor simply prefers that it be written a different way.

That style of editing violates an important, though unwritten, principle: the reporter "owns" the story. At one level, that statement is inaccurate. Formally, the newspaper "owns" the story. It hired the reporter to do the work, and it has a right to use it or not. The newspaper and its editors do not, however, have a moral right to do as they wish with a story. The work is based on the reporter's information gathering, and his or her byline appears on it. Informally, the reporter really "owns" the story. The story is "on loan" to editors, who ensure that standards of fairness, accuracy, balance, clarity, comprehensibility and the like are met. The reporter's ownership is tempered by institutional needs. Good editors accept responsibility for the story. They represent the institution and the readership. Reporters can do what they want within limits set by the institution and administered by editors. In so doing editors, particularly copy editors, are acting as "readers' representatives."

2. Suggest, don't dictate. And be ready to adjust, compromise or make another suggestion. This approach is a key element of coaching (see below), but many excellent editors who would not call themselves coaches use this strategy. As a copy editor, I found that making a suggestion was almost always better than merely questioning the wording of a lead or another paragraph. It opens a dialogue whose logic is similar to the logic of the philosophical dialectic of thesis–antithesis–synthesis. A benefit is that the result is often better than the reporter's original words *or* the copy editor's suggested rewrite.

Why do this? Suggesting rather than telling demonstrates that the reporter's view is valued and doesn't usurp the reporter's power. Copy editors don't have to ask about everything. They don't have the time, and it's not necessary. But on changes that might be arguable, such as tone, word choice and sentence structure, discussing problems and suggesting changes can be very productive. People like to choose. They like to have a say in what they produce. Writing coach Donald Murray said he often would make several suggestions when he was working with writers.[4]

3. Ask the right questions. Stories should not run with major flaws or holes. But ask yourself whether you (or the reporters) have the time to address relatively minor points that would be nice to have for comprehensiveness but that are not essential, especially if they require additional reporting. For example, the copy editor who mechanically asks a reporter to provide the age of any source quoted in a story is likely to develop a reputation as a carping nitpicker. Often, the age of a source is useful information in news stories, but sometimes it really doesn't matter. And it can be difficult for the reporter to track that information down. Copy editors who have been reporters often have a better sense of what is possible in the time available and what really is impractical given daily deadlines.

4. Pick your battles. Some proposed changes are too minor to argue over, and a tendency to pick fights over every word choice can reinforce the reputation of a copy editor as "a common scold," as McIntyre puts it. Arguing over nothing also can work to a copy editor's disadvantage when serious issues arise. You don't want to be seen as Chicken Little; you want to make sure that people listen to you when it's important. Sometimes good enough is good enough.

When do you agree to disagree and take it to the next level? Matters of fairness, taste and libel are often a good reason. Anything that might spare the paper serious embarrassment is a good bet. As a copy chief, I once argued a grammar point through several levels of editor. It was a dangling modifier in the lead of a three-part series, the first series the newspaper had written from Vietnam since the end of the war. The reporter did not want to change it, and the assigning editor and his supervisor agreed. I pursued the issue because I felt a grammatical error in the lead paragraph of the showcase article on the front page of a million-copy Sunday paper would not look very professional. I was prepared to take it to the top. It was changed.

5. Make "the reader" an ally. Of course, you as a copy editor don't have a special "lifeline" to the reader. Neither does the reporter. And, of course there is no such thing as "the reader." Readers of general circulation periodicals, such as newspapers, are not the same and typically are not even similar in age, race, sex, educational background, life experiences and interests. As an editor, you should have a pretty good idea what makes a story hard to read or insensitive or unclear. And you certainly have the reader in mind when you suggest changes to make the story more accessible and understandable. But even if the logic of appealing to "the reader" is questionable, the strategy can be valuable anyway. It can sometimes defuse a situation that has degenerated into "my word against yours" or agreeing to disagree. By appealing to a third party, one that both reporter and editor are supposed to be serving, it is possible to bracket the personalities out of a conflict and speak more directly to the issues.

6. Give in occasionally. On a story that has many problems that you and the reporter have been able to solve through discussion, you might back off on a point or two of disagreement. This can be a useful strategy even when you suspect your change would improve the story. Sometimes preserving the relationship is more important than letting a slightly cluttered passage or a minor ambiguity through. Again, use common sense. Don't let anything serious, such as an inaccuracy, through.

7. Rewrite when necessary. Plenty of stories can be improved, but make sure that what you're doing or suggesting reflects improvement that you and the reporter can agree upon. Too many editors rewrite merely because they themselves wouldn't have written the story that way. That's not a good enough reason, and it often creates unnecessary and unproductive tension. As suggested in the first tip, copy editors should be able to defend any change they make to a story and be able to articulate substantive reasons. Such reasons include accuracy, clarity, comprehensiveness, grammar, spelling, punctuation, flow, organization, and the like. Writers, on the

whole, don't mind being edited if they understand why changes should be made. Most realize that they are not perfect, and they want to improve. What irritates writers greatly is seeing their stories substantially rewritten for no apparent (or a never articulated) reason. What makes them even angrier is hearing an editor say, "I didn't like it" when they ask why a lead was changed or why a story was rewritten.

8. Don't come into the saloon with guns blazing. If the lead is a big problem, don't begin a conversation by saying "This lead is incoherent!" Start with minor fixes and points that are clear-cut; move on to potentially more difficult issues. This approach is similar to a strategy articulated by Ken Metzler in his textbook on interviewing.[5] Metzler points out that skilled interviewers often start with small talk and easy ego-reinforcing questions and move in stages to areas that are more complicated and potentially troublesome.

9. Save their butts. Sometimes that's all you can do to get prickly reporters or prima donna columnists to realize that they are better off with you than without you. This strategy takes time, but time is generally on the copy editor's side. The nature of daily newspapering, indeed one of the main reasons copy editors have job security, is that mistakes will be made. Sooner or later, the problem writer will make a serious mistake with a name or some other fact, and if you're vigilant, you can catch it. It's worth mentioning it to the writer, but do so casually, not in an "I told you so" or "Gotcha" tone.

10. Make friends. It is easier to have a good working relationship if you have a friendly or at least a collegial relationship. Don't always talk shop with colleagues. Discuss other things—sports, if you're not on the sports desk, or fishing, music, politics or restaurants. Talk about your kids. Organize a staff softball game or a barbecue. At small papers, staff members from different departments often attend get-togethers or spend time outside of work together. Many editors and reporters who work for small papers are about the same age and at a similar stage in their careers. In fact, many reporters at those papers are editors, and vice versa. Interaction outside of work is often much easier because there aren't as many options in a small town. At larger papers, which are more bureaucratic and have more specialized staff positions, interaction outside of work (and inside it) often is difficult to maintain. Reporters and copy editors can be 25 or 65. Some are not long out of college; others have grandchildren. The possibility of outside interaction is worse at morning papers, where many reporters work a traditional day shift and many copy editors work what is called a swing

shift at a mill (from 3 to 11 or 4 to midnight). Mismatched schedules even color professional out-of-work activities. For example, Society of Professional Journalist chapters often offer excellent professional programs that can help bridge gaps between different departments. But if you work for a morning newspaper copy desk, you'll probably miss most of those sessions. They'll be scheduled when most of the staff (i.e., reporters) can attend. That serves the greatest number, but it doesn't help copy editors. News organizations themselves can arrange training sessions at times when all staff members can attend.

PEOPLE-MANAGEMENT IDEAS

Copy editors can adopt approaches for dealing with people that have been used by enlightened managers in many fields. Here are a few:

• Praise in public, criticize in private. This prescription has taken on the status of a mantra in business/management circles, but it remains an underused strategy in news organizations. Daily journalists tend to spot a problem and react. Often vocally. And deadline pressures exacerbate the problem. Many journalists of an earlier era, particularly editors, were uncharitable in their criticism. Some were just mean. They acted as though yelling at or even swearing at reporters was the path to reporter enlightenment. Some reporters did learn their craft that way. Clark and Fry report the experience of Jon Franklin, a two-time Pulitzer Prize-winner who said he learned to do the job right by sheepishly listening as an editor tore his stories to bits. Franklin also said he got an ulcer in the process.[6] Clark and Fry point out that there's a better way, and their book is a lengthy articulation of that better way: coaching.

Copy editors are starting at a disadvantage; critiquing is a big part of the job, and it might be the most important part of the job. And nobody likes to be criticized, even in a profession where criticism is expected. One strategy to make the inevitable criticism go more smoothly is to not always criticize. Nothing, other than tradition, is stopping copy editors from congratulating reporters who write a good lead, report a telling detail or provide a particularly clear explanation of a complex issue. How you praise is very important. As Joe Grimm, the Detroit Free Press recruiting and development editor, says, "drive-by feedback" praise is ineffective. Don't just say, "Great story," as you pass someone in the hall. Make it specific—tell the reporter exactly what you liked about the story.[7] Besides being a nice thing to do, offering specific praise is a good management strategy; it encourages the writer to do more of the same.

Some newsrooms seem like war zones. Reporters see the copy desk as enemy territory, and copy editors see the reporters' area as the same. Both sides have a natural aversion to crossing enemy lines. Moreover, design of space with a department, such as the copy desk, can make things more difficult. At most newspapers, copy editors work side by side, and a discussion with a reporter at the copy desk is not very private. One strategy is to leave the security of the copy editing desk, pod or lair and walk over to the reporter's desk to talk about a story. Copy editors who make a habit of crossing the line can improve relations with reporters while they solve a specific problem with a story.

The wrong way to solve the "criticize in private" problem, indeed a solution that can create greater problems, is to use e-mail. Electronic communication is certainly private, but anyone who has spent time on discussion lists knows that e-mail comments all too easily can be taken the wrong way. A seemingly innocuous comment can be taken as a personal attack and quickly descend into name-calling and ad hominem attacks. What's worse, e-mails can be forwarded to others, further escalating a conflict. It is easy to get angry over e-mail; it's more difficult to get angry in person. Face-to-face communication preserves the multiple levels of human interaction, such as expression or even body language, that are used by skilled professionals to communicate respect, even while they are criticizing a person's work. E-mail can be used productively in newsrooms, to double-check a minor point or to check in with a supervisor on deadline, but using it to discuss substantive criticism is a false economy.

Another way to implement this management strategy is to not mark up mistakes and put them on bulletin boards. This practice is common at many newspapers, and it always breeds resentment. No reporter (or copy editor, for that matter) likes to see his or her mistakes circled in red and displayed in a public place. A reporter might learn to avoid making the mistake in the future, but the reporter also will learn to resent the person doing the markup. It is, and always has been, a bad idea. A better idea is to collect some typical mistakes, remove identification and use them for overall staff training or workshops.

• Criticize the work, not the person. This is a tricky issue because journalists have so much invested in their work. Criticism of a reporter's writing ("This lead is unclear") can easily be misinterpreted as criticism of the person ("You can't write clearly"). Criticism in public makes it worse. It is difficult to not view public criticism as an attack on the person.

The previous strategies, which can greatly improve editor–reporter interaction, lean heavily on individual initiative and have an ad hoc quality. There also are more structured ways to improve those relationships.

CROSS-TRAINING

The idea is simple: Walk a mile in their shoes. Some papers have taken a page from the management book on team-building and have instituted cross-training. A copy editor might work for a short period as a reporter or a designer, or a reporter might spend some time as a copy editor. This approach has several obvious benefits. It increases scheduling flexibility if staff members know multiple jobs, but, more important, it gives staff members firsthand experience with the pressures and challenges of jobs held by others. Copy editors who have been reporters are in a better position to discuss stories with reporters and assigning editors. They've been there and done it. They have faced similar problems with sources, deadlines, writer's block, and so on that the reporters they now deal with face. Trading places yields understanding and credibility. Familiarity breeds understanding, not contempt. Should all copy editors have reporting experience? Some top editors refuse to hire a copy editor who has not been a reporter. For the rest, who probably are a substantial majority, it's pretty much moot. Even if managers prefer to hire copy editors with reporting experience, the supply and demand are out of balance. Technological change, primarily the need for additional copy editors to handle pagination, and the increasingly difficult time many papers have attracting good copy editors in the first place have made this question largely irrelevant. Newspapers can no longer afford to insist that copy editors have reporting experience, as many once did. But they can make adjustments.

The Philadelphia Inquirer, for example, occasionally hired copy editors right out of college (usually after an internship or two). Because the newsroom management realized the value of reporting experience, those copy editors would spend some time early in their careers in reporting positions, usually in suburban bureaus.

Even if you can't swap jobs, you can learn about the other positions. One suggestion is to go to lunch with reporters, photographers or others and talk about what they do.

EDITING PROTOCOLS

Different publications have different corporate cultures as far as the level of editing that is expected and/or acceptable without discussion, but few have written these "rules" down. Some well-known metropolitan newspapers have a reputation as "reporters' papers," and others are known as "editors' papers." The Washington Post was probably the best-known example of the former category, and the New York Times of the latter. Most papers are somewhere in the middle. The situation is further complicated because reporters who work for the same publication can react very differently to editing. Some don't fret over substantive reorganization, even wholesale rewriting, while others are wedded to every comma they type and sometimes even complain about style changes. Sometimes a copy editor finds out that he or she has broken an unwritten rule only when a reporter hollers or writes an impassioned memo to the managing editor.

Roy Peter Clark and Don Fry, in an excellent book called "Coaching Writers," discuss one possible solution to the problem. They talk about "editing protocols," which they define as "nothing more than a set of guidelines" that reporters and editors can follow in making changes to copy, particularly late in the editing process.[8] They report the results of a 1989 Poynter Institute seminar, in which a group of copy editors drafted a list of "38 typical changes that copy editors are often called upon to make at the last-minute." The protocols are broken into three sections:

1. Changes in which consultation is not required. Examples are correcting a misspelled word, clarifying attribution and making minor cuts for space.
2. Changes in which consultation is desirable. Examples are paraphrasing a quotation, moving a sentence or section, unless they are important.
3. Changes in which consultation is required. Examples are changing a lead, revising for fairness, revising the tone of the story and holding a story.[9]

A small number of newspapers have written protocols; many have unwritten ones that copy editors learn through trial and error. Protocols differ because papers have different histories and organizational cultures. Some encourage strong, open criticism and aggressive copy editing. Others seem to discourage it. Some encourage copy editors to criticize the organization or tone of a story but not whether a story should run at all. Some feel that copy editors' are fact-checkers, style fixers and headline writers and that substantive questions should be addressed by others in the editing chain.

A written protocol can be a valuable tool, as long as it doesn't become a straitjacket. It is of no use if staff members—copy editors, assigning editors and reporters in particular—don't know it exists. That sometimes happens. As Clark and Fry point out, protocols are best used as guidelines. They can stimulate discussion about the editing process in a newsroom and can help improve relations between departments. "But," they caution, "any protocol that gets in the way of common sense or efficiency is not worth much."[10]

Any protocol that suggests discussion of one issue or another is moot if a copy editor can't get in touch with the reporter. This problems occurs often at papers where reporters and editors work different shifts. One of the easiest ways to ensure that discussion can happen is to get a phone number where the reporter can be reached or have the reporter call in later.

COACHING

An approach known as the coaching movement takes a somewhat different approach. It sees the editor–reporter relationship primarily as one of consultation. Clark and Fry, who teach at The Poynter Institute, have explained the approach in "Coaching Writers." They point out that consultant Donald Murray was the first to use the term in the context of newspaper editing and that the movement has grown in popularity in the 25 years since Murray began working as a writing coach at The Boston Globe.[11] Now a sizable minority of newspapers have a staff position that includes the word *coach* in the title. Newspapers can find dozens of consultants who offer coaching services in both writing and editing. An online discussion list, newscoach-l, is written by and for coaches; most of the more than 100 members are either part- or full-time writing coaches at their newspapers.

Clark and Fry aimed their book primarily at assigning editors, but the ideas can be applied more broadly. Many of the techniques can be employed by copy editors in their relationships with reporters, and some of the ideas can be translated to the relationship between copy editors and their supervisors on the desk. Training editor Michael Roberts of The Cincinnati Enquirer says, "I think anyone can be a coach—peers, bosses, even skilled subordinates coaching upwards."[12]

Clark and Fry draw a key distinction between coaching and fixing:

> "Every editor must learn to fix stories, but fixing is not the same as coaching. Coaching is the human side of editing, fixing the literary side. In other words, the editor coaches the writer but fixes the story."[13]

What is important, they say, is helping the writer learn to improve the story. In practice, that means the responsibility for revision rests with the writer, not the editor. The editor's responsibility is to help the writer see what revisions will improve the story. The benefits of this approach, they say, are long term:

> "Fixing has an important short-term benefit: getting the story up to the standard at which it can appear in the paper. Coaching feels better and lasts longer. . . ."

Coaching can build a reporter's confidence, but "crude fixing undercuts the confidence of the reporter." By crude fixing, they are referring to the all-too-typical example of a reporter waking up to read a very different story in the newspaper than the one he or she turned in the night before.

> "Fixing may turn writers and editors into adversaries, whereas coaching unites them as partners."[14]

A few other ideas from coaching are careful listening, consultation throughout the writing process, and an emphasis on working with writers rather than telling them what to do.

Clark and Fry say that coaching means that editors will have to spend more time early in the process, but they point out that the time spent on the front end means a great deal of time saved later. A two-minute discussion about the focus of a story early in the writing process can save 20 or more minutes of last-minute reorganizing or rewriting.

Coaching can help in plenty of situations. At one small-circulation afternoon daily, the city editor often heavily rewrote stories. He had been a talented reporter and was probably the best writer on staff, and his rewrites clearly improved the stories. The readers benefited, but the reporters fumed. The city editor did not give them the opportunity to rework their own stories, and he never explained why he rewrote them. A city editor facing deadline pressures might reasonably conclude that it is quicker to rewrite than to discuss or negotiate changes with a reporter. In the short term, the city editor is correct. Afternoon newspapers work on very tight deadlines, and editors have long used those pressures to justify their seemingly arbitrary actions. But as Clark and Fry point out, that style of "fixing" can waste time in the long run, because the reporter will not change by osmosis. If an editor can afford to spend some time on the front end, explaining the problem and letting the reporter address it, that reporter is less likely to repeat the mistake in the future. In the long run, it saves the city editor time.

COACHING AND COPY EDITING

It is easy to see how coaching can improve the relationships between reporters and assigning editors. But how does this apply to copy editors, who are at a different stage in the editing process? Can they also act as coaches?

Yes and no. The nature of the editing process, which in almost all newsrooms places copy editors right at the point of production, means that some of the approaches used in coaching will not work. Copy editors will not be able to consult with reporters early in the writing process, they will generally not have as much time for consultation as assigning editors might, and they might not have the luxury of letting reporters do their own revisions, particularly near deadline. Sometimes there's only time for fixing. Besides, there is a different dynamic between copy editors and reporters than there is between assigning editors and reporters. Copy editors typically are not in a supervisor–supervised relationship with reporters, as assigning editors are. Some of the techniques suggested by Clark and Fry work largely because they remove the hierarchy from that relationship.

But copy editors can apply some coaching ideas to their interactions with reporters. Asking, listening and suggesting are three of those strategies. For example, suppose a copy editor wanted to change the following lead, which appeared on a front-page analysis story in July 2002. The copy editor thinks the two paragraphs, really just two sentences, are too long to read easily and contain more information than they need to:

WASHINGTON—With the stock market plunging the other day and surveys depicting Americans as increasingly worried about the way the Bush administration is dealing with the economy and corporate fraud, Treasury Secretary Paul H. O'Neill, the administration's main voice on economic issues, was in Kyrgyzstan.

Mr. O'Neill's absence—after a trip to Africa in late May and before a trip to South America late this month—reinforced the view on Wall Street and in political circles here that President Bush's economic team was not responding sufficiently to growing economic and political pressures.

A typical "fixing" approach is to tighten the lead, move the unnecessary information lower in the story and call the reporter over to the desk to approve the rewrite.

WASHINGTON—Last week, the stock market was plunging and Americans were growing more worried about the Bush administration's handling of the economy and corporate fraud. Meanwhile, Treasury Secretary Paul H. O'Neill was in Kyrgyzstan.

Mr. O'Neill's absence reinforced the view on Wall Street and in political circles here that President Bush's economic team was not responding sufficiently to growing economic and political pressures.

A coaching approach takes a different tack. The copy editor first asks the reporter why he thought it important to include all of the information in the lead. The reporter might have a reason that the copy editor didn't consider. He might not. If not, the copy editor could suggest removing X, Y and Z from the lead, or turning the long first sentence into an itemization:

WASHINGTON—The stock market plunged the other day. Surveys showed Americans increasingly worried about the economy and corporate fraud. And Treasury Secretary Paul H. O'Neill was in Kyrgyzstan.

Mr. O'Neill's absence reinforced the view on Wall Street and in political circles here that President Bush's economic team was not responding sufficiently to growing economic and political pressures.

The reporter looks at the new lead and says, "I see your point about the length of the lead, but your first graf reads too much like another story we ran about the market, not about how the administration is dealing with it. And I'd like to make sure people know why O'Neill is important." The copy editor agrees. The reporter sits down and crafts a new lead, removing X and Y but leaving Z in because it's important and doesn't get in the way:

> WASHINGTON—As the stock market plunged and Americans grew more worried about the Bush administration's handling of the economy and corporate fraud, Treasury Secretary Paul H. O'Neill was in Kyrgyzstan.
> The absence of Mr. O'Neill, the administration's main voice on economic issues, reinforced the view on Wall Street and in political circles here that President Bush's economic team was not responding sufficiently to growing economic and political pressures.

The reporter retains control of the lead, and the copy editor has helped make it more readable. The lead rewritten by the reporter isn't very different from the lead using the "fixing approach." The benefit is that the reporter did it. It takes a bit more time to use the coaching strategy, but not that much longer, and the payoff, as Clark and Fry suggest, is worth it.

When do you coach and when do you edit? The not-so-simple answer is coach when you have the time and edit when you don't. And sometimes unnecessary discussion can waste time by turning into unnecessary negotiation. Some editing points are simply not worth negotiating when time is short. Copy editors should edit, and if that means fixing what needs to be fixed, so be it. That's what they get paid for. But it doesn't mean that running roughshod over a writer's work is OK.

Copy editors too can benefit from the coaching process, especially if they have a supervisor, a copy chief or a slot, who acts as a coach. Some slots are every bit as heavy-handed as the most insensitive city editor. If they don't like a headline turned in by someone on the rim, they simply rewrite it without discussion. Like the city editor in the example above, the slot expects the copy editor to understand why without explaining it. This "crude fixing" of headlines can lead to the same ill will that "fixing" a story can. Headline writing is part of the craft of copy editing just as writing a lead is part of reporting. Copy editors want to feel they have ownership of their work, just as reporters do. Slots who take a coaching approach, asking questions and offering suggestions so that the copy editor can do the rewrite, will be teachers as well as supervisors. If there's no time to coach, and often there isn't, the slot should make time after deadline to explain why the headline was changed and offer the copy editor the opportunity to redo it for the next edition.

THE COPY EDITOR–SLOT RELATIONSHIP

Not all newspapers have copy chiefs or slots. More of them should. A slot at a midsize paper might supervise a few copy editors; a slot at a large metropolitan daily might supervise 10 or 15. But a slot is more than a supervisor. He or she is also a teacher. A slot teaches copy editors how to do the job the paper wants them to do. A good slot can also teach reporters and assigning editors.

What makes a good slot? Some management consultants suggest that it's more important for supervisors to be good leaders than technical experts. Supervising copy editors is somewhat different. To retain credibility with the rim, a slot needs to be as good or better a wordsmith—and a good leader. A good slot needs to have excellent copy editing and headline-writing skills as well as good people skills. A copy chief with poor people skills makes life miserable for copy editors on the rim; a good leader who is not a good technical copy editor is not an effective coach or a constructive critic. The best slots are people who can both do and teach.

THE COPY EDITOR–DESIGNER RELATIONSHIP

It's 10 p.m. on a Friday; deadline for the first edition of the Sunday paper is several hours away. The copy desk still has not seen page layouts for a special year-in-review section. Why not? The designer, who works in the art department, is hanging onto the pages, trying to make the designs perfect. The copy desk is running out of time, and the slot complains to the news editor. The rim typically needs the last couple of hours to finish Page One and edit late stories. Finally, around midnight, the designs appear, two hours before the pages are to be set in type. The copy desk slaps headlines and captions on the stories and outputs the pages because it needs the rest of the time to finish its other work. The designer is pleased; the section looks good. The copy editors are angry; they have not had time to write good headlines. They know they could have done a better job if the designer understood their jobs as well as his own.

Why does this happen? A simple case of an inconsiderate designer and newsroom management unwilling to get involved? Perhaps. More likely it's a lack of understanding of the other's needs, in particular how long it takes to do a credible job of writing display type for a special section. The desire on the designer's part to create the best possible (most artistic and functional) designs is understandable, but the desire of the copy desk to craft the best possible words to flow into those designs is a legitimate concern as well. Even if the copy desk somehow works a miracle and delivers great display type, hard feelings will be a byproduct.

Designers need to understand the rhythms of copy editing and the limitations copy editors face. Every copy editor has a war story about the one-column headline that needs to have the name "Druckenmiller" or "Schwartzkopf" in it.

Copy editors, likewise, need a better understanding of the issues designers face. They need to treat designers as journalists, an approach that often is missing from editor–designer interactions. Several items from a list of "22 Things Never to Say to a Newspaper Designer" give a flavor:

"The story and pictures will be in tomorrow. Can't you start now?"

"We have to make a last-minute switch and there's no art with the cover story. Can you pull something together real quick?"

"We've worked on this story for a year. You have three hours."[15]

The copy editor–designer relationship is one that cross-training can dramatically improve.

THE COPY EDITOR–PHOTOGRAPHER RELATIONSHIP

During a break in a copy editing workshop at a midsize daily in the Northwest, I was called aside by the photo editor, who shoved a tear sheet into my hand. "Tell them about this one," he said, pointing to a feature centerpiece about after-school activities at a school for the deaf. He had circled a small headline that accompanied a photo showing the color guard leading the Pledge of Allegiance in sign language during a football game. The headline, which was at best confusing, read:

Cheerleading
stays the same

He'd written in red:

1. They're not cheerleading
2. It isn't the same—they sign.

He was angry. His photographer had provided accurate caption information, but the copy editor blew it. The headline might have been trying to suggest that cheerleading is still cheerleading, even at a school for the deaf. But it didn't read that way, and as the photo editor pointed out, it wasn't even a picture of cheerleaders; it was the color guard.

The photo editor and the other photographers considered themselves visual journalists. They got the correct information as well as the shot. When the picture appeared with incorrect information, it reflected badly on the photographers as journalists. There's a history here that copy editors should know about. Few editors and reporters are aware of the resistance news photographers faced in their struggle to get editors and reporters to think of them as journalists. For many years, they were considered little more than technicians.[16] One finds photographers complaining in trade journal reports as late as the '90s that they were still being treated as second-class citizens in the newsroom.[17] Design consultant Ron Reason's compilation of "Things Never to Say To or About a Photojournalist" reflect the slights many have heard. For example:

"Are you just a photographer, or do you write, too"?

"We need to fill this page; get one of the photographers and tell them to go find something."

"No, you can't come on the interview. The subject will never open up with a photographer around."[18]

Underlying most of the comments is a dismissive attitude toward the photographer as journalist.

Tensions can arise in newsrooms because other journalists fail to treat photographers as equals. Copy editors, who often interact with photo staff members about sizing, cropping, choice of photos and caption information, should be aware of the history and the issues and should work on improving the relationships.

CONCLUSION

Technical ability, whether in writing, editing, photo or design, takes you only so far. Newspapers are organizations that depend on teamwork, and people in different departments need to learn to play nice. Quality newspaper work depends as much on relationships as it does on technical skill. But the relative insularity of departments in publishing organizations and poor interaction between members of different departments can have serious effects on the quality of the work produced and on the smooth running of the organization.

Many journalists are working to make things better. Professional meetings, institute workshops and in-house newsletters are picking up on the problem, devoting time and resources to such discussions. Tips and strategies from coaches and excellent editors have been reaching a broader audience. It's a good trend, one that should continue. Relationships are much better now than the days when interaction flowed in one direction—from editor to reporter—and most of it was monosyllabic, primarily the word "No."

8 ◢ ◢ ◢ ◢ ◢ ◢ ◢ ◢ ◢ ◢ ◢

Introduction to Display Type

What is "display type"? The simplest definition is "the bigger type." It is a catchall term that some papers use to refer to the headlines, decks, captions and other forms of presentation type written by copy editors. The term may be new, but the idea is old. Newspapers have used larger and/or bolder type for many years. Headlines, which first were set in relatively small point sizes because of the cost of paper and other printing materials, have grown in importance to the extent that they now take up a significant fraction of a typical page. Adding other display elements, such as secondary, or "drop," headlines, summary decks or paragraphs, captions, and liftout quotes, means newspapers might devote 10 percent of their "news hole," their available space, to display type. Given that commitment in space and cost, copy editors should take great care with display type. Yet at many publications display type is treated superficially, with little regard for any criteria other than whether it fits in the space and can be written in time to meet deadline.

Naming of display type elements often is inconsistent from publication to publication. What a newspaper copy editor calls a *headline*, a magazine editor calls a *title*. Even within newspapers, the same element can go by different names. At some papers, the shorthand for headline is spelled *head*; at others, it's spelled *hed*. For example, many papers call the 14- to

18-point display text that appears between the headline and the lead paragraph of the story a *summary paragraph*. Other papers refer to the same feature as a *deck*, a *nut graf*, a *blurb*, or any of a number of other names. To complicate things further, at many papers and magazines, a *nut graf* is not a display element at all. It's the paragraph in a feature story that follows the lead and transition, a story element that summarizes the focus and sets up the story. *Liftout quotes* at one publication are *pull quotes* at another. The line at the end of type on a section front that tells the reader where to find the rest of the story is variously called a *jump line*, a *turn line* or a *continuation line*. The words underneath or alongside pictures are called *captions* at many publications. At others, editors refer to them as *cutlines*, a term that dates to the era of photoengraving, when back-shop workers turned photographs into halftone engravings called *cuts*.

About the only newspaper display element on which there is general agreement is the term *headline*, though there sometimes is disagreement about whether a given form is actually a headline or something else.

FUNCTION OF DISPLAY TYPE

The most well-known and important function of display type, of course, is to summarize the story. Headlines and decks, in most cases, "tell the story." Captions explain the photos and sometimes provide additional important or interesting information that does not fit into other display-type elements. Liftout quotes and other display elements provide secondary information as well as offer readers what many designers call "points of entry" to the page.

Display type also has important visual functions. Newspaper designers talk about "breaking up the gray." Bigger and bolder type breaks up masses of small, low-contrast body type, thereby making pages more visually interesting and inviting. The relative density of large-pointsize headlines contrasts with the relative lightness of body type. Contrasting elements are particularly important on newsprint, which is of lower quality, and thus offers less contrast than the better grades of paper typically used in magazines or books. Moreover, designers use variations in size and boldness of display type to help give readers a map of sorts—to tell readers what stories are most important, what is secondary, what is serious and what is lighter in tone.

Well-written display type is crucial for "scanners" or browsers, those readers who actually read very little. Scanners look over pages to catch the gist of the news without reading all, or sometimes even any, of the story. Well-written and well-conceived display type can act as a headline service, providing enough of the story for casual or busy readers to get some grasp of the news. It can also "sell" the story and help turn scanners into readers. This function of display type has become more important in the last several decades as changes in work and leisure have severely limited reading time for many people.

AN APPROACH TO DISPLAY TYPE

Display type is powerful and should be handled with great care. It can color the reader's view of the story before the story is read. Good display type can create a strong impression, poor display type can create a weak impression, and erroneous or misleading display type can create a misimpression of the story. Display type, particularly the headline, is the first text the reader sees, and, in many cases, it's the only text a reader pays attention to. A great deal of thought should go into display type, what it says, how readable it is, how understandable it is, how it looks.

In writing display type, a copy editor should understand that the whole is often greater than the sum of the parts. Headlines, decks, captions and liftouts carefully crafted to work together can tie important aspects of a story package together, presenting information in a way that individual elements cannot possibly do. In so doing, the parts should neither conflict with one another nor be unnecessarily repetitive. Some news organizations strongly discourage the repetition of even one key word in two elements of display type on the same story. Others seek to avoid use of the same word in headlines on different stories on the same page. Within a headline, copy editors generally shun repetition. It wastes precious space. If a headline order is too tight to convey the essence of the story, some repetition might be crucial to enhance clarity or prevent misunderstanding. But in rare cases repetition can be necessary or even creative. Here's a headline that appeared in The Register-Guard of Eugene, Ore., during the recount controversy in the Bush–Gore election:

**Gore builds his case
as Bush builds his team**

Repetition is what raises this headline out of the ordinary. Many papers would not run the headline as is because of the repetition, or they would try to find a synonym for one of the *builds*. That would be a mistake; the word *builds* is the right word in each clause. Publications that stick to rules at all costs often lose the opportunity to provide readers a very good headline. Some publications enforce criteria for headlines and captions that others find unnecessary or even counterproductive. The next few chapters will examine some of these rules and discuss which are worth saving and which should be re-examined.

Display type ultimately serves the story. The story is what's important; display type presents it and provides entry points into it. In most newsrooms, copy editors are the only staff members who have control over all of the words that present the story. Their goal should be to use display type effectively—to provide as much information as clearly as possible and to select information in a way that is representative of the story.

Display type can be a minefield. Because the copy editor works with fewer words than the reporter does, the chances of writing hyped or misleading headlines are great. Readers often comment about headlines they feel are incorrect, misleading or miss the point. Here's a headline on a story about a 2002 wildfire, known as the "Biscuit fire," in southwestern Oregon near the California border:

Biscuit fire could put out
the lights in California

That looks serious, especially given the widespread power outages Southern California suffered through the summer before. The lead, however, tells a different story:

> Oregon's largest wildfire in more than a century threatened power lines feeding several Northern California towns Sunday as crews tried to stop a slow creep along its southeastern flank.

The headline should have said "some lights in California." or even "in N. California."

Beyond headlines, other elements of display type, even elements as seemingly innocuous as liftout quotes, can convey misimpressions when they are taken out of context. A striking or extreme opinion that appears as a quote in the body of a story can be seen for what it is: a relatively mi-nor element, one that's not typical but worth mentioning in the whole of the story. When the same words are pulled out and set in larger type as a liftout, they can take on an importance far greater than they warrant. Copy editors often are tempted to find the "best" quote for a liftout; they need to remember that the bar is higher for them—the quote must not invite read-ers to conclude that the quote is representative of the story.

Display type has been undergoing much change, and no doubt it will continue to be fertile ground for design and typographic experimentation. Styles of headlines, captions and other elements come and go, as do type-faces. Sometimes, it seems, design experts are either reinventing the wheel or perhaps marketing the past as the future. Headlines written as multiple decks never died in The New York Times or The Wall Street Journal, but at most dailies, multiple-deck headlines were eliminated by the mid-20th century. Redesign experts felt decks did not look modern and clashed with modular design, which became the norm in the last three decades. Toward the end of the century, multiple decks began making a comeback at several well-known papers. An example is The (Baltimore) Sun, which typically uses more than two decks on front-page headlines. Whether this trend will continue to grow or wither again is anyone's guess. Taking a long view on design trends in newspapers, one is tempted to agree with Yogi Berra, who said, "It's déjà vu all over again." Copy editors, unless they also are design-ers, can do little but watch the show and make the necessary adjustments.

Writing display type has become more complicated and will probably continue to become more complicated. This trend is good news for busy readers, who appreciate the fact that they can find out what's going on without spending a lot of time reading stories, but it's not so good news for busy copy editors, who find they have a lot more work to do to write and coordinate display-type elements in an era of shrinking newsroom budgets and staff cuts. Writing good display type takes practice, and good criticism is the best way for the inexperienced to learn. Some copy editors seem to have a knack for turning out high-quality display type quickly. Others struggle with it. But all copy editors can learn to write better display type.

9

Headline Basics

In the late 19th century, philosopher Charles Sanders Peirce developed a threefold way of understanding the function of language. Peirce, who is regarded as one of the foundational thinkers in the field of semiotics—the study of signs—said signs can act as icon, index or symbol.[1] Not all signs have all functions. Words, for the most part, have only one: they refer to an object or a concept. They have a referential, or symbolic, function; in other words, they carry meaning. A highway sign that depicts a curve in the road has both an iconic and a symbolic function. The curved line on the sign is an icon—an image, of sorts, of the actual twisting road. The sign itself also has symbolic meaning—there is a curve ahead, so pay attention and slow down. Another type of road sign might have a stronger indexical function. A one-way arrow, for example, has a pointing as well as a semantic function.

Peirce was a philosopher and scientist. He did not discuss headlines, but if he had, he might have looked on them as a semiotic trifecta. Headlines have all three functions. They have an iconic function, that is, they provide a clue about the importance of the story. Large headlines, headlines at the top of the page and headlines on the front pages of sections communicate importance. Headlines also tell the reader where to begin the story. That is an indexical, or pointing, function. It's probably easiest to see this function in its absence. When poor design separates the headline from the beginning of the story, readers are left to flounder—to search for the beginning of the text. Finally, headlines tell the story, or at least offer strong clues about the content of the story. This is a symbolic, or referential, function. Headlines typically summarize the story's main point or points.

In a semiotic sense, headlines are very powerful communication devices because they work at multiple levels—probably more than Peirce's three. Headlines have extremely high readership—researchers often point out that headlines are all that scanners or casual readers see when they page through a newspaper. Headlines also provide important cues for committed or thorough readers. On Web pages, headlines often are treated as links—readers choose to follow a link on the basis of what the headline says. Unfortunately, the care and time editors take in writing headlines is often minuscule in proportion to their importance to readers. Many times heads are written as an afterthought—a few words slapped atop the story and squeezed or expanded through the magic of desktop publishing software to fit the space and make the edition.

HEADLINE HISTORY

It's difficult to imagine a newspaper page without headlines, but, historically speaking, headlines are a relative newcomer. Newspapers of the late 18th and early 19th centuries often did not even use headlines. Headlines sometimes were difficult to distinguish from the story itself. They appeared in the same point size as the story, though sometimes in bold face. Paper and type fonts were expensive relative to the other costs involved in newsgathering and printing.[2] The printing technology of most of the 19th century also made it difficult to run large headlines, particularly multicolumn headlines. The column rules—the lines between columns that can be seen on microfilmed editions of newspapers from the 19th century—were more than a device to visually separate columns that were spaced close together. They did have such an effect, but they also played an important role in keeping the thousands of pieces of metal type locked into the page forms that were used on the presses of the day. "Breaking column rules" for a multicolumn headline was asking for mechanical trouble during printing.

Even major news events of the day—the election of a president, for example—bore headlines that seem embarrassingly tiny by today's standards. For a variety of reasons, including lower-cost paper, technological advances in printing and new competitive pressures, headlines began to appear in larger type. Many early headlines were written as labels, sometimes multiple labels. The decks often were written in different combinations of bold and light face, and in different styles, such as all caps or caps and lowercase. The New York Morning Journal's lead story on June 3, 1889, was a report on the devastating Johnstown (Pa.) flood. It ran under the following one-column headline:

AMID THE DEAD.
A Glimpse of the Hor-
ror at Johnstown.
A VALLEY OF DEATH.
1,500 Corpses Found—Un-
counted Thousands in Ruins.
A GHOUL LYNCHED.
Swarms of Drunken Roughs
Despoiling the Slain.

The headline uses labels such as "A VALLEY OF DEATH" as well as statements in a subject–verb construction, such as "1,500 Corpses Found." The number of lines roughly reflected the importance of the story.

Some big-city papers, such as Pulitzer's New York World and Hearst's New York Journal, developed a tradition of multicolumn headlines, and even banners—headlines that stretch across the width of the page—in the late 19th century, a time when metropolitan papers competed intensely for readers.

With the widespread adoption of stereotyping, a process that enabled papers to mount a lead cast of a complete page of type on their presses rather than the actual type itself in a page form, more multicolumn headlines began to appear. Newspaper pages began to use more horizontal page elements, calling for different types of headlines. Eventually, papers dropped many of the additional decks seen in those late 19th and early 20th century pages, instead letting one multiline headline carry the story.

Today, some newspapers tend toward vertical looks, with more one- and two-column, multiline headlines and the accompanying tighter headline counts; many follow more horizontal approaches, with four-, five- and six-column, one-line headlines common. Most are a blend of horizontal and vertical story elements and, as a result, papers use headlines in almost any column width. Computer typesetting has made it easy to design pages with type wraps and headlines specified at nonstandard lengths, known historically as "bastard" measures. As a result, many papers regularly deviate from their underlying page grid, especially for section fronts. In the late 20th century, many papers seeking a "new" look again began running multiple decks in descending point size, though typically in widths greater than one column. Such overall design changes mean that copy editors find themselves writing headlines in an almost dizzying array of line lengths and point sizes.

HEADLINE RULES

Headline rules also have evolved. Early headlines used simple past tense, as news stories did and still do. Headlines also appeared with ending punctuation, typically a period. Tense and punctuation rules began to change in the late 19th and early 20th centuries. Headlines now no longer have periods at the end; but other punctuation, such as question marks, which are necessary for comprehension, continue to be used. Single quote marks are used instead of double to save space. The simple past became a "historic present," which lent a greater feeling of immediacy to the news columns. In the 20th century, radio and later television laid claim to breaking news, offering far greater immediacy than a newspaper could. But the historic present has continued, and today one of the few ubiquitous headline rules is the use of present tense for events that occurred in the immediate past.

Mayor wins re-election

The headline speaks of yesterday's news in present tense, while the lead says, "Mayor Jane Washington won re-election yesterday. . . . " Most headlines are written in simple present tense, or in passive voice:

Arsenic
is found
in wells

Present-tense, active-voice headlines are preferable, but the limitations of line length and the goal of keeping related words together often make a passive-voice verb expedient. Occasionally, present perfect is used, sometimes with the auxiliary verb dropped.

**Mayor taking a vacation
after a bruising primary**

When one is referring to actions that have been taken or events that have occurred beyond the immediate past, headlines may be written in past tense.

**Sept. 11 tragedy kept
tourists from city
for several months**

**Silt from dam project
hurt fishing last spring**

Given the information the first headline seeks to convey—that the World Trade Center depressed tourism for several months—the present-tense verb "keeps" would not work. The past-tense headline on the river story also is appropriate, because it is speaking about a continuing action in the past. Past-tense headline are rare, because most news stories refer to events that happened yesterday.

Additional rules distinguish headline style from traditional news style. Most of these departures from AP style allow headline writers to save space.

- Numerals less than 10 are acceptable in any use (at many papers).

**Council approves
9-member board**

- More abbreviations are allowed in headlines (at many papers).

**Quake in Calif.
damages school**

- Easily recognizable abbreviations often are acceptable as nouns as well as adjectives (at many papers), and the percent sign (%) is acceptable, rather than "percent," as AP style specifies for text.

**N.J. turnout
exceeds 60%**

- A comma can be used in place of the word "and" if space is tight.

**Quake damages
school, church**

**Mayor, council
agree on taxes**

HEADLINE CRITERIA

Most newspapers subscribe to what might be called a "theory of headlines" that includes several criteria. A good headline should be:

- Specific. It should tell the story. The typical news headline is written to summarize the story as carefully and completely as possible. Sometimes, though, a headline should be more general, suggesting the theme rather than summarizing an action or issue. Feature stories often demand such an approach.
- Comprehensive. A headline should be as complete as possible in a handful of words.
- Clear. A headline should not confuse readers. It should be direct and to the point.
- Carefully attributed. If necessary. In most cases, sources are as important in headlines as in text.
- Graceful. To the degree possible.
- Faithful to the tone of the story.

Headlines should *not* be:

- Inaccurate.
- Misleading, that is, promise more than the story delivers, or invite the reader to draw an incorrect conclusion.
- Clever at the expense of clarity, tone or appropriateness.
- Agrammatical or break in awkward places

The skills headline writers use to meet those often conflicting demands are similar to those a reporter employs in crafting a good lead. But the key difference—what makes writing headlines both difficult and rewarding—is that the writer must do the job with four, five, six, or sometimes as many as eight words. The extreme brevity of headlines raises the bar considerably, so far that newspapers typically treat headlines as a task best done by specialists, editors of one title or another, rather than reporters.

Headline writing is more art than science, and a knowledge of rules and techniques helps tremendously. With practice and some coaching, copy editors can become quite good at headline writing. Many find it to be the most creative aspect of the job. Here is a closer look at those criteria.

SPECIFICITY

In general, specificity is good. Headlines tell the story. Many readers scan headlines to get a summary of the day's news, and headline writers should respect their wishes. Specificity is an important "user-friendly" criterion.

City Council holds
monthly meeting

Even an inexperienced copy editor realizes that this headline is inadequate. It is weak because it fails to capture the importance of the story—it is not specific. The council always holds monthly meetings. That isn't news. But too many copy editors fall into the trap of taking the headline only a small step farther:

City Council votes
on tax measure

A glance through many daily newspapers (and Web sites), turns up too many headlines of that sort. They offer a measure of specificity but less than most copy editors have within their grasp. "It fits; it's accurate; it'll do" is a mantra that has become more pronounced as editors have taken on many page makeup tasks once done in the composing room. Headline writers can do better, and it doesn't take much longer to do so.

Council increases
property tax 10%

An extra minute or two yields a headline that treats readers with the respect they deserve. A tax increase is news; a sense of the magnitude is crucial. That extra minute is time well spent.

Here's a headline about budget problems that ran under an overline, a label that said: "Springfield schools."

Programs may face budget ax

The headline is accurate but vague. It lacks specificity. The writer can provide a much greater sense of the story:

Music, sports, jobs may be cut

Here's another example:

Court lets
grading
practice
continue

One-column headlines are not easy, but this one can be improved considerably. Here are a few alternatives that fit in the same space:

Court
upholds
student
grading

Students
can grade
papers,
court rules

Students
can grade
kids' work,
court rules

The last one is the most specific, though some papers would shun the use of the word *kids* as too slangy. That's a matter of local option, but as the two other alternatives indicate, it's easy to make this headline more specific.[3]

A problem some headline writers have is an inability to determine when it is important to be specific, when specificity isn't necessary and when it's simply the wrong approach. A feature story that appears with a very specific, newsy headline is an example of the problem. A news story that cries out for a straightforward subject–verb–object treatment but winds up topped by an ill-conceived flight of verbal fancy is an example of the opposite problem.

COMPREHENSIVENESS

It seems silly to speak of thoroughness or comprehensiveness when the typical headline contains about five words. It's a good goal to keep in mind, though. Headlines should be as complete as they can be, tell as much of the story as possible and preserve important qualification. The following headline was not as complete as it could be:

Man's death resulted from inexperience

Thoroughness in this sense relates to both specificity and attribution. The headline does not provide enough information to lead readers to recall the original event, a news story the week before about a man who drowned while trying to rescue two girls caught in a strong river current. The headline also lacks attribution. It's an assertion from an emergency services official, but it reads as a self-evident truth. The following headline is more informative. It uses passive voice, but the tradeoff is worth it:

Inexperience cited in would-be rescuer's death

Lack of thoroughness often emerges as vagueness, and it can be seen in the extreme. The worst case is the "no news" headline, which summarizes an issue using words that on their face add up to self-evident truths.

Investigators find more evidence

A reader might reasonably ask, "Isn't that what they're supposed to do?" The headline says nothing. It is so vague as to be useless. An example from "The Lower case," a monthly feature of the Columbia Journalism Review also makes the point:

Plane too low to the ground, crash probe told

It's easy to see what the editor was trying to say—a plane had been flying too low—but in the context of a headline, which is really no context at all, it reads like an absurd truism.

CLARITY

Headlines should convey the meaning of the story as clearly as possible given the constraints of line length and point size. Here's a headline that fails the clarity test because it uses unnecessary jargon:

City's old train station may become a multimodal hub

City planners might understand the concept of a "multimodal hub," but few others will. Here's a better approach:

City wants to make old train station a hub for buses, too

Now everyone who reads the headline will know what that story is about. What about the following headline?

Dead baby
had visited
ERs twice
in six weeks

What is that story about? It's a fair question, because often a headline is all that a reader sees. Here's another version of the same headline, which would have fit in the same space:

Baby who died
of battering
had been seen
twice in ERs

Some headlines are easy to write (editors say they "write themselves"), and others are much more difficult because the facts they need to summarize are very difficult to convey in a few words. Here are two one-column headlines from different papers on a Washington politics story from the Clinton presidency:

**Videos
of coffees
released
to media**

**Tapes of
Clinton,
donors
released**

The second is clearer, though it had to violate a headline rule to make it fit. Many papers prefer to not let a preposition end the first line.

Often problems of unclarity stem from the use of "headlinese." *Headlinese* might be defined as words that no human being would utter in context but that headline writers use because they fit into tight spaces. Verbs tend to be the main culprits.

Headlinese verb	*English translation*
Raps	criticizes
blasts	really, really criticizes
inks	signs, as in a bill
nixes	votes no, turns down
keys	is crucial in causing
nabs	arrests
jinxes	confounds, in some way, or confuses

Even casual newspaper readers can find many more. Glance at enough sports pages and you'll soon find examples of the verb *lift* used in headlines. *Lift* is a perfectly reasonable verb in many contexts, but "Iverson lifts Sixers" is not one of them. A rough translation would be: "Iverson's performance spurs Sixers to victory." Why *lift* instead of *spur*, which itself approaches headlinese? In the days before computers, when copy editors had to count characters to determine whether headlines would fit, the *l, i, f* and *t* counted as one-half unit each. Most other lowercase letters were a full unit. The word *lift* fits in very tight counts, in little more than half the space that a word such as *spur* would take. In the age of computer typesetting, it still does. Fitting is important, but sense-making is even more important.

Occasional headlinese is probably a necessary evil, and many of the best headline writers occasionally lapse into it, but too much is like bur-lesque. On rare occasion, though, headlinese can be so bad that it actually becomes good, as this headline, which was mentioned on an irreverent Internet mailing list for journalists named BONG-l, demonstrates:

Foote heads arms body

The headline was about a British diplomat named "Foote" who was chosen to lead a disarmament team. It is not clear that such a headline ever ran, but if I had had the opportunity to write it, I surely would have done so, even though it played on his name. And I would tell my grandchildren about it.

AMBIGUITY

A related clarity issue arises from the tendency toward ambiguity in head-lines. One could almost state the problem as an axiom: As the word count drops, the likelihood of ambiguity increases. The English language is re-dundant; a reader can often make sense of a sentence even if some of the words are dropped. But it's tougher with a headline:

Russian discounts rumored deal

If you think about it long enough, you can unravel the meaning of this headline. To save you the trouble, here's the lead:

> Russia's U.S. envoy said Monday that he has seen no evidence that Iran has formed a new alliance with the Palestinians against Israel. . . .

The problem with the headline is that three of the four words can serve as a different part of speech, depending on context. *Russian* can be an adjec-tive as well as a noun, and *discounts* can be a noun as well as a verb. One can think of contexts in which *Russian discounts* make sense, such as Rus-sian discounts on vodka or steel. The situation gets murkier with the word *rumored*, which can be a verb as well as an adjective. The obvious solution, substituting the word *denies* for *discounts*, creates another problem. *Denies* has a different shade of meaning and would be misleading. Here are two other approaches:

Mideast deal rumor is discounted

Envoy says Mideast deal unlikely

Both lose some specificity—the source of the statement—but they gain some clarity. Neither rewrite is completely satisfying, but headline writers need to get used to making tradeoffs.

One word that can be read as two different parts of speech can create confusion, even in a headline with quite a few words:

Bush administration logging success
in short time at revamping forest rules

The word *logging* can be read as an adjective modifying *success* or as a verb form with a missing auxiliary form (*is* logging). Most readers who stumble when they see this headline will eventually figure it out (The Bush administration *is* logging success), but they shouldn't have to. A clearer approach would be to replace the word *logging* with a less ambiguous verb, such as *finding*. As a bonus, readers won't go Ouch! when they realize that the unclarity stems from a poor attempt at a play on words (*logging* . . . *forest*).

Copy editors should think twice before they omit articles and auxiliary verbs in headlines. Those little words traditionally have been considered "padding" by teachers and some headline writers, but they are often crucial for comprehension in headlines. Dropping them can create confusion.

Free historic trail tours a festival highlight

The headline would be much clearer if the *a* became *are* or *are a*.

Sometimes, a missing part of the verb *to be* or an article can create a misimpression:

Disgruntled workers like time bombs, report says

This headline appeared on a trend story following several deadly rampages by employees. Without the verb *are*, the headline can be misread in an ironic way. Here's the same problem from "the Lower case," this time caused by a missing article:

Officers finally getting shot at promotion exams

Words that can be misread as different parts of speech or in two differ-ent ways sometimes create headline problems by inviting readers to laugh when they shouldn't be laughing. Words that have multiple meanings can be troublesome. Again, a few examples from "The Lower case," where such headlines live in infamy:

Lawmaker
backs train
through Iowa

Prosecutors say Simpson had an hour to kill

Air Force considers dropping some new weapons

U's food service
feeds thousands,
grosses millions

Phrases or clauses that can be read more than one way often lead to unintended humor:

Panda mating fails; veterinarian takes over

Lansing residents
can drop off trees

If you read the last story, you'd realize that it's about discarding Christmas trees. But when you see the headline, which you see before the story, you can't help but think about monkeys.

An adjective can be read in the wrong time sequence:

Exemplary postal worker
shoots two friends at work

Clearly the headline writer meant that the employee had been considered an exemplary worker before the shooting, but the relative brevity of head-lines can invite the ridiculous interpretation.

MISLEADING HEADLINES

Headline writers must take care that their words do not go beyond the facts of the story or are not sufficiently qualified. The limited number of words in a headline is no excuse for a headline that is misleading. Several years ago, a United Parcel Service strike played havoc with business shipping and led to layoffs at UPS as well as at businesses that depended on the shipper. An AP story focused primarily on layoffs; it quoted one small-business owner who said she would have to close her mailing service franchise business, which depended on UPS. One paper ran the following headline:

UPS strike
destroying
businesses

The story did not support the verb *destroying*, a very strong word. One example is not enough to support such a blanket statement. Possibly the headline writer took a cue from the lead:

NEW YORK—Small companies say the United Parcel Service strike is killing business and pushing some to lay off employees and close their doors.

The original story sent by AP might have had more supporting information about business closings. The newspaper, which had a policy against continuing stories from Page One, might have trimmed the story to fit the 8-inch hole. It's also possible that the AP lead went too far. If so, it should have been rewritten. The problem is that even if there was more support for the assertion in the original version, readers would never see it. An additional problem in this headline is that it can appear biased. Both sides in a labor dispute worry about how their positions appear to the public. The headline above might elicit sympathy for business owners and anger directed at those unionists who are "destroying businesses." If the story supported the assertion, it would be defensible. But the story doesn't. A better approach would be:

UPS strike
is hurting
businesses

or

**UPS strike
is leading
to layoffs**

Most headlines are expected to tell the story. Misleading headlines may tell more than the story or less than the story. Several months after Enron declared bankruptcy, Kenneth Lay, the embattled chairman of the energy company, canceled an appearance to testify before a Senate committee. Lay, who had agreed to testify voluntarily, said he changed his mind because he feared he would not be able to get a fair hearing. The following headlines appeared in Northwest dailies:

Enron chief's lips are sealed

Enron chief cancels Senate appearance

The first headline is catchier, perhaps even a bit flip. The second head is straightforward. Which is better? My vote is for the second, but not because I dislike catchy headlines. The problem with the first is that it tells more than the story does. To say a person's *lips are sealed* in the context of a hearing may suggest that he decided to exercise his Fifth Amendment right against self-incrimination. If the headline invites a reader to draw that conclusion, it is misleading.

Another problem is accurate headlines that inadvertently upset readers. Readers come to the newspaper with different sets of experiences, and some may read things into headlines that the copy editor never considered.

**City takes
steps to set up
gay registry**

This headline appeared on a story about a city's efforts to create a procedure so that gay and lesbian couples as well as heterosexual unmarried couples could document their relationships. The intent was to create a record so that people could support claims to benefits and rights that often are denied such couples because they are not considered families. There are some problems with the headline—to many in the gay/lesbian community, the term *gay* refers only to men, not to women. And the headline failed to mention that the process also would be available to heterosexual couples. A more serious problem was the word *registry*. The word is accurate; it is the term that other cities use to refer to such documentation systems. But out of context—always a danger in headlines—the word read to some in the gay/lesbian community as Big Brother—a government intrusion on their privacy, echoing practices in regimes such as Nazi Germany. Of course, when they read the story, they realized that their first impression was incorrect. But headline writers should not depend on the story to clarify, or to disabuse a reader of a misperception. The problem is a tricky one in headline writing. It requires trying to put yourself in the place of different readers and trying to see how a headline might appear from their perspective. One strategy is organizational—the more diversity a newsroom has, the more likely someone will pick up on such problems before they are printed.

ATTRIBUTION

If an assertion cannot stand alone in a lead, it should not stand unattributed in a headline. Space limitations are no excuse. Headlines have high readership, and stories often don't. Copy editors usually can find a way to work attribution into the headline, even if it means writing a less specific headline. The following headline is an assertion that requires attribution. The headline provides it:

**Local police
abuse rights,
marchers say**

If the headline were only two lines long, attribution is still needed. Here are two headlines in the tighter space:

**Protest targets
police brutality**

**Protesters allege
police brutality**

The first headline does not suffice; police brutality can be read as a fact rather than an assertion. The second, because it contains attribution, makes clear that the accusation is an assertion. Attribution is necessary whenever an assertion or a statement is made that is not established fact.

Be especially careful with trend stories or reports of research that tend to make a general claim:

America is a healthier nation, for now

That headline is a flat assertion, but it reads as fact. The story was based on a survey that found improvement in public health. One study is almost never definitive in health sciences. The finding of one survey is often contradicted by the next one. The headline needs attribution:

Americans' health improves, survey finds

Attribution in a summary or a subsidiary headline is not enough. Many headline writers try that approach from the beginning; they should leave it as a last resort. Placing attribution in subsidiary display type, to be sure, is better than no attribution, but it is not wise unless there is no alternative. Visually, the big type carries the weight—and therefore the iconic importance. A better solution is to provide the assertion and attribution (or assertion and denial) in the head and to use the summary type to provide the detail you could not place in the main head. The following example demonstrates the problem and a solution:

New fat substitute poses dangers
A consumer group says olestra
is not safe. The manufacturer
defends the product.

Fat substitute dangerous, group says
A consumer organization says
olestra is not safe. The
manufacturer defends the product.

The second headline/deck combination is better. Unlike the first, it attributes the assertion in the same line of large type. Both approaches provide additional detail in the deck. Chapter 11 says more about this issue. A related problem is the headline that attempts to play on words but inadvertently reads as unattributed opinion:

Whiting quotas are fishy

Timber directive has hollow ring

A fair question to ask of those headlines is, Says who?

Preserving attribution is one of the most difficult aspects of headline writing. A copy editor must do in five words what the reporter has 20 or 30 words to do. Assertions, statements and opinions that require attribution in the story require it as well in the headline. One could argue that attribution is even more important in the headline than in the story, given that the headline is all that many people ever read and the story has more opportunity to provide attribution later. Headline writers must strive for specificity and thoroughness in headlines. These demands often conflict, yet all are important. The solution, often enough, is compromise. Be less specific than you can to preserve attribution, or be less specific in the attribution to enhance thoroughness.

GRACEFUL HEADLINES AND "SPLITS"

When newspapers began to run multicolumn, multiline headlines regularly, many adopted a rule that grammatical elements should be kept together on the same line of a multiline headline. A copy editor who broke those rules (actually a set of rules) produced a headline called a "split" or "break." At many newspapers, the copy desk supervisor would not accept a split headline and would direct the copy editor to rewrite the headline to follow the rule. There were exceptions, such as this banner headline in the San Francisco Chronicle in 1898:

BATTLE SHIP MAINE BLOWN
UP IN THE HARBOR OF HAVANA

That headline is not very graceful; one suspects that grace might not have been the primary concern for such a dramatic news event. And there always have been papers that have not followed rules on splits religiously. But journalism students and novice copy editors have long been taught to follow the lead of some of the most-respected papers, such as The New York Times, which take great pains to avoid splits. The idea is worth some discussion, because more split headlines seem to be appearing in print, even in papers that have long frowned on them.

The general rule is simple: Keep related words together. For example, an adjective should be on the same line as the noun it modifies. Here's a headline that violates the rule:

> **Electricity**
> **grid choke**
> **points costly**
> **to ratepayers**

It's difficult to read from the first line to the second and worse between the second and third. At the very least, *choke points* should be together on one line. An alternative:

> **Electrical grid**
> **choke points**
> **are costly**
> **to ratepayers**

This version is better. The auxiliary verb *are* helps the flow, but *Electrical grid* still is awkward because it modifies *choke points*. Another alternative:

> **Choke points**
> **in power grid**
> **are costly**
> **to ratepayers**

This headline fits in the same space, eliminates both splits and is much easier to read. It typically takes an extra minute or two in most cases to avoid the split, but it's time well spent. The rewritten headline is less awkward and usually clearer.

Here's a multicolumn headline that breaks awkwardly:

> **Cops call foul on Medina girl's computer**
> **death threat against Orioles baseball star**

The story was about a teenage girl in a Seattle suburb who as a joke wrote an e-mail message to her boyfriend that included a death threat against

Cal Ripken Jr. The boyfriend was a fan of Ripken's. The Internet service provider screened the message and passed it on to police, who took it seriously and assigned officers to guard Ripken during a game in Seattle. The split makes a long, complicated headline—one that packs a series of adjectives before the noun *threat*—even more difficult to follow. At the very least, the words *computer death threat* belong on the same line for clarity and readability. There are many ways of rewriting it; one version that uses most of the same words is:

Cops call foul on computer death threat made by Medina girl against Orioles star

Eliminating the split makes the headline easier to track. Many papers would insist on using the word *police* instead of cops, which they consider tabloid slang.

Another rule is that verb forms should not be broken between lines.

Diamondback slugger has donated millions to charity

Rewritten without a split:

Arizona slugger has given millions to local charities

Infinitive forms are used in headlines as a shorthand for future tense. They should not be split.

Arizona slugger to give millions to charity

could be rewritten without a split:

Diamondback slugger will donate millions

A prepositional phrase should not break between lines, particularly with the preposition left hanging on the end of the first line.

40 county prisoners sent to new state prison in Stayton

Rewritten without the split:

40 county prisoners sent
to new Stayton state prison

When an adjective can also be used as a noun, an adjective–noun split can be confusing, forcing readers to backtrack and try again:

Activist picks up litter
campaign for Arizona

The headline writer was trying to be clever, using *picks up* as a verb for a story about an activist who shifted her attention to an anti-litter campaign. But because the first line reads as a perfectly good statement on its own, readers will pause after *litter*, expect another statement to follow, then go back and reread when they see it doesn't.

Sometimes adjective–noun splits make headlines sound silly:

Hospital
ends sex
unit plans

This is very easy to write without the split:

Hospital
ends plan
for sex unit

Here's one more that appeared in print:

Senator blasts federal air
regulations as too costly

And the rewrite:

Federal air-quality rules
are too costly, senator says

Some newspapers allow splits in smaller headline point sizes and in single-column headlines, where it's often difficult, if not impossible, to avoid all splits. In recent years, some newspapers have relaxed the rules on splits in any headlines. I have asked a number of editors why, and they tend to offer two explanations:

- It's too difficult or too time-consuming to follow the rules.
- It doesn't matter. A reader can still understand split headlines.

I have found little in modern newspaper research that argues one way or the other. I think in the absence of such research, newspapers should consider the practices used in other forms of media that rely heavily on headlines, for example, advertising. Split thoughts in advertising headlines are rare. They are even more rare in outdoor advertising—highway billboards. It seems to me that ad copy writers are on to something. A highway billboard must be read at a glance, while a driver or passenger is moving along a highway at high speed. The big type must be clear and understandable, or else the reader will not get the message. David Ogilvy, a famous advertising executive, said that when you've written the headline, you've spent 80 cents of the client's advertising dollar. In other words, the headline must draw the reader in, must be clear, may be clever, and so on. Newspaper headline writers are not spending the client's money, but their intent is the same as billboard copy writers'—they are trying to capture the attention of readers whose eyes are racing past the elements of a page, often at high speed. Split headlines, because they are more difficult to comprehend at a glance, might invite readers to pass on by.

I also believe there is a headline aesthetic that is worth preserving. Headlines look as well as read, and headlines that do not split thoughts look better. From a readability standpoint, a headline is easier to follow when related elements appear on the same line. It is more graceful. It is also more difficult and somewhat more time-consuming to write. This is one tradeoff I think should be made in favor of taking the time. I recommend avoiding splits if at all possible.

OTHER TRADITIONAL RULES

Here are three rules that many editors view as gospel but that could use another look:

- Don't write question heads.
- Don't "pad" headlines with articles and auxiliary verbs.
- Fill the space.

Some newspapers discourage or even ban headlines that are stated in the form of a question. It is true that a question head can be a cop-out, but there are some stories that can best be captured with a question. An example is a news analysis that examines pro and con arguments on an issue, such as abortion. A question headline in this case can solve a space problem if the headline is too short to capture the essence of both sides. An analysis piece might ask a question, such as "Is Iraq hiding nuclear weapons?" and then provide evidence pro and con. An investigative piece might ask a question. In such cases, a question approach might be the right choice for the headline. An outright ban on question headlines may handcuff copy editors. The overriding question is, What does the story say? If the answer is a question, then a question headline might be the right approach. Just don't overuse the device.

One rule that some editors follow but that should be dropped is the prohibition on what is disparagingly called headline "padding." The practice—dropping articles and auxiliary verbs—was mentioned before in the Clarity section. Some newspapers treat it as a headline rule, but in many cases dropping such words makes headlines awkward or confusing enough to require a second or third read. For example:

Warmer weather hot
for local businesses

This headline appeared on a story about how summer weather creates a demand for certain products, such as lawn chairs, picnic accessories and swimwear. It's much easier to read with the verb *to be* included:

Warm weather *is* hot
for local businesses

The rule prohibiting "padding" should be dropped because following it can make a headline unreadable:

Free historic trail tours a festival highlight

Free historic trail tours *are* festival highlight

Consulting a popular career choice

Consulting *is* a popular career choice

Historically, many newspapers tried to fill lines of a headline to within a character or two. Some, such as The New York Times, retain very strict guidelines on spacing. The Times, in fact, still "steps" many headlines, so that each line of a multi-line headline is indented from both the left and right margins. For example:

Green Party in New Mexico
Goes from Gadfly to Player

This attention to detail works for The New York Times, but most other newspapers do not have the time or staff resources to worry about such things, even if they would like to follow Times style. Also, the Times uses what is called "upstyle" for headlines, capitalizing all words except prepositions of few characters and articles. Most papers once used that style but switched to "downstyle" decades ago. Downstyle follows the capitalization criteria stories use: the beginning word in a sentence and proper nouns.

Many newspapers also have relaxed their traditional rule on filling the lines of a headline, perhaps as a result of the increased value placed on white space as a design element in newspapers. Criteria on filling the headline space vary from paper to paper. If a generalization is possible, those with more airy designs appear to allow more flexibility in filling or not filling lines. Those with tighter, or grayer, designs, appear to favor headlines that neatly fill the column. I think local option is going to prevail. A wise approach is perhaps a compromise. Don't write lines that are very short relative to the other lines of a headline; don't worry too much about filling lines tightly.

TONE

Tone can be as simple as the difference between a news story and a feature story. A headline writer shouldn't put a newsy headline atop a softer feature story. Readers will take a cue from the headline and expect a news story. For example, the headline on a profile of a young pianist who won a prestigious award should not say "Pianist wins XYZ prize." Such a headline would be appropriate if the story is a news item announcing the prize. On a profile, the headline should reflect the story as written, perhaps focus on her age, or motivation or the challenges she has had to overcome.

The opposite, writing a feature headline on a news story, is also generally a mistake. When the news is important, literary allusion or other flights of verbal fancy are the wrong way to go. For example, when a rain-swollen river causes a dam to fail and the flood waters wash three houses away, the headline shouldn't say "When it rains, it pours." The headline should convey the news, and the tone of the headline should match the tone of the story. Anything else is usually jarring. Chapter 12 has more examples.

A related tone issue might be called force or power to attract attention. "A headline should grab the reader" is a prescription that many students have heard. It is often stated with the same level of moral certainty as a parent's admonition "Eat your peas; they're good for you." The truth is more nuanced.

It isn't a crime to write a routine head on a routine story. Some headlines, for example, need only tell the story as succinctly and plainly as possible. Headlines on minor events or routine meetings on Page 12-B do not need or deserve sparkling treatment. Headlines on news briefs should be as informational and direct as possible. Headlines on Web pages have an even greater burden because the headline often serves as a link to another page that carries the text of the story. If a Web headline is not clear, readers will not have the information they need to make a choice to follow the link.

Sometimes a stellar headline works well on a routine story. But, more generally, if a headline attracts too much attention, it may be disproportionate to the importance of the story. This is not to suggest that dull news headlines are fine. They all should be clear and informative. It's merely to suggest that copy editors should strive to write the most attractive headlines on the best or most interesting stories and that a great headline might oversell a routine story. Overselling can be a problem. If all headlines try to attract attention equally, none of them will. The reader will feel as though he or she is strolling through the midway at the county fair. Everybody and everything cries out for your attention; consequently, nothing stands out.

Heads on prominently displayed stories, heads on features or brites designed to lighten up a page and readers' spirits, and heads on major events have a more legitimate claim to attention.

TABLOID VERSUS BROADSHEET

Some metropolitan tabloids (half-size newspapers that do not have a horizontal fold) take greater liberties with abbreviations, slang and idioms than broadsheet (full-size) papers typically do. They have a sassy tone, often even on serious news stories. This loosening of rules is, in part, the result of tighter headline counts and larger headline type. It also has to do with tabloid "attitude," which values bluntness, informality, even flippancy. "Pres Oks" might be used instead of "President approves." The difference can best be seen by comparing a broadsheet and a tabloid headline on the same story. Here's a headline that ran in The Philadelphia Inquirer, a well-respected metropolitan broadsheet, on a story about the wreck of a tank truck carrying sulfuric acid:

Acid tanker tips; part of I-95 shut all day

The wreck was front-page news in both papers in the city. The major north–south route through the region was shut down, tens of thousands of commuters were rerouted and 100 residents were evacuated. The following headline appeared in the Philadelphia Daily News:

ACID TRIP

Tabloids can go too far with flippancy or cuteness. Some might say "Acid trip" was inappropriate for a serious story, even in a tabloid. Others would disagree, saying that the nature of tabloid journalism calls for such headlines. Few broadsheet dailies would allow a headline writer to refer to a couple of morticians as "working stiffs," as the Philadelphia Daily News did. I'm not sure the tabloid should have used it. Not all tabloids have headlines written in tabloid style. Newsday and The Christian Science Monitor, for example, write headlines that are more like The New York Times and The Boston Globe than they are like the News York Daily News or the Philadelphia Daily News.

OVERALL APPROACHES

How do you write headlines? Some teachers and copy chiefs suggest an analytical approach—thinking of the story in terms of its key nouns and verbs and building the headline from those. That can be good advice, particularly if it forces you to think in terms of strong subject–verb–object headline statements. When the purpose is to provide information as clearly and concisely as possible, it is difficult to beat a subject–verb–object structure.

Many headline writers favor a more holistic approach. They ask them-selves, "What's the story about?" and try to answer it as briefly as possible. The answer would typically be a sentence, sometimes a phrase. I find this approach valuable with students who sometimes develop headline writer's block. I ask them to tell me, in their own words, what the story is about or what is important. You might think of what you would tell a friend about the story if you had only a few words to do so. Sometimes the headline "writes itself" when you think of it this way; other times it doesn't quite work because of the restrictions of line breaks and length. With a basic concept, though, it's easier to come up with variations that will fit the specs. Often that approach shifts your perception from focusing on specific words to focusing on ideas and leads to a good headline.

One size doesn't fit all. Sometimes it's better to try different ap-proaches and see which works best. A copy editor might find that an ana-lytical approach is better for news heads and that a more holistic approach works better for features.

If you're stuck, change your approach, rather than beat yourself up until you find the right word. Sometimes you just can't make an active head work in the count, but a passive structure just falls into place. Sometimes copy edi-tors will agonize over headlines because they can't find a verb or a noun that helps tell the story and fits in the space. I see too many copy editors reach for the thesaurus, convinced that all they need to do is find that special word to make the headline work. Sometimes they do find the right word, but many times there is no right word. The head needs to be recast.

In general, I think copy editors should not use a thesaurus to write headlines. Many copy editors and teachers of editing would disagree, and I'd agree that at times a thesaurus can be helpful. But using it often can be inefficient and counterproductive. Most copy editors have a general store-house of words they can use to tell the story and have no need to search for that special word. A second problem is that the word one finds in a thesau-rus often is not quite the right word, or it might be too arcane for headline use. Headlines should flow freely and be understandable at a glance, much as billboards along a highway are designed to be read. That special word buried in subparagraph 3 on Page 187 of the thesaurus might give some readers pause. A third problem is that reliance on a thesaurus can waste time. The thesaurus gives the illusion that there is a right word. Copy edi-tors sometimes waste precious minutes trying to find it.

A better approach is to study different newspapers, particularly well-edited ones, to develop a better sense of good headline words and to observe what experienced headline writers do. You'll often find strong verbs that you knew but didn't think of using in a headline. Some headline writers seem to have been born with an ability to capture a story well and invitingly in a few words; others struggle with the task. But paying close attention to how good headline writers work, and seeking a mentor either at your own publication or another, can help inexperienced headline writers become very good ones.

TIPS AND STRATEGIES

• Proofread headlines carefully. In fact, proofread them more carefully than you proofread text. Some computer systems allow copy editors to see the headlines they write in the same size and font as they will appear in print. In many systems, headlines appear on screen no larger than normal story type. It's easy to miss a typo or fail to catch a misspelling when you see it on a computer screen in normal point size. Headline mistakes are much easier to see when they are printed in 36-, 48- or 72-point type, and they are embarrassing. Readers pick up on those mistakes and often write letters to the editor complaining about them. Here are some headlines that appeared in print, some in "elite" newspapers:

Months of sparing [sparring], now Simpson's trial

Malcom [Malcolm] X's daughter arrested

Typhoon death tool [toll] is expected to climb

Dispite [Despite] fears and concerns, Navy is a good neighbor

These students are learning to 'parle [parlez] vous' at age 2

**Relays fair [fare]
well for men**

Occasionally, typos are extremely embarrassing:

**Survey says
teching [teaching] is
top priority**

Deng returns
to pubic [public] view

• Besides checking for typos and misspellings, make sure that your headline cannot be read in any way you don't want it to be read. Copy editors know what the story is about before they write the headline, and because they are immersed in the context, they can fail to see an alternative meaning that a reader, who sees the headline first, might see. To reduce the likelihood of seeing one of your headlines featured in "The Lower case," you should try to look at each headline with fresh eyes, as a reader would. It is difficult to do that, but one suggestion, if deadline permits, is to write a headline, put it aside for a short while, shift your attention to another task, then go back and reread the headline before sending it along in the production process. Having a slot or copy chief read over headlines also can help, but chances are that person is in the same position, having read the story first.

• Watch regionalisms. Some words tend to be used in a certain part of the country but not in others. If you grew up in that part of the country, you might assume that the word is just as common elsewhere. An example is the word *spendy*, which is used as a synonym for expensive in the Northwest. I recall being surprised to see that word appear in text and headlines in Oregon; I had never seen or heard it used in the Northeast.

• Don't succumb to a technological mind-set. As minutes tick away toward deadline, it can be convenient to think that you can electronically manipulate any set of words to fit a given headline space. This is one of the insidious downsides of technological progress. Electronic type manipulation can save important minutes if used sparingly and wisely. But it's too easy for copy editors to become addicted to letterspace reduction (kerning), point size changes and expansion or contraction of the letterform. It might save seconds or minutes on a given page, but over the long term it can lead to a mind-set that anything can be squeezed or expanded to fit. The more such practices become the norm, the more copy editors become production workers rather than craftsmen and craftswomen.

• Never say never. Consider breaking the rules if you have a good reason, but remember that good reasons are generally in short supply. And you'd better be able to explain why your idea justifies bending or breaking a publication's rules.

Matthew Arnold called journalism "history in a hurry." Headlines could be called journalism in a hurry. Today's headline styles represent a blend, or perhaps a hodgepodge, of various traditions with an occasional new wrinkle made easier by computer typesetting. Headline writers have to deal with a cornucopia of headline forms, type sizes and column widths. Headline styles include "overlines," "kickers," "underlines," "hammers," "slammers," "combinations" and "side-saddles," to name a few. Which of these you might use depends on your publication. Another entire class of headlines, called "designed" heads or "art type," makes use of shading, shadowing, tilting, varying of point sizes and other electronic manipulations. Practically every combination imaginable can be found in one paper or another. To add to the confusion the same style of headline goes by different names at different papers. At one newspaper, for example, a "deck" might refer to one line of a multiline main headline. At another it refers to a subheadline (a secondary headline in smaller point size that is independent of the primary headline). At a third paper, a "deck" might refer to a text paragraph that appears between the headline and the lead of the story. A fourth paper might call that text paragraph a "summary paragraph," instead of a "deck." The best lesson for copy editors is to not worry too much about what a particular headline style is called. What's important is what the headline says.

10

Headlines
The Next Level

Every Christmas, a retrospective story about Mideast tension originates in the West Bank town of Bethlehem, the biblical site of Jesus' birth. Some of the specifics change from year to year, but the underlying theme—of never-ending conflict—is the same. Many newspapers run the story, often on the front page, and copy editors face the same challenge every year: how to convey the essence of the story, yet not echo the headline that ran last year, and the year before. A copy editor at The Philadelphia Inquirer wrote a very good headline on that story in the early '80s:

O little town
of little faith

It captures the essence, reflecting the sense of despair that pervaded the story. The use of "O little town" alludes to the reason the story was running: turmoil in a place of religious significance to U.S. Christians during the Christmas season. One could perhaps take issue with the headline as Western-centric, or even Christian-centric, but I think such criticism would be misplaced. The headline was written for a U.S. readership, and it captured both the sense of despair and the longing for peace that the story conveyed. It had grace, even rhythm. It did not repeat the reporter's words; it amplified them. It was quite an accomplishment in six words. I felt it was an excellent headline, and many of us on the copy desk congratulated the writer. Then we all went back to work on the next edition.

Newspapers run great headlines but not very many. The relative scarcity of superior headlines probably has to do with the time pressures newspaper copy editors face and the volume of stories they process. The editor who wrote the Bethlehem headline also was working on several other stories and headlines in the hour or so before deadline. Such pressures usually lead to headlines that are adequate, perhaps even good, but few that are great. Some copy editors are content to produce workmanlike headlines; that level of quality might be all that their publications expect. Others strive for more. How do copy editors—and their news organizations—move the bar from good to great in headline writing?

The question is really two questions:

1. What distinguishes great headlines from good or adequate ones?
2. What distinguishes great headline writers from good or adequate ones?

The answer to the first question is not particularly satisfying: You know great headlines when you see them. They draw attention to the story by capturing its essence, typically through wording, turns of phrase, imagery or ideas that the reporter might even wish he or she had considered. They just seem to connect better; they tell the story perfectly, often creatively. Many are almost lyrical, but many others are not. A great headline doesn't have to be fancy, drawing on literary allusion or figures of speech. It doesn't have to be clever, though many great headlines are. It can be a straight news head that precisely and gracefully tells the reader as much as possible in a few words. Really good headlines are the pinnacle of a headline writer's art, and the opportunity to write them is one of the things that make the job most interesting.

The answer to the second question is ambiguous. Some excellent headline writers seem to have a natural gift. They appear to have an innate ability to identify stories that cry out for a stunning headline and then find the right combination of words to make it happen. They might have learned the skill, but they probably can't tell you exactly how they learned it. To some degree, you can't teach the ability that they have; you can, however, learn from them, and if you're a slot, or copy chief, you should nurture it and encourage its use.

Other great headline writers do not start out at the top. They learn the craft by watching how the best headline writers approach the job. They let their minds wander and play with word associations but always within the boundaries of newspaper constraints, primarily time and space. They know how to use humor, subtlety, even on rare occasion ambiguity, but only where appropriate. They see that metaphor, allusion and imagery can be powerful tools, but they also realize that headline writers must take care to use the tools wisely or else they turn out clichés. They are aware that an inappropriate metaphor or an ill-conceived allusion can cheapen a story. They try to write the big type with pace and rhythm, and they avoid the use of headline jargon and words that momentarily interrupt the flow. They also realize that one person's winner can be another's clinker, and they often ask for feedback from their colleagues so they can avoid the mistake of assuming that everybody else will like a headline if they do. They can distinguish good from great, and they know that the difference between a good headline and a great headline may, oddly enough, be greater than the difference between a bad and a great headline. Some near-misses are pretty close to heads that sing. They also have learned one of the most difficult lessons for headline writers: Not every story needs or deserves a great headline. They know when to go for the gold and when the reader is better served with silver, bronze, or even a durable grade of steel.

The missing piece is typically the institutional support provided so that copy editors can write creative headlines. That support includes sufficient staffing so that copy editors actually have the time to concentrate on headlines. It also depends on the development and maintenance of a copy desk structure that nurtures good headline writing. Copy chiefs who constructively criticize their copy editors are an essential part of that structure, though some smaller papers provide similar feedback through other newsroom positions, such as news editor or managing editor. Creativity in headlines also depends on the support of newsroom managers. Top managers can set the tone for a news organization, and nothing encourages excellence in headlines as much as honest congratulations from the executive editor for a particularly creative effort.

CREATIVITY AND HUMOR

All creative headlines are not humorous, but many headlines that draw a smile are creative. Humor is used in newspaper headlines much as it is in advertising headlines: to attract the reader and make the reader feel good about the "content." It is probably not used as often (by some estimates, about 40 percent of ads use humor), but it can be used as effectively.

Puns and word plays, for example, can be very creative. Or they can be very bad. Ad copy writer Bruce Bendinger says: "The pun is not the lowest form of humor. The lowest form of humor is a smart-ass ad that wastes the client's money."[1] Copy editors are not selling a product—at least not in exactly the same sense that an ad copy writer does—but the basic idea is common to both forms.

Old Volkswagen ad campaigns are legendary in advertising. One ad, in particular, can serve as a model for the sort of creativity in humor that headline writers can strive for. The ad showed a group of nuns waiting to pile into a VW microbus. The text of the ad was a disarmingly simple headline:

Mass transit

It was a text and visual pun that still is used in advertising courses as an example of creativity. Headline writers can come up with creative, inviting plays on words. Here are a few that I think worked well:

Chemist's accident
started 50-year trip

—on a story about the inventor of LSD

Fawning over flora

—on the opening of a major garden show

Betting on pairs
Couples in the real-estate game

—on a story about husband-and-wife teams in real estate

Economist sees the forest and the trees

—on a university economist in the Northwest who argues that the shift to a high-tech economy should be accompanied by a shift away from policy that favors timber-industry interests

The last headline might strike some as hauling out a tired old cliché. I find it creative because it accurately captured the essence of the story by using a familiar turn of phrase that connected closely with the story. The creative part is that the phrase in this case is both literally and figuratively true. It's also true, however, that what is considered creative often depends on the eye of the beholder. For example, I liked the following headline, which appeared as an object of ridicule in "The Lower case":

Steals clock; faces time

Unfortunately, truly bad or tired plays on words appear all too often. The main problem is not that they are bad in and of themselves. Headline writers should avoid them because they are predictable and they draw attention to themselves and away from the story. A good play on words invites you into the story. A bad, trite or clichéd play on words pushes you away. It might not waste the client's money, but it certainly wastes readers' time and tries their patience. I'd argue that the following are all bad:

Businessmen high on hemp products

Global demand puffs up tobacco profits

Plan for a fence
has neighbors railing

Dogs bone up
on police work

Timber sale gets the ax

A concrete solution
found for pitted bridge

Here are a few concrete suggestions for avoiding the most predictable plays on words:

1. Avoid plays on railroad terms, such as:

Rail project back on track

Rail project off track

Train project derailed

Company uncouples rail projects

2. Avoid plays on airport or airplane images:

Airport project takes off

Airport project grounded

Airline profits soar

Airline profits plummet

Airline finds unfriendly skies

The problem with these headlines, as with many others, is that they have been used too often. The first time, or maybe even the first 10 times, they seem clever. They aren't clever any more. Writing headlines based on tired old word plays is like telling your friends the same joke over and over. Friends avoid you when you do that because you're boring. Readers might too.

3. Avoid mixed metaphors, such as:

Fishing workshops
on tap this month

4. Don't play on words that sound like the right word but have nothing to do with the right word. Cooking pages are ripe for such tripe.

The pear facts about anjous

The pasta-bilities are endless

Avoid them because they're just dumb. The typical reader reaction is "Ouch!" The following headline reflects a similar, but more troubling, problem:

HANS down, driver safety
the most vital concern now

This was the headline on a story about the Head and Neck Support (HANS) system, which was designed to protect race car drivers from serious injury. This type of play—using an unfamiliar abbreviation because it sounds like a word in a common turn of phrase—is almost never good, and sometimes the timing makes it highly inappropriate. The headline appeared on a sports section front in 2001 on a story inspired in part by the controversy surrounding the death of racing star Dale Earnhardt, who was not wearing a restraint when he crashed. Word play on serious topics is almost never appropriate.

Sports pages often boast the most creative and clever headlines in the paper. When a stormy day caused scores to rise at the British Open golf tournament in 2002 and dashed the Grand Slam hopes of Tiger Woods, the following headline appeared:

British field gets blown away
Tiger can't
hack it in
bad weather

On the same section front, when the leadoff hitter rose to the occasion and provided the hits to propel the Los Angeles Dodgers to victory, the headline read:

L.A. taps into unlikely power source

The headline plays off Southern California's power problems of the previous summer. Such a headline might have struck many readers as insensitive if it had appeared during the serious power crisis. A year later, after the problems eased, it appears clever, and even if a reader doesn't catch the play, it still tells the story. The broader point is that what is acceptable in headlines can be a moving target. A headline writer's best ally is common sense.

Some word play, however, descends well into the pit of insensitivity. Consider the following headline, which appeared on a well-known newspaper Web site:

Shack attacks

It echoes a phrase sometimes used to refer to basketball star Shaquille O'Neal. That might be cute in a basketball story, but it does not belong at the top of a stand-alone caption about a 1998 confrontation between Israeli police officers and Palestinians over tin shacks built by settlers in the Muslim Quarter of Jerusalem's Old City.

Or the headline:

Dorm encourages
a handy language

This appeared in a Page One teaser at the top of the page referring to a story about the residents of a college dormitory who decided to learn sign language. It's simply inappropriate humor. Or the headline "Boweled over," which appeared with a photo and caption for a successful fund-raising event for the Gastro-Intestinal Research Foundation. The list of unfunny attempts at headline humor would circle the Earth at the Tropic of Cancer.

Offbeat police stories are a minefield. Sometimes clever headlines are appropriate on them; other times they are not. Good judgment is the key. Consider the following lead of a police blotter story that appeared in a college newspaper:

> A woman upset over having to drive her drunken roommate home sprayed her friend with gasoline from a convenience store pump Sunday, then killed her by lighting the gas stream on fire, police said.

Most people would agree that such a story is no place for humor. The headline that appeared read:

Guess she's not the
designated driver type

The level of violence in the story isn't even remotely funny. Good judgment is the key, and the college copy editor who wrote that headline failed to exercise it. In other cases of unusual police stories, humor might be appropriate. Here's another lead:

> A man who had been "imbibing," as Springfield firefighters delicately put it, jumped into a pit toilet at Clearwater boat landing and spent the night there because he couldn't get out.

Is the following headline appropriate for that story?

Man spends night in deep doo-doo

The answer is: It depends. If the man had been injured, probably not. If the man had been named, perhaps not. But the man was rescued the next morning, none the worse for his experience, and the story was written in a tongue-in-cheek manner. The victim was not named in the story, no doubt to save him embarrassment. Given the circumstances, I think humor is OK. The key question to ask is whether anyone is harmed by such a headline—or any headline that uses humor.

In assessing potential harm, copy editors need to think of readers as well as subjects of stories. What some people consider funny, others might consider crude, insensitive or even scandalous. Copy editors need to consider whether it's worth offending some readers to give others, even most, a chuckle. Here's an example that, based on reactions in workshops I've presented, strikes about half as funny and half as inappropriate. The story was about a tractor-trailer load of live chickens that overturned on a highway, spilling much of its cargo. The headline was:

Poultry in motion
Tipped rig dumps thousands of chickens

That headline draws laughter from some people but rubs others the wrong way. When I ask how many would have run it in their papers, the feathers fly. About half say yes and the others no, and most are very passionate about their view. Many of the chickens, after all, were killed by the accident, and some people don't see humor in that. One more example appeared on a brief story about astronaut John Glenn, who requested Metamucil wafers for a nine-day spaceflight.

Glenn may need help
releasing payload

Many people will grin; others might find it crude. How can you judge whether to use such a headline? One suggestion is to try it on a number of colleagues. Another is to keep your audience in mind.

Headline writers have a natural tendency to reach for images and for plays on words. That's fine; it's important for copy editors to stretch their literary wings in what amounts to a telephone booth. But, alas, there is a tendency to sometimes reach too far, and it's just as important to resist that tendency. One needs to balance creativity and discipline. Headlines should match the tone of the story. If a headline is serious, readers will expect the story to be serious. If a headline is playful, readers will expect the story to be playful.

WRITING CREATIVE HEADLINES

Are there secrets to writing creative headlines?

Here's an example of a routine wire "brite," a short, offbeat story that moved on a national wire service years ago. It was used in newspapers throughout the country because it was unusual, not because anyone outside of Kansas needed to know what happened.

> KANSAS CITY, Kan.—A bank robber conducting a performance of the prison choir at a businessman's meeting over the weekend took the end of the concert as his cue to exit. In the commotion that followed, the organist slipped away, too.
>
> Authorities from the U.S. Penitentiary at Leavenworth have been seeking John Wagner and Steve Rose since they escaped Saturday after the 20-minute concert.
>
> Wagner, 38 had just finished conducting the 21-voice choir at a Jaycees luncheon meeting. The choir is made up of convicts with excellent records. . . .

This story provides a good opportunity for a headline writer to be creative. Here's the headline that ran:

At Leavenworth, they break out in song

It's a play on words that would draw a smile from many readers at the breakfast table.

What type of thought process leads to "breaking out in song"—the idea that makes the head attractive? Newspaper headline writers typically don't analyze what they do; they just do it. Advertising copy writers *have* thought more about the process that leads to creativity in the big type, and newspaper headline writers can take a cue from them. Copy writers often use a process of word association, or even free association. It's a process that starts with less focus and moves toward concepts that will allow them to attract attention in a way that meets the strategic goals of the ad campaign. Newspaper headline writing does not require that level of strategic thinking, and it is done much more quickly than ad copy writing. But the techniques used by copy writers are similar to the techniques used by many good headline writers. They let their minds wander for a while.

The chain of associations that led to the Leavenworth headline might go something like this:

Prison (chorus)
Bars, behind bars, bars on a scale . . .
On the run
Man on the run (for those who remember Paul McCartney)
On the lam (cliché, dead-end)
Jailbreak
Jailbirds, free as a bird, free as a songbird
Break out
Break out in song

Typically, a headline writer will follow a few side trails that lead to dead ends before hitting on the idea. One secret is to not worry about space constraints at the beginning. It's better to think about ideas and associations first, then worry about finding the combination of words that executes the idea and fits in a given headline space. The idea is the key; implementation is important, but there's usually a way to make a good idea fit.

Of course, the idea must be appropriate; a clever idea that is insensitive is worse than a dull headline. Is the tone suggested by "breaking out in song" appropriate? Prison escapes are not, on the whole, a topic to joke about, but this one is harmless. Or, perhaps, it's harmless at this point. If someone had been taken hostage, injured or killed in the escape, any clever headline would be inappropriate. If that had been the case, the story probably would not have run nationally—it would have been a local crime story, of interest only to people in that region. This story ran because it met the criterion for newsworthiness best articulated by Arthur Brisbane, William Randolph Hearst's lieutenant: It elicited a "Gee Whiz!" reaction. Better yet, it was humorous.

Here's another example, from a Page One story in The Philadelphia Inquirer. The story explored the growing trend of suburban communities to control the appearance of houses and yards in certain developments through the use of restrictive covenants on property deeds. The story listed many examples, including a suburban development whose rules allowed wooden play structures in back yards but not metal swingsets. The headline that appeared was the following:

A swingset? There goes the neighborhood

This head is a bit flip, but it matched a major theme of the story, which focused on the controversy about the expansion of Big Brother-type rules that many residents found extreme, even ridiculous. It also highlights a technique that can be very effective in such cases: focusing on a key example to make the larger point of the story. The idea is similar to a reporter's choice of an interesting, representative anecdote for a lead on a news feature. The anecdote is a specific incident chosen both because it is compelling and because it is representative of the story as a whole. The other point suggested by this headline is that it's OK to break the rules if you have a good reason. The awkward break between lines was atypical for this newspaper, which takes great pride in headlines that are graceful and do not split thoughts. But the idea worked so well that it was readily approved by the copy chief and the news editor, and it drew a congratulatory note from the executive editor the next day.

Another example of an excellent, highly creative headline was written by a high-school freshman on a workshop newspaper. The story was a profile of a costume designer whose ability to see the humor in everyday life complemented her creativity in costume design. The headline, which had to fit in a very tight count underneath a short liftout quote, was:

Life's a stitch

The short quote that appeared at the top of the package explained a bit more about the story and gave a taste of her personality:

> "I've been all over the world.
> Well, my costumes have, anyway."

The headline writer found a turn of phrase that connected well with the focus of the piece—her work as a costume designer—and offered a glimpse at her personality at the same time. Not bad for three little words. The quote provided some of the necessary context.

This example, and some of the others, reflects one of the main strategies headline writers use when they want to be creative. They take a familiar turn of phrase that might even be a cliché and place it in a new context, sometimes by turning it upside down.

MISGUIDED CLEVERNESS

Sometimes cleverness is the wrong approach. A few rules are worth following. For example, do not use subjects' names for headline wordplay. This rule is worth following 99 percent of the time. When Olympic short-track speed skater Apolo Anton Ohno fell in the final of the 1,000-meter race in Salt Lake City, the headlines were predictable:

Oh-no!

Get it? Things got worse when Ohno won a gold medal in a different event a few days later after the skater who crossed the line first was disqualified. It was "Ohno, Oh yes!" Get it?

Rarely, if ever, should you use a person's name in a play on words. People are sensitive about how their names appear in print, and headline writers should be sensitive too. People don't choose their names, and copy editors who think it is appropriate to exploit a coincidental connection between a name and a news or feature story should reconsider. It seems particularly insensitive when the play is based on an English reading of a non-English name, such as "Ohno"—who is an American of Japanese descent. A second reason to avoid such plays is that they are tiresome and predictable.

An entertainment story about how singer Bonnie Raitt still enjoys touring after 30 years bore the headline "Singer keeps coming back for more," which was good. The overline, however, wasn't. It said:

Raitt of return

That play on her name adds nothing but confusion. It's hard to grasp the meaning without a second read; it's difficult to even see the word play. Raitt may be returning, but that has nothing to do with the banking term "rate of return." There really is no good reason to use the singer's name that way. Here's another:

Music festival
Shedds offices
to make home
in old church

The translation is as follows: A Northwest music festival is moving its administrative offices into an old church that has been renovated at considerable cost to provide a performing arts space. The building is called The Shedd Institute in honor of an ancestor of one of the principals involved in funding the project. Playing on the name is not funny. Worse, it makes the headline confusing. It fails one key test of headline cleverness: It is distracting rather than attracting. Unfortunately, such plays are all too common. Here are two that made it into print:

This Moses wrote the Bible on jeeps

Mark of distinction

The second was a large-type headline on a lengthy, serious retrospective story about the career of former U.S. Sen. Mark Hatfield. The tone of playfulness is just wrong.

Likewise, one should not play on a company's name in a headline. It is potentially insulting, generally predictable, sometimes misleading and typically jarring because the tone created by the wordplay does not match the tone of the story. This problem manifests itself often in newspaper business pages, and it is not clear why it happens there so often. For example:

Agripac-ing it in

This headline appeared on a story about a local cannery, Agripac, that was rumored to be ready to shut down. The headline, which attempts to play on the idea "packing it in," is even difficult for readers who live in the region to understand. Here's another example:

Group Dynamix

This headline appeared on a profile of a computer game developer named "Dynamix." It was a fairly straightforward business story marking the eventual takeover of the company by a conglomerate. The term from which the headline drew, "group dynamics," for its word play, had little, if anything to do with the story.

One can find many examples of trite and predictable headlines. How many times, for example, have the words "pipe dream" appeared on business-section headlines about pipe manufacturers, or "sweet success" on stories about candy companies? One would think that business page editors and copy editors would have a better grasp of the seriousness with which their sources and readers view the subject matter. Perhaps headline writers feel that business stories need brightening up. Such plays would appear far less often if copy editors had to face company executives, as reporters do, and interview them for the next story.

JUDGING CREATIVITY

Consider two garden-page headlines that attempt to be clever. The first appeared on a story about the difficulty of keeping some aggressive plants from overtaking a garden:

Give them an inch, they'll take a yard

The second appeared on a column about how one needs Olympic drive and determination to eradicate certain weeds:

No guts, no morning glory

Both headlines are quite clever, and anyone who makes an honest attempt to brighten up a standing feature such as a garden column deserves praise. There is a subtle issue, however, that makes the first headline a winner and the second a loser. The first headline takes and reinterprets an old saying in a new light. It is exactly the point of the story. The second sounds good; it's also a reinterpretation of a familiar saying, and morning glory, as any gardener knows, is very difficult to get rid of. The problem, though, is that the headline literally says the opposite of what the column says. The point of the column is that you need to have guts to get rid of weeds like morning glory. If you have no guts, you will have a yard full of the weed. One might argue that I'm being too literal in criticizing that headline. I'd counter that accuracy remains a fundamental criterion in all headlines and that a copy editor should not suspend that rule because a turn of phrase sounds good. It violates what is perhaps the most reasonable assumption readers have when it comes to headlines: The big type tells you what the little type says, or at the very least, the big type doesn't contradict the little type.

To avoid such problems, copy editors can take a page from the Olympics rulebook. Judge a clever headline by averaging two marks, as is done in figure skating. The first is for technical merit, the second for artistic expression. Both garden-column examples get high marks for artistic expression. But the "morning glory" headline gets thumbs down from the judges for technical merit—after all, it's wrong.

It's possible to boil down the rules for cleverness to three tests:

1. Does the headline pass the "ouch" test? In other words, does it invite people in rather than make them groan and push them away?
2. Does it pass the "sweet old Aunt Jane" test? Is it insensitive? What would you think if the subject of the story were your own kindly aunt?
3. Does it pass the "figure-skating" test? Is it technically correct as well as clever?

THE TWO FACES OF CREATIVITY?

Management theorists often suggest that creative failure should be rewarded. They point out that it is difficult for people to improve or advance if they don't take chances. Does the same apply in headline writing?

Yes and no.

Headline writers need to take chances, or else they can get stuck in the rut of predictability. But they need to take chances *prudently.* Copy editors need to not take chances for the sake of taking chances, to not play with words for the sake of playing, to not push the envelope just to say they pushed it. Headline writers also need a safety net, because at times the downside of creative failure might be greater than the danger of failing to take chances. It depends on whether that near-miss might offend readers or invite them to feel that the newspaper is acting in bad taste. If that happens, the damage to the credibility of the organization might be worse than the harm of stifling an editor's creativity.

A copy chief who acts as both a sounding board and a teacher is the best safety net. Newspapers that do not have such a position are missing an excellent opportunity for headline quality control as well as copy desk staff development.

Another strategy is to test iffy headlines on trusted colleagues and, if possible, on people who are not working next to you on the desk. A "trusted colleague" is one who will tell you honestly when your headline doesn't work. Sometimes that approach doesn't work. People who work in the same newsroom often tend to think alike. Years ago, when newspapers were typeset by production workers, a copy editor might bounce a headline off a compositor or engraver to get a better sense of whether it might appear insensitive to people outside the newsroom. The same goes for literary allusions or popular culture references. University-educated copy editors might agree that an allusion works, but readers might see if differently. Sometimes it's wise to get the view of someone who might not be university-educated, perhaps a member of the front-office clerical staff. On a pop culture reference that's crucial to an understanding of the headline, it might be a good idea to see how it plays with older employees. Time constraints limit an editor's flexibility in seeking other views, but on iffy headlines, it can be time well spent.

CHALLENGES AND OPPORTUNITIES

In headlines, it's a tossup whether time or space is the biggest challenge. Despite the flexibility of electronic type, the limitations of line length in print often do not allow you to write the headline you might choose if length were not a criterion. There are several strategies to get more out of a tight count.

1. Electronic Type Manipulation

Computer typesetting has given copy editors much more flexibility in making headlines fit than their predecessors ever had. Copy editors now can squeeze or expand type on the horizontal dimension, reduce or enlarge fonts on the vertical dimension or adjust both dimensions. They can shrink intercharacter white space or expand it. Limited typographic adjustment is OK (and what adjustments are allowed vary from publication to publication), but copy editors should avoid the temptation to squeeze or enlarge a headline simply to make deadline. The result can be a design disaster, with headlines that are supposed to be the same size looking very different, or headlines that are supposed to be 6-points different looking essentially the same. Overmanipulation of headline type can defeat the consistent look that well-edited publications strive to maintain. Consequently, many editors have found that abuse of typographic tools can become a problem.

Publications adopt different guidelines on electronic manipulation. Some allow the increase or decrease of point size. Others allow horizontal compression or expansion of the letterform. Some allow kerning (white-space reduction between characters) or word space manipulation (similar to the expansion or contraction of spacing that line justification produces). Some allow designers to manipulate type but don't let copy editors do so. Standard desktop publishing packages such as QuarkXPress make such manipulations easy, and systems used at large papers, such as CCI, Unisys, Harris and Atex, also allow such manipulation.

Beyond the impact on design, a cavalier attitude toward typographical manipulation can subtly change the attitude that copy editors bring to their craft. In effect, it can help shift one's attitude from a craft mind-set to a production mind-set. In studies of the impact of pagination on copy editors, I have observed many newsrooms in which headlines get short shrift. Copy editors/page designers have come to rely on the wizardry of computer typesetting to make anything close fit. They leave little time for headline writing, spending too much time on page-makeup considerations that once were the province of back-shop workers. When it comes time to write the headline, they slap something onto the electronic page and manipulate the type to make it fit. The result is a subtle, or perhaps not-so-subtle, erosion of the craft of headline writing. Historically, editors wrote headlines and compositors typeset them. Computer typesetting has eliminated many of the distinctions between journalist and printer that had developed over a century or more, but copy editors should try to retain a sense of craft, even in the face of looming deadlines and staff cutbacks. Using electronic gimmicks to make the first headline that comes to mind fit is not the mind-set of an editor. It's a production mind-set.

2. Harnessing Ambiguity

Many great memorable headlines are humorous, but a great headline does not need to be humorous. In fact, cleverness without humor can make for excellent headlines. One strategy is to suspend the rule on clarity and to deliberately write a headline that can be read two ways. The challenge is to make sure both readings provide a window into the story. So if a reader catches the first meaning, that's fine; if the second meaning, that's OK too. If a reader catches both meanings, you've got a winner. The danger is writing the sort of headline that appears in "The Lower case" because the second meaning is silly, off-color or inappropriate. The benefit for a headline writer is that ambiguity in effect lengthens the headline. If you can write a headline that has two meanings and both meanings convey what the story says, you've effectively doubled the headline count. Here are three examples:

A league that shoots for more

—on a package of story and photo about a youth development league that uses basketball to teach kids leadership and other values.

Developer steps across line

—on a story about a builder testing the urban growth boundary limits.

An ouch of prevention

—atop a centerpiece photo spread of schoolchildren grimacing while they get immunizations at a city clinic.

Most headlines do not lend themselves to ambiguity. In general, news headlines are not the place to employ ambiguity; clarity and specificity are too important. Those headlines should tell what happened as completely and clearly as possible.

Features and trends are a better bet. Here the goal is not so much to tell what happened as much as to give a sense of the piece, perhaps a hint of some of the complexity. Use this strategy sparingly, but when it works, it can work wonders.

TIPS AND STRATEGIES

- Edit headlines. Headlines should be edited by another person, just as copy is edited. Deadline pressures and newsroom organization sometimes make it more difficult to give heads another look. In systems that do not have copy chiefs, it is a good idea to pass headlines through another copy editor before they are preserved for posterity in newsprint. Web headlines also should be edited. It might seem that mistakes are less serious on the Web because, unlike in print, a Web headline can be corrected on the fly. But understaffing in Web operations can keep editors from making changes quickly.

- Coach headline writers. Coaching is an important role within a copy desk; here the coach is the copy chief or slot, and the person coached is traditionally called a "rim" editor.[2] Slots should be teachers as well as supervisors, and teaching rim editors to write better headlines is one of their most important duties. Unfortunately, many fail to accept this responsibility. They simply recast a headline in much the same way a city editor might rewrite a paragraph without consulting the reporter. A better way is to offer feedback, perhaps in the form of a suggestion, and let the copy editor rewrite the headline. Deadline pressures sometimes make this process difficult, but even in those cases, a slot should make an effort to debrief a copy editor on why the rewrite. Time, as usual, is the challenge.

Most copy editors enjoy writing excellent headlines—it might be the most rewarding part of the job. What distinguishes great headlines from good or adequate ones? You know them when you see them:

The man who would be King

Because it appeared in a magazine, the preceding was technically a title, not a headline. It ran in a University of Oregon student magazine called Flux, and it appeared above a large picture of an Elvis impersonator in his tacky outfit. As a headline, it breaks a rule many newspapers follow: to write headlines in s–v–o (subject–verb–object) structure. That's a good rule for many stories, particularly news stories, because it is the most efficient and clearest way to summarize information. But in the case of a feature story—a profile of a local Elvis impersonator—a better goal is to capture the flavor, which this headline does. It's a label that puts a well-know phrase in a new context. Some of the best newspaper headlines break the rules, or, perhaps more accurately, bend them to suit the story. Good newspaper headline writers look to other media for ideas, to magazines and to advertising. Here, newspapers should take a cue from magazines and use labels if they fit the story and capture the essence.

Why a whole chapter on headline creativity?

Because creativity is important—to readers as well as to headline writers. Writing these headlines has always stimulated copy editors; it is the place where they themselves can be creative rather than helping others be creative.

The trick is to balance creativity and discipline—to know when to let fly and when to hold back.

11

Other Display Elements

Years ago, it was easy to discuss newspaper display type. The two categories were headlines and cutlines. Now it isn't so easy. Newspapers use a wide variety of display-type forms, including various headline combinations, such as main and deck heads, multiple decks in descending point size, liftout quotes, and overlines and labels on packages and special reports. They also use such display elements as fact boxes and at-a-glance boxes to summarize information presented in stories or to provide additional information. The text for these boxes is sometimes written by copy editors, but often it is prepared by reporters or assigning editors and processed through art or graphics departments before it gets to the desk.

The expansion of the role of display type serves two main purposes. The headlinelike items that accompany stories provide additional "points of entry," which are considered by many designers essential in capturing the interest of casual readers. They also act as design elements, providing contrasting type to break up gray blocks of text and contributing to a newspaper's individual look.

The trend toward multiple points of entry also has created more work for the copy desk, whose members write most of this display type and typically edit what they don't write. Beyond headline skills, copy editors who write and edit these new forms of display type must learn to think holistically, to coordinate the multiple elements that accompany a story. The various pieces of display type, which can easily number four or more on a single story, must not be repetitive yet must work together to provide as much information as possible about the story. The overall impression of the display type should be greater than the sum of the parts.

MULTIPOINT-SIZE HEADLINES

Newspapers today use many combinations of headline point sizes on individual stories. Look at 10 papers at random, and you'll probably find six or seven different styles. Many set large main headlines with smaller "drop" headlines or decks. Others do the reverse, setting a smaller point-size headline atop a larger primary headline. A few have returned to the past, using the type of multideck, descending-point size headlines common in the late 19th century. Many also shift fonts in secondary headlines, sometimes setting the smaller deck in a different font or a contrasting face of the same font, say italic versus Roman.

Some news organizations have developed in-house criteria for writing combination headlines, but an examination of many newspapers that use such headlines suggests that there are some general rules. One is that type appearing as headlines—whether main or secondary—should be written according to headline rules. No ending punctuation is used, split thoughts are avoided, numerals lower than 10 are acceptable, articles and auxiliaries can be dropped if needed, and so on.

Another rule is almost too obvious to state: The main or dominant headline should reflect the primary element or focus of the story. The biggest type is the first type a reader sees, and it should tell the story. Choosing a good focus for secondary or subsidiary headlines is not so straightforward. What you should write depends on the space you have available in the main as well as the secondary headlines and on what you need to say to convey the essence of the story. Some stories can be summarized well in a few words; some cannot. For a story whose main point can be summarized well in the biggest type, a copy editor might write a secondary headline that summarizes a different element of the story.

**City Council approves
150-unit development**
Action is delayed
on tax proposal

The first headline reflects the most important news of the meeting; that information would probably be in the lead sentence of the story. The main headline is long enough to capture the essence of this point, so the drop, or deck, headline can be used to highlight another important matter: the tax proposal.

For stories that are difficult to summarize in tight counts, a copy editor can use the deck to amplify or explain the main headline.

Council approves
subdivision plan
150 units planned
for Laurel Estates

Here are additional examples of the same approach, which is a very common strategy in headline–deck combinations:

Curriculum
experiment
begins in fall
Anthropology will be first
to offer 4-credit courses

School district delivers bad news
102 Springfield employees get pink slips

Sometimes the strategy can be used in a feature approach even when the headline is long enough to tell the story:

Good golly, Molly's got opinions
Texas writer Ivins sees humor in politics

All-Stars, fans fit to be tied
Classic ends in 7–7 deadlock when both teams run out
of pitchers

The main headline on the latter, which was a large-point-size banner across the top of the sports page, could have said, "All-Star game ends in a tie." That would have placed the news more directly in the main headline. But the headline writer chose to take a more featurelike approach, making a play on words in the big type, and letting the secondary headline provide the details.

A somewhat different approach is to build a partial quote into the subsidiary headline to capture some of the emotion reflected in the story or to better reflect the story's tone, as in the next example.

Council approves
subdivision plan
'I'll see you in court,'
key opponent vows

Magazine-style headline and deck combinations, which appear frequently on centerpiece packages, use another approach. They use an attractive label or phrase for the largest type and rely heavily on the secondary type to provide clarifying information. The big words, which often use elaborate and creative typography, should act as a theme for the package, tying the story and photos together.

Blast from the past
Scientists using old documents and modern computers put a possible date to a huge Northwest quake

Cheers and jeers
Some applaud rally squads while others prefer to push 'em back, waaaaay back—to the dark ages from whence they came

Kicking butts
The Great American Smokeout is here, so put out that cigarette and get ready for the first day of your nicotine-free life

The tendency in many of these heads is toward flipness, which is appropriate in many cases. Flipness is not essential, though. The big type can play it straight and still work well:

Back from the edge
The Fish and Wildlife Service will celebrate the recovery of the bald eagle and the gray whale

The elements of multideck headlines should not depend on one another too closely, because it's jarring to read phrases or clauses set in different typography as units. Some newspapers disagree, but I believe that a secondary headline should read as a separate headline statement even when it amplifies a previous headline. The main headline should not "read into" a secondary headline, as the example below does:

Council approves
apartment proposal
Delays action
on tax increase

This combination headline is, in effect, a single sentence. One subject (council) has two verbs. This approach appears to be efficient. It might allow a headline writer to squeeze more information into a headline. The problem is that the two headline sizes don't look like one sentence, because sentences don't shift point size around the middle. A better approach would be to write the secondary headline in passive voice, so both pieces of the combination read as separate clauses:

Action delayed
on tax increase

An alternative is to use a synonym for *council* such as *board*, *body* or *panel*. Be careful, though, not to stray too far into headlinese.

Attribution, if necessary, should be in the main headline. Some newspapers take the position that attribution in a secondary headline or even a summary paragraph is sufficient. I believe that approach is a mistake. The problem is that display type has an iconic function, as suggested in Chapter 9. Size matters; it typically reflects importance. Attribution that appears half as large as the assertion visually downplays the importance of the source. A related problem is that readers might ignore the deck, reading the statement or assertion as commonly held truth. If a statement or assertion needs to be attributed in the lead of a story, it generally needs to be in the headline itself. For example,

Pollution leaking
from paper mill
State says plant
discharging waste

It is safer and more responsible to build the source of the allegation into the main head. An "official report" is not necessarily established fact:

Paper mill leaking
pollution, state says
Investigators report
high level of acid

In this case, the attribution appears in the big type, and as a bonus, the drop headline can be used to provide additional information. An alternative is a passive-voice construction, which sometimes allows the headline writer to get another detail into the headline:

High level of acid
reported in waste

Some editors prefer to avoid passive voice in headlines at all costs. I would relax that prohibition if the payoff is worth it. For example, sometimes the main headline does not provide enough space to properly attribute an assertion. In such cases, it generally is possible to suggest attribution through use of a passive-voice verb and to use the summary paragraph to clarify it:

Pollution
reported
near mill
State says tests found
acid in waste discharge

SUMMARY PARAGRAPHS

Much like drop headlines, summary paragraphs offer the copy editor the chance to provide more information in display type. And, as with multideck headlines, a copy editor must coordinate the elements and tailor the approach to the needs of the story. If the headline cannot adequately reflect the story because of space limitations, an editor can use the summary paragraph to amplify it or to provide important qualification. If the headline is long enough to capture the essence, the summary paragraph can provide additional information.

**Crowding leads college
to tighten standards**
Next year's freshmen
will be asked to meet
a minimum GPA of 3.25.

Dark clouds looming over baseball
Steroids and talk of a strike dampen a
festive part of the season—the All-Star break.

Summary paragraph style differs from paper to paper. Indeed, the element itself goes by different names. It is variously called a "summary paragraph," a "deck," a "key[word] deck," sometimes even a "nut graf," a term that many papers use to refer to something very different—a summarization section near the top of many feature stories. Stylistic differences abound as well. Some newspapers drop articles in summaries, much as headline style allows; others don't. Some papers use ending punctuation on summaries; others don't. Some use keyword identifiers at the beginning, often in bold face; others don't. Keyword identifiers make display type more difficult to write if the newspaper shuns use of the same word twice in display type, as many do. If a word is important enough to highlight as a keyword, it probably should be in the head or summary text. I believe it is best to treat summary paragraphs as text, using articles, auxiliary verbs and ending punctuation. Summaries typically are written in point sizes much smaller than headlines. They look more like text than headlines, and they read better as text.

**Serena
defeats
Venus**
Younger Williams is
No. 1 in world, at
Wimbledon and at home

Here is the same summary rewritten as text rather than in headline style:

The younger Williams is
No. 1 in the world, at
Wimbledon and at home.

The difference is subtle, only two articles and a period, but readability is much better.

As with multideck headlines, a summary paragraph can be used to provide additional information or even to highlight a quote that lends color to the headline. Here's a combination in which the main head tells the story well enough and the summary paragraph is used to provide additional information:

**Film actor
Rod Steiger
dies at 77**
From Al Capone to the
Pope, his portrayals
were compelling.

Like secondary headlines, summary paragraphs should not be used to provide attribution that belongs in the headline. Because of the great difference in point size between a headline (say 72-, 60-, 48- or 36-point) and a summary paragraph (14- to 18-point), an important attribution can get lost or passed over in the smaller display type, and an assertion that might be debatable can appear to be established fact.

Sometimes a summary paragraph can be used to support a brighter, feature-style headline on a news story. For example,

Nobel winner's ex-wife had a theory, too
She had demanded
half of "any Nobel Prize"
the economist might win.

The headline could have been written in a straight-news fashion:

Nobel winner's ex-wife gets half of prize

But it would not have been as inviting. "Had a theory too" is a nice touch. The summary paragraph in this case provides those details and lets the copy editor write a bright, clever headline on a story that does not demand straight news treatment.

Summary decks (as well as subsidiary headlines) should not contradict the main headline or raise confusion in a reader's mind. This seems too obvious to state, but some display type combinations fail this test. The following head–summary combination raises more questions than it answers.

**City may
relax code
for sake of
homeless**
A designated shelter idea
unravels as councilors
consider options.

The main headline is vague, and a reader's reasonable conclusion is that the summary paragraph clarifies or explains the vague headline. The headline suggests a positive action, but the beginning of the summary suggests a negative result. One needs to read the story to make sense of the headline, which is always a clue that something needs to be rewritten. The story makes clear that a city proposal to create a shelter for homeless campers ran into too much opposition. As a result, council members discussed other options, including some that would require a relaxation of city land-use rules. Here's a better head:

**Homeless
shelter
proposal
hits snag**
Opposition leads the city
to consider alternatives and
examine land-use rules.

This headline flips the ideas around. The main headline summarizes the main point; the summary paragraph amplifies it and introduces the second element. Technically, "homeless shelter" should be on one line. In many one-column headlines, the tradeoff between a split and comprehensiveness favors comprehensiveness.

LIFTOUT QUOTES

Many newspapers use quotes set in larger type to give readers additional points of entry and designers additional typographic elements. If well chosen, liftouts can add life to display type and visual contrast to a page. If poorly chosen, they add little and can often detract from the overall impression of a story. Liftouts and other display elements should not be used merely to solve design problems. In too many cases, stories that have no appropriate liftout quotes are designed for liftouts, and the result is large type that serves more as a point of distraction than a point of entry. A well-chosen liftout quote can help tie the package together. Here is a headline and liftout on a 1995 story about the freeway killing of a German tourist, the second in six months.

Tourist's slaying in Miami stirs outrage

"They did everything
right, and the husband
was still killed. It's just
something we have to face.
It's reality in the city
of Miami."
—Sgt. Diego Ochoa,
Miami Police Department

The liftout provides another element. It offers additional information about the crime as well as a sense of resignation on the part of the police spokesman. Here's another combination of head, deck and liftout:

Monster blizzard threatens East Coast

Three people are killed by tornadoes in Florida
as the massive storm begins its trek north.

"This could be the
worst storm of the
century. . . .
We're not crying
wolf this time. It's
really coming."
—National Weather Service

This liftout is used well. The head provides the basic news, the deck provides important detail, and the liftout provides support for the head as well as a sense of drama. The elements play off one another but are not redundant.

One important consideration is that a liftout quote be representative of the story. Just as with headlines, when text is bigger and bolder, it speaks louder, and it takes on greater importance in readers' perceptions of stories. Often the best or most dramatic quote is a good choice for display, but sometimes the most striking quote is not the best option. Here is an example of a liftout quote that runs the risk of casting the story in a misleading light:

Portland's prepared for 'Operation Summit'
Dressed all in black
and identifying herself
as Judy ("Like Garland,
except I'm not dead"), she
decided she wasn't terribly
interested in the summit.
"Old trees suck," she said.

At first glance, this liftout is difficult to follow because of the introductory clause and the parenthetical insert. But Judy's quote at the end is certainly an attention-grabber, and it probably was chosen for that reason. The story was a lengthy look at what people in Portland, Ore., thought about the high-profile summit on old-growth forest issues that President Clinton attended in the early '90s. It was an advance story, and it quoted many Portland-area people who had credible, intelligent things to say about the meeting and its importance. The only extreme comment in the story was Judy's "Old trees suck." Using that quote in display type can present a distorted view of the story. In fact, one can conclude, based on the headline and the quote, that people in Portland could care less about the summit. The story largely said the opposite.

CAPTIONS

Photo captions are the Rodney Dangerfield of display type. To echo the longtime comedian's trademark line, captions "don't get no respect." After headlines, captions are generally considered the most widely read display type. They are smaller in point size than summary paragraphs and liftout quotes, but readers are attracted to captions before the other display type because the photos capture their attention. A typical sequence of reader attention is headline–photo–caption. Sometimes, it's even photo–caption–headline.

Whether they are read first or second, captions are so important that one would expect news organizations to take great care in writing them. That, unfortunately, is not the case. No research I'm aware of supports the following assertion, but I suspect, based on 30 years of careful news reading, that word for word, captions contain more mistakes than story text. An understanding of common newsroom practices illuminates why errors can occur in captions. Readers, however, don't care why mistakes are made. They just see mistakes and think the publication is poorly written or edited.

In copy flow, captions are often treated as an afterthought. Mistakes can occur because caption information is incorrect or sketchy or because photos or page designs are late. Copy editors often simply pay less attention to captions than to other display type, particularly headlines. Mistakes occur because captions get less editorial attention than even the most insignificant story gets. At many small newspapers, the only person who reads a caption before it is printed is the person who wrote it. There is no better recipe for trouble. Everyone needs an editor, even a copy editor. At papers that have a slot–rim desk structure, a caption generally gets two reads: by the copy editor who wrote it and by the copy chief. At large papers, which have more specialized jobs, a news editor or a supervisor might take an additional look, but deadline pressures often make it impossible for those editors to give captions a careful read. In contrast, even a three-paragraph brief cobbled together from a news release is usually read by at least three people and often more: the reporter, the assigning editor, the copy editor and, if one is available, the copy chief.

Photo editors sometimes argue that captions are so important that they should be written by a dedicated caption writer. I think that approach would create more problems than it would solve. The caption should be written by the same person who writes the headline and other display type to ensure that all elements work well together. And one caption writer would not have time to read all stories carefully. The only practical way to solve caption problems is to pay more attention to them.

CRITERIA FOR CAPTIONS

Caption writing is an art, one based at least in part on rules. Like headlines, captions should be active, specific and informative. Typically, they need to explain what is happening in the photo; sometimes they don't need to do so because it is obvious. In general, captions should:

- Make the photograph understandable.
- Be readable.
- Be integrated well with other display type.
- Correspond to the tone of the story.

Caption criteria tend to be fairly consistent from publication to publication. Newspapers tend to follow similar rules on verb tense, identification of subjects and use of articles. Captions tend to follow text style for wording but headline style for tense, though there are exceptions to both. Captions, like headlines, typically use the historic present. The logic of using the historic present in captions is understandable—you are usually explaining what's going on in the photo as if it were happening. But there are many exceptions. Present tense is generally used to explain the action taking place in a picture. Consider the following caption for a photo that might be used to illustrate a dry spell in farm country:

Jimmy Jones stands knee-deep in corn in a drought-parched Iowa field.

Many captions do not need a time element; the assumption is that the photo is current. When it is important to provide the time element in the caption, the historic present is less logical and often appears jarring:

Jimmy Jones stands knee-deep in an Iowa cornfield on Tuesday, a day before heavy rains broke a four-week drought.

Using "stands" to refer to an event that the same sentence clearly shows occurred in the recent past is problematic. You don't "stand on Tuesday," you "stood on Tuesday." One way to eliminate the inconsistency is:

Jimmy Jones stands knee-deep in an Iowa cornfield. On Wednesday, heavy rains broke a four-week drought.

One can still argue that there is an inconsistency in tense between the sentences, but it isn't as jarring as an inconsistency within a sentence. Another approach, which some news organizations use to avoid the problem, is to address the action with a phrase instead of a full sentence.

> Jimmy Jones standing knee-deep in an Iowa cornfield on Tuesday. The next
> day, heavy rains broke a four-week drought.

The New York Times Manual of Style and Usage, 1999 edition, offers good
advice:

> "Captions about fresh news may be written in the present tense (Firefighters
> carry an injured crew member from the wreckage of the cargo plane). But if
> the caption includes a past time element like yesterday, the verb must change
> to a participle (carrying) or to the past tense (carried) an injured crew mem-
> ber yesterday. A caption recalling history or old news can use only the partici-
> ple form or the past tense."

As with writing headlines, copy editors need to use common sense in
choosing tenses. For example, captions written on file photos used to illustrate a trend or news feature story often make more sense in past tense.
Here's a good approach for a file shot of one of the worst wildfires of the
2002 season that might be used for a story predicting fire danger for the
2003 season:

> One of last summer's most devastating fires threatened the community of
> Show Low in Arizona. The wildfire threat in much of the West is expected to
> be as great this year.

A passage from The Philadelphia Inquirer style manual provides a clear
statement of what captions should do:

> "Simply stated, the caption should explain the picture so that the reader is
> left with no reasonable questions. The caption should not stress what the pic-
> ture has already made obvious, but it should supply information the picture
> cannot. For example, a picture can show a football player leaping for a pass,
> but it probably cannot show that the result was the winning touchdown. The
> caption should say so."

Older versions of the AP Stylebook had a section on captions. The 1986
version says, "The caption's job is to describe and explain the picture to
the reader." Copy editors often can place the photo better in the context of
the story by providing additional information:

> Jimmy Jones, who is 4-foot-2, stands knee-deep in corn in a drought-parched
> Iowa field. In a normal rain year, the corn would be up to his chest.

The additional contextual information helps make the point the photo is illustrating. By providing the boy's height, one has a better idea of the corn's height, and by adding the final sentence, readers who are not farmers can better understand the significance of the photo.

IDENTIFICATION

A glance at various newspapers will show there is some variation in the style used to identify people in picture captions. Some, for example, use commas to set off words that clarify identifications; others use parentheses. But all approaches try to make it clear to the reader which person is which in the picture. Perhaps the most common approach is to identify subjects from left to right using parenthetical inserts:

Jimmy Jones (left) and his brother, Jason, stand knee-deep in an Iowa cornfield.

Common sense should prevail in identifications. Occasionally, it's better to identify a person who is not leftmost first. If a person in the right side of the frame is a more dominant subject in the photo or is more central to the story, it probably makes more sense to identify that person first.

Here are a few more suggestions:

- Make sure that the people who are identifiable are identified. But if a person is barely identifiable and it is not important to name him or her, do not do so.
- Do not insult the reader's intelligence. For example, if two boys and a girl are pictured and there is no possible confusion over names, there's no need to say Johnny (left), Jimmy (center) and Ginny (right). It's enough to identify Johnny (left) and name the other two.
- Make sure that someone who is identified in the caption has not been cropped out of the photo.
- Remember too that objects often need to be identified as much as people do. A piece of equipment that is mentioned in the story might need to be identified in the picture.

If caption information and the story disagree on names or other facts, don't automatically assume the story is correct, as some copy editors tend to do. It is true that some photographers are not as careful about accuracy as reporters generally are, but many photographers are extremely careful with the information they provide, more careful than reporters. The reporter's creed, "Thou shalt not assume," is as valid in caption writing as it is in reporting.

TYPES OF CAPTIONS

The simplest caption is the nameline on a "mug," or head, shot. Some styles use last name only; some use the full name. Often, however, newspapers use a style of identification and exposition for mug shots. Some, for example, use the second line to provide an individual's title or other information about a person:

John Sidgmore
Chief executive of WorldCom

Other papers allow more flexibility in the choice of a second line, perhaps working an important piece of information from the story into it, or even a short quote:

John Sidgmore
WorldCom executive will testify

Head shots that accompanied two examples provided in the section on liftout quotes are examples. The first accompanied the "Tourist slaying" story:

Uwe-Wilhelm Rakebrand
Shot while driving on freeway

The second was a shot of the Nobel laureate whose ex-wife claimed half his prize:

Robert Lucas Jr.
"A deal's a deal"

Copy editors have a tendency to dispatch these simple captions with little thought. That's a mistake. A well-written exposition line can add to the overall package if done well. A poorly written one can create serious problems, even appear to contradict the story. Here are two examples that were misleading or confusing.

In late 1995, when the Unabomber's identity was still unknown, the AP moved a story about a profile developed by the FBI. The headline and caption read:

Unabomber not likely to keep promise

John Douglas
Bomber probably keeps a diary

At first glance, which is all many people ever give a page, it appears from the combination of display type that John Douglas is the Unabomber. Readers keeping up with the news would realize that the Unabomber had not been captured, but others might do a double-take and think for a second that the story was reporting an arrest. A better approach would have been to use the second line to identify Douglas as the FBI profile expert.

Another example occurred on an item about Courtney Love, the singer whose husband, Kurt Cobain, shot himself to death. The headline and caption read:

Rocker tried to kill herself before husband's suicide

Courtney Love
She was "going to blow my head off"

There is no way to make sense of that caption until you read the story. "She" and "my" refer to the same person—Courtney Love—but the caption is impossible to track. Rather than try to shoehorn a dramatic quote into an inadequate space with confusing pronouns, the copy editor should have identified Love more prosaically, say as rock star Cobain's wife. Again, common sense is the key.

ONE-LINE CAPTIONS

For many newspapers, this type of caption, also known as a "singleton," is the workhorse. Despite their brevity, one-line captions are supposed to meet the general criteria for captions, that is, they need to explain the picture and identify the subjects. Often, one line is enough. All too often it isn't. The problem is greatest in singletons on small photos, such as two-column pictures. As a result, many newspapers allow these captions to be written more in headline style, with articles and auxiliary verbs dropped. For example,

Jimmy Jones (left) and brother, Jason, stand knee-deep in Iowa cornfield.

Such captions are harder to read. Caption type is small and is read as text, not as a headline. Dropping words should be a last resort. Often it's possible to find an elegant way around the problem:

Jimmy (left) and Jason Jones stand knee-deep in an Iowa cornfield.

FULL CAPTIONS

Multiline, often multisentence, captions are used by many newspapers when a single line is insufficient. Others use full captions as their standard. In writing these captions, a good approach is to explain the picture and provide identification first, then use the remaining space to provide additional information.

Jonathan Doe, a paid petitioner from Portland, solicits signatures for an initiative proposal outside the Fred Meyer store at Southeast 39th Avenue and Hawthorne Street. Oregon Employment Department rulings mean paid signature gatherers must be treated as employees and not independent contractors.

Some full captions are written for photos that run without stories. Those photos are known as "standalones" or sometimes "wild art," a term that many photographers shun. Typical examples are photos of spacecraft blasting off, weather-related photos and accident and fire photos. Pages need photos or graphics, and sometimes the only image available is a standalone. In some cases they are used because they are simply very good pictures (e.g., weather or colorful flower or sunset photos). In other cases, editors feel that an event should be covered, but it isn't important enough to warrant a full story (e.g., blast-offs). In still other cases, the photographer happened by a news event and collected enough information for a short item.

The caption must serve as a ministory for standalones. The technique is almost like broadcast writing. You must tell as much of a story as possible in several sentences, clearly and concisely. As with other full captions, a good approach is to explain the picture and identify people first, then use the rest of the space to provide enough information. The approach is the same for photos that refer to a story inside:

A helicopter drops water on the Cache Mountain fire, one of two that threaten resort communities in the Sisters, Ore., region. Firefighters gained ground in the Cache Mountain fire, which destroyed two resort homes in Black Butte two days ago and remains a threat to others. Story on Page 3-B.

CHOICE OF PHOTOS

Copy editors often are not in a position to select photos for publication, but they typically are in the best position to determine whether a photo does not work well with a story. Much as in using liftout quotes, copy editors should make sure that photos chosen to accompany a story are appropriate and are not misleading. Every copy editor has had the experience of writing a caption on a photo that doesn't connect well with a story—the smiling file shot of the bank president who has just been charged with embezzling funds or the photo of a robbery victim grinning. Unfortunately, one cannot write "shown in happier times" to address the discrepancy between photo and story. Inappropriate photos can also be the source of legal problems, particularly in the area of privacy law (see Chapter 6). Sometimes the only reasonable approach is to ask that the photo not be used. Because they read the stories carefully and write the captions, copy editors are in the best position to see such discrepancies.

Sometimes the problem is more subtle. Photographers and photo editors naturally want to use the most striking or dramatic shots. Sometimes, however, such photos can be misleading. For example, a photo of the one act of violence in a lengthy demonstration that was otherwise peaceful might not be the most appropriate photo to use with the story, even if it does have the most action and is the "best shot." In such cases, a copy editor can ask that the photo be changed. Often, however, copy editors will lose those battles. A fallback position is to make sure to write a fair caption, one that places the action in the broader context of the event.

TIPS AND STRATEGIES

• Avoid editorialization, whether intentional or inadvertent. The Philadelphia Inquirer stylebook offers sound advice:

> "The caption writer should not make assumptions about what someone in a picture is thinking or doing, or try to interpret the person's feelings from his or her expression. *Club-swinging police officer* . . . may cast an onus on the officer, but *Eyes blazing defiance, the demonstrator* . . . may shift the prejudice in the opposite direction. The reader should decide what the clubs and the eyes convey after being told the simple facts of the situation.
>
> On the same principle, the caption writer should avoid characterizing the picture as beautiful, dramatic, grisly or in any other way. . . . "

• See it first. One of the best tips on caption writing is what the AP called its "Cardinal Rule" on captions: Never write a caption without seeing the picture. Copy editors will find that the opportunity to violate this rule presents itself occasionally because of technical production glitches and late photos. Writing a caption without seeing the picture, even to achieve the laudable goal of meeting a deadline, is like asking for a correction. Failing to see a photo crop, for example, because one never saw the photo can lead to an egg-on-the-face explanation the next day. In one case, because of a design problem, a file photo of two people getting on a train was used to illustrate a story. One subject was the focus of the story; in effect, the photo was serving as a head shot. But in the last-minute rush, the photo was not cropped. The second figure in the photo was of a prominent member of the community who had died a year before. In another all-too-common occurrence, the caption is written for a photo that is replaced by another. Writing captions without seeing the photo leads all too frequently to serious embarrassment for the publication as well as for the caption writer. Publishers might disagree, but this is a case where missing a deadline is justifiable.

• Remember that images speak louder than words. When the photo seems to be saying one thing and the caption or story another, the reader will tend to believe the photo. The visual channel tends to be more realistic than the verbal channel, a fact that is well known to television news professionals. After all, the audience can "see for themselves." As a practical matter, this means that copy editors must realize that their ability to use a caption to explain a discrepancy between the photo and the story is limited.

• Study publications that write captions well. Two magazines widely respected for caption writing are National Geographic and Sports Illustrated. Both publications devote substantial time and energy to caption writing. Readers can glean many of the important points of National Geographic stories from the captions, and the captions are integrated with the other display type and the text about as well as any other publication does it. Sports Illustrated captions exhibit a trademark crispness and flair, which fits the subject matter well. The captions, which are written for a sports-savvy readership, often place the photo squarely in the context of the story, and they do so with an amazing economy of words.

The trend to create more display-type points of entry has made newspapers more accessible to readers. Done carefully, this type can add to a story's impact and understandability. Done poorly, it can add to confusion. Extra care must be taken in writing all forms of display type: headlines, decks, liftouts and captions. Mistakes are as easy to make, if not easier, in display type as in regular text. But they loom larger.

12

Words and Images Together

Here is a headline-writing task: You have a long profile of an artist that will anchor the front of the feature section. A large photo of the artist, an 85-year-old woman sitting in her meditation space, dominates the package. A smaller photo shows a weaving, one of the artist's works, which are considered by art critics to be quite good. There is some smaller display type underneath the headline. It says:

> She is a weaver/artist
> in a spiritual quest for freedom.
> She calls her works "clouds."

Your job is to write the headline. The type is large, so you have only three or four words to work with. I've given this task to students in many classes and to professionals in workshops. They come up with a variety of ideas, typically labels such as "Weaver of dreams" and "Spinner of clouds." Those aren't bad, and there probably are better ideas. After a few minutes, I show them the page and the headline that ran with the story. They gasp. Here it is:

Fruits of her loom

The newspaper might as well have said, "A portrait of the artist in her BVDs." This unbridled cleverness, which appeared in a highly regarded metropolitan newspaper, should have been cut off at the pass, if not by the copy editor, then by the copy chief. The story and the photos say "respected artist"; the headline says "underwear." The headline is silly, but even worse it is disrespectful.

This example offers several lessons. One is that even good newspapers make mistakes if they don't pay attention. If students and professionals are appalled by that headline, why didn't an editor at the paper raise a flag? The second is that cleverness and humor can be abused and that the result can be hurtful. The third, which is the primary focus of this chapter, is that the display type should complement the other story elements, not contradict or clash with them. All the pieces should work together to present as complete a picture as possible. They should not create a puzzle for the reader. The display type should match the story in focus and tone. If a headline is serious, readers will expect the story to be serious. If a headline is playful, readers will expect the story to be playful. And a headline should not be ridiculous if the story isn't, as in the artist story.

The worst examples of conflicting, or discordant, elements are those that use humor inappropriately. In the winter of 1996, a serious flood spawned by heavy rain and early snowmelt threatened many communities and cities in the Pacific Northwest. It was a continuing story—day after day, newspapers and television stations reported the damage to upriver communities and the predictions being made for the impact on the larger cities downriver. Several days into the story, one newspaper ran a story reporting that communities in low-lying suburbs had suffered substantial flooding and that the river might crest at a 100-year level a couple of days later in the city itself. If that happened, it would spill over a substantial portion of the downtown area. A large photo showed two people standing in a flooded apartment, obviously distraught. The headline said:

Too much rain, it's plain

The story says the situation is bad and getting worse. The photo says tragedy. The Page One headline says, "Look at me; I'm clever. I can make a rhyming headline that echoes that famous Broadway show tune line 'The rain in Spain. . . . ' " The next day was almost as bad. The main photo showed two people wading across what had been their lawn to reach their home. The six-column headline read:

Water, water everywhere

Editors casting their nets for imagery landed Professor Henry Higgins one day and Samuel Taylor Coleridge the next. And several days later, after the worst had passed, President Clinton made a quick trip to visit the region to look over the damage. The headline read:

Clinton to flash by floods

"Flash by floods?" Get it? That headline is supposed to be clever, but there's a time and place for cleverness. Bad news is not an occasion to be clever. There's also an element of commentary in the headline. It suggests that Clinton was in a hurry—he just stopped by to make an appearance. In all three examples, the headlines did not match the tone of the story in seriousness. The cleverness, in effect, trivialized tragedy and invited readers to conclude that the newspaper was insensitive.

More recently, a fairly strong earthquake hit the Seattle area, injuring more than 250 people and causing substantial damage to buildings. One newspaper ran a large photo of a pickup truck smashed by falling bricks. Smaller photos showed an injured pedestrian, a badly buckled sidewalk and a woman trying to reach family members by cell phone. It was a well-designed and well-executed package, except for the headline:

Quake, rattle, a heavy toll

Again, the headline trivializes tragedy. The story says destruction; the photos say serious damage, injury and concern. The headline says, "Ain't I clever?" Natural disasters are serious; they are no place to play word games or to come up with a turn of phrase that calls to mind an old rock song. Headlines need to match both the facts and the tone of stories. So why do such mismatches happen?

Editors and newsroom managers often agonize over the wording of headlines on major news events. Good, focused, informative headlines don't seem to be enough. They want more. They squander minutes, sometimes hours, searching for that special image, allusion or turn of phrase that seems to transcend the event. Then they congratulate themselves. One could argue that all of this is largely a waste of precious editing time that could be spent making sure the news of the event is well written, accurate, consistent and not repetitive. To be sure, you want an accurate headline that captures the magnitude of the event. But, paradoxically, the biggest news really does not require the best headline. There is no need to write a compelling headline, or worse, to be particularly creative, or clever, or eye-catching when writing a headline about an event such as the Sept. 11 tragedy, or a major earthquake, a devastating storm or a major election. The news itself is compelling, far more than the headline could ever be or needs to be.

In many major news events, the big, bold headlines serve primarily a graphic purpose: They anchor the front page and provide a sense of the magnitude of the story. They attract attention more by their size and position than by anything they say. In such cases, the news, not the headline, is what draws people to the newspaper. So why waste a lot of time over it?

Besides, there's another downside. The San Francisco Examiner generated a lot of discussion for its huge one-word headline—BASTARDS!—on the World Trade Center story. That headline was nothing if not compelling, and one could argue that it captured at least some of the emotion many Americans were feeling. But there were some compelling reasons not to use it. First, it's pure in-your-face opinion. Even the enormity of the World Trade Center devastation doesn't give a news organization leave to pass off opinion as news. Second, that type of headline compels people to talk about the headline itself. It draws attention to itself and to the (gutsy?) editors who decided to run it. That's not what a headline should do. Headlines should not shift attention from the news to the people who edit the news.

HEARING THE MUSIC

In writing display type, the copy editor needs to be a conductor, making sure all of the elements work together in harmony. Many times, however, one or more of the elements is out of tune.

Sometimes, it's just a failure to look at all of the pieces holistically, as a reader would. Or to understand that words that are appropriate in the context of the story might appear misleading, unintentionally humorous or insensitive when they appear in large type underneath a photograph that tells a different story.

Two weeks into the 1993 standoff at the Branch Davidian compound in Waco, Texas, which culminated in 78 deaths, federal agents shone bright lights on the fortification one night. They did not explain their reason, other than to say it was a tactical maneuver. Papers across the country ran daily stories about the continuing battle between federal agencies and the sect headed by David Koresh. One newspaper ran the following head-line:

Authorities try tactical maneuver

The summary deck, in much smaller type, mentioned the lights. The head-line was accurate, though it was somewhat vague. Unfortunately, the headline ran with a prominent three-column photo of a Waco resident holding a banner displaying the words "Kill Koresh," The headline was about 42-point; the words on the banner appeared about three times as large just underneath the headline. The juxtaposition created a problem because readers do not always visually separate elements the way copy edi-tors do mentally. They could easily read "Kill Koresh" as the tactical ma-neuver, or perhaps think that someone at the paper was making an edito-rial statement. One might argue that no one would read the words on a banner depicted in a photo and think they had something to do with the headline. I disagree. I've showed this example to journalists who worked on copy desks during that period, and they all see the connection. It's true that they have the benefit of hindsight; Koresh indeed was killed when au-thorities attacked the compound not long afterward. But someone should have noticed it at the time. One point for headline writers is that they need to look at the big picture—how all of the pieces might look to a reader. A headline that is acceptable without a photo might be better re-cast if the photo tells a different story. A second point is that clarification in smaller display type is often not enough to prevent readers from leaping to unintended conclusions.

In 1993, Hurricane Emily, a fairly strong storm, was big news on the Eastern Seaboard for a few days because it appeared to be headed for land-fall. Tens of thousands of people were evacuated from coastal areas. In-stead of clobbering coastal towns and surging inland, Emily brushed North Carolina's Outer Banks and veered back out to sea. It destroyed a few buildings, but the big story was that the East Coast was largely spared the destruction of a powerful hurricane. The headline one paper ran was accu-rate:

East Coast 'dodged a bullet'

The summary deck read:

> After striking a
> glancing blow, Hurricane
> Emily heads to the
> North Atlantic.

That display type captures the essence of the story. "Dodged a bullet" is in quotes because it was taken from a National Weather Service spokesman's quote in the second paragraph. But the photo accompanying the story showed several buildings that were flattened in the Outer Banks town of Buxton, where the storm did hit. The juxtaposition creates a contradiction for the reader. The headline, which is accurate, says the hurricane did not tear up the East Coast. The photo, however, shows substantial damage. The small display type in the summary deck is not enough to explain the confusion. The photo and the big type speak louder. One way to solve the problem is to hold the photo on the ground that it highlighted the extreme case. But, as a photo editor would argue, it's still the most newsworthy picture, and it's difficult to make a persuasive case otherwise. Flattened buildings are still flattened buildings, and they make a better photo than buildings that are still standing on the East Coast.

The solution, which is in the copy editor's hands, is to write a different headline, one that addresses the photo without overstating the destruction. Flipping the elements in the head and deck around yields:

Emily strikes glancing blow

The summary deck reads:

> The East Coast "dodged
> a bullet" as the hurricane
> headed to sea after
> hitting the Outer Banks.

This approach works much better with the photo. Using the partial quote "dodged a bullet" might not be the best approach in either the head or the summary, because it echoes the top of the story too closely. It might not be an issue in this case, but lifting a key passage can annoy reporters who find their turns of phrase or well-chosen quotes expropriated for the headline. And it can irritate readers too because they wind up reading the same words twice quickly.

Sometimes display type appears out of synch because a sentence, phrase or partial quote that works well in the body of the story does not work very well when it appears in a headline. A headline that appeared on a food-poisoning story is a good example. A woman became critically ill from E. coli after eating a taco salad at a local restaurant. In the story, the woman, who talked about her ordeal several days later while still recovering in the hospital, was quoted in the story: "I filled one of those fried tostadas with hamburger meat and beans, sour cream, guacamole, onions and cheese—all that good stuff." The headline writer chose to use a fragment of that quote to tell the story:

Taco salad: Lot of good stuff and E. coli

A photo of the woman, who was 62, accompanied the story. In the picture, she is lying in a hospital bed, still looking very ill, with her husband comforting her. The photo creates a different context. The quote, which made sense in the context of the victim telling her story, appears extremely insensitive when pulled out of that context and used right above a photo of the poor woman. The newspaper changed the headline between editions. The new version read:

E. coli: A life turned upside down

This headline is much more appropriate. It reflects the seriousness of the story—the woman was hospitalized for a week—and it is much more sensitive to her experience.

A related problem occurs with a mismatch between the expression of a subject in a photo and what the story says. If you spend enough time reading newspapers, you'll see a file photo of a beaming politician that appears on a story about his indictment. Or the opposite situation: a serious or frowning face on a happy story. Readers find it hard to believe that editors do not notice such incongruity. Many times editors do notice, but they fail to make the case strongly enough to do something about it. The only sensible solution is to find or take a better photo, or to even suggest that the photo not run if that's the only one available. Unfortunately, the pressure to break up a column of gray type with a head shot, even one that is inappropriate, is sometimes too great.

GRAPHICS AND HEADLINES

Newspapers use graphics extensively today, in part because of the influence of USA Today. Type for graphics needs as many reads as story type does, yet it often gets less attention. Like photos, graphics capture attention, and as in captions, mistakes in graphics loom larger. They are part of the package, and they need to complement the other elements.

Apparent contradictions can occur between headlines and graphics. During Clinton's first term, a Knight-Ridder News Service story examined the administration's record on appointing women to policy posts. The story pointed out that 37 percent of Clinton's appointees to top governmental positions were women, a much higher percentage than George Bush's 24 percent, which ranked second. The story also mentioned that except for Hillary Clinton, women were absent from Clinton's inner circle. A bar chart accompanying the story showed Clinton clearly ahead of his six predecessors in appointing women. The headline, which was in a tight two-column hole, said:

Women missing in Clinton circle

The deck said:

While the president has
increased the presence of
women in government, few are
among his closest advisers.

But the graphic "says" otherwise. It clearly shows Clinton way ahead of the rest in appointing women. All are accurate, but the combination looks contradictory. In a later edition, the paper rewrote the display type:

Women gain at White House

Although the president has
appointed many to high level
posts, women are still closed
out of his inner circle.

Again, all are accurate, but the focus is flipped between the head and the deck. Which is better? I'd say the second. Given the limited size of the headline and the fact that the graphic clearly showed a significant difference on appointments, the rewrite produced a package of display type that better captured the essence of the story, was more consistent, yet still provided the qualification. This example suggests that headlines can be very powerful in coloring one's view of a story. A Democrat could look at the second head and be satisfied; a Republican could look at it and say it was soft on Clinton. It also points out the need for copy editors to see all parts of the package before they write display type.

Besides editing stories, copy editors should edit the graphics that accompany stories. Reporters and assigning editors often provide too much information to fit into a graphic, and the graphic artist needs to rewrite or summarize. Sometimes the artist writes the type based on his or her own research. Artists get busy and make mistakes. They need editors too, and, like reporters, they deserve to have someone else carefully check what they've done. Copy editors can also ensure that graphics contain important standing elements, such as a compass point on a locator map. They should see that tone or hatching on bar charts is correct and that important reference points from the story, such as a stream near a toxic waste site, are included. Copy editors should look at graphics as a reader would and make sure that the information can be understood quickly and easily.

A copy editor is in the best position to make sure that story and graphic agree and that both have the latest information. Communication is often poor between editors and graphic artists, and physical distance often exacerbates the problem. In large news organizations, graphic artists often work in a different office than others in the newsroom, sometimes on a different floor. A similar problem exists at newspapers whose Web sites are in different parts of the same building, in a different building, or even across town. Physical barriers to communication can lead to problems. Communication is vital, and nothing beats face-to-face discussion.

ORGANIZATIONAL PROBLEMS

Why do problems with discordant or contradictory elements occur so frequently? Perhaps it's a tendency to focus on one thing at a time—to see the trees but ignore the forest. The tendency is understandable, given the way newsrooms are organized into specialized departments. A division of labor—separation into reporting, editing, photo, design and graphics departments—is probably necessary to produce such a complex product in the short time available. But readers do not understand newspaper departments, nor should they have to, and they do not care how newspapers organize their troops. Most have a pretty good idea that editors and reporters perform different tasks, but beyond that many don't distinguish the work of a copy editor from that of a reporter. Even some journalism students are surprised to learn (usually in editing class) that reporters don't write headlines.

Copy editors need to keep the reader in mind when crafting display type, because it is the display type that binds a package together—that links photo and graphic and text. Readers tend to look at the elements sequentially, say, a photo first, then a headline, then maybe the caption, then the text. But they also look at the story package as a whole, and they have an expectation that all the pieces will work together and not contradict one another and that they will combine to present as complete a picture of the story as possible. Readers deserve as much. It's up to the copy editor to make it happen.

The specialized structure of newsrooms makes integration, or coordination, of elements difficult. It may seem that the news editor or the designer is the best person to look at all of the elements together. I'd say the copy editor is probably in a better position, because the copy editor has read the story more carefully than the news editor or the designer probably had time to do. But editing at this level requires a broadening of horizons. Copy editors who see themselves as word editors and headline writers but fail to see themselves as visual journalists will have a difficult time. By paying more attention to visual considerations, they will have a better chance of spotting problems with mismatched combinations of images and words.

Editors have restructured newsroom positions over the last several decades—sometimes to take advantage of technology changes, sometimes to deal with their demands. At many papers, the design function has become more specialized—and removed from copy desks, where it had been placed for many years. This has created new opportunities as well as new problems. Visual journalists, in particular photographers, photo editors and designers, need to realize that the elements under their control—the images and the juxtaposition of elements—must serve the story.

Designers must pay attention to words—and to what is possible. Designers have to realize that looks aren't everything. That elaborate centerpiece package will not be as compelling as it should be if it is impossible to write a good headline in the space allotted. Copy editors too need to understand the conditions facing visual journalists. In the case of an "art type" headline, I'd suggest having a copy editor and a designer get together early in the process to come up with labels that both like.

TIPS AND STRATEGIES

- Be the reader. Try to look at the story package as a reader would. In writing display type, remember how readers scan a page: photo, headline, caption, display, text.
- Remember that readers see large pictures first. Big color photos are especially eye-catching. If a photo conveys an impression, it is difficult for text to overcome that impression.
- Pay close attention to banners and signs in photos. A photo accompanying a protest story from Germany prominently showed a banner bearing the German word for "shit." That one was caught before publication by a copy chief who happened to be familiar with German.
- Learn from colleagues in other departments. If you get the chance for some cross-training, say in design or graphics, take it. The more you know about the challenges, the opportunities and the rhythms of those departments, the better you'll succeed at your own job. You'll have a better idea of what is doable, and your criticisms and suggestions will be better informed.

Making the words and images work together is an art, and it is one that can be learned. Often, all it takes is stepping back and looking at the elements the way a reader might. Here's an example of a missed opportunity. Eugene, Ore., has the same problem many other college towns have: disappearing street signs. A feature story in the local paper looked at the problem of sign theft, pointing out that the sign most often stolen was for Nirvana Street. Another hot item was a sign for Corona Street. The story ran with a photo of a street department supervisor standing underneath a sign for Corona Street. The headline read:

**Sign thieves find avenue
to bliss in Nirvana Street**

That's not bad, given what the story said, but the prominence of the Corona sign in the photo creates a problem—or an opportunity. Here's a headline that covers both bases:

Sign thieves seek Nirvana,
but they settle for Corona

This headline is better because it addresses the elements readers will see as well as those they will read, yet remains true to the essence of the story. The unanswered question is why Nirvana? Because of a longing for Eastern spirituality or because of the rock group?

13 Page Design

This chapter is a brief introduction to basic principles common in newspaper design. The pages used as examples reflect basic structural ideas; they do not demonstrate some of the more elaborate design and typographic elements that many newspapers now use. Those who would like to explore newspaper design in depth should consult one of several excellent newspaper design manuals, such as the one written by Tim Harrower.[1]

FUNDAMENTALS

Newspaper design is the visual implementation of news values and judgment. That's one definition. Another is that "design puts art in the service of communication."[2] Design consultant Mario Garcia says, "As far as I am concerned, there are no 'theories' of newspaper design. Not in the abstract sense of the word, anyway. Newspaper design is deep rooted in practical realities, and is more an organic than an abstract process."[3]

From an editor's perspective, design serves content. It presents a road map and provides visual cues about what is important and what is less important, what is serious and what is playful, what is related and what is unrelated. Designers use a variety of techniques to make those distinctions:

- Modular design. All stories and packages of stories are arrayed in rectangles.

- Variation in the size of one element relative to the others. A center-piece package is typically the largest element on a section front; a metropolitan brief is several column inches deep inside the paper.
- Position on a page or within the paper (above the fold or below it, front or inside). Elements at the top of a page and on section fronts are generally more important than those at the bottom of pages and inside.
- The use and play of photos and other graphics. Photos and graphics can draw attention, and they can be used to tie related elements together or to separate unrelated elements.
- Typography (large vs. small, bold vs. light, Roman vs. italic, art type vs. standard headline typography). Stories with larger and bolder headlines are generally more important than those with smaller headlines, Roman headlines often suggest news, italic suggests features. Art type (specially designed) headlines suggest special packages.
- Other devices, such as rules and boxes. Boxes can group related items; rules can organize or separate them.

For much of the 20th century, "page design" often was synonymous with "page makeup," especially on inside pages. The copy desk would send stories and generic-size headlines based on length of copy, and a compositor in a "hot type" back shop would "design the page" by placing the larger elements at the top and fitting the rest together like a jigsaw puzzle. An editor would typically look over the result and perhaps make suggestions or rewrite a headline to make the page work better. Pages that were designed in the newsroom, generally section fronts, were usually done by editors who also had other duties, such as assigning stories, editing copy and writing headlines. At many weeklies and small dailies, editors with other duties still design pages. At many midsize and most large newspapers, page design is now primarily done by specialists called "designers." Professional organizations, in particular the Society of News Design, and journalism training organizations such as The Poynter Institute, have helped make design a newsroom specialty over the last several decades. Many newspapers have restructured their editing staff, creating separate copy desks and design desks, or some variation. Many university journalism programs, which decades ago offered page layout training only as part of a broader copy editing class, now offer specialized courses in page design.

The professionalization of design and the growth of design desks have produced newspapers that are more creative, more visually sophisticated and more consistent-looking, all of which benefit readers. The occasional negative result is the inadvertent creation of a wall between departments that need to communicate and work together. Designers and editors should be on the same page; too often they aren't. Some newspapers have created teams and other structures to enhance interaction between reporters, designers, photographers and copy editors.

Design should not be an end in itself. Design that is self-indulgent or overly embellished does not serve content, and thus does not serve readers. Designers are journalists first and artists second. Because they are visual journalists, designers can often help editors and reporters think in terms of producing content that will be visually compelling within the limitations of the size and shape of newspapers and the technology used to produce them. News values and decisions should not play second fiddle to presentation issues. The desire to create an artful design should not dictate coverage, story length or photo use. That's putting the cart before the horse.

Some argue that designers should play the central role in a newsroom. I feel that is a mistake. Design is a relative newcomer as a newsroom specialty, and some of the more extreme claims made for design as the central player in modern newsrooms are perhaps better seen as struggles over turf, the same struggles that other positions engage in. It is best to think of the designer as one of several important players, not *the* key player, in the newsroom. By any reasonable calculation, including sheer numbers, reporting would have to be considered *the* most important role in a newsroom. But such discussion is silly and almost always counterproductive. A news organization needs all of its parts to make the whole.

Modern newspaper page design in the United States is based on a handful of ideas related to fundamental visual principles of balance, contrast, harmony and rhythm. You can also think of them as do's and don'ts. Here are the do's:

DO'S

1. Use a Dominant Visual

The visual, sometimes called a "center of visual interest" or "dominant art," can be one photo or more, or a graphic, or a combination of those elements. The dominant visual directs reader attention. It says: Look here first! A single dominant visual is probably best. A combination of smaller images can be confusing, but sometimes it can be effective, such as a collection of faces of stock traders showing various emotions on a day when the market tumbles.

Many newspapers follow this principle on section fronts but abandon it on inside pages. As a result, the fronts look clean and focused and the inside pages often look like a jumble.

Figures 1 and 2 show the difference between a section front with a dominant visual element and one with photos about the same size.

Figures 3 and 4 show the difference between a dominant visual on a small inside page and two competing visuals.

2. Make Pages Modular, If Possible

Modular design, or design in rectangles, is a relative newcomer to newspaper design. Its roots are modernistic, reflecting the idea in art and architecture that form follows function. Much of the art of Dutch painter Piet Mondrian, whose work influenced the modernist school of architecture, looks a lot like modular page design. Many Mondrian paintings look like simple gridworks of lines crossing at right angles. Kevin Barnhurst, who has written several books on newspapers and visual design, points out that the essence of modularity was mathematical. Design was based on an underlying grid of evenly spaced columns; elements could also cover multiple columns of the grid. This created rectangles, often in an overall vertical arrangement. U.S. newspaper designers, he said, retained the rectangles but often ignored the regularity of the grid, sometimes setting type in "bastard measures."[4] They also liberally used horizontal elements, such as strips of stories that spanned the entire page. In the last two decades, some newspapers have returned to the idea of a grid that determines the widths of all elements. Gannett newspapers, following the lead of USA Today, adopted a seven-column grid. Others work on six or even 12 (allowing typographic elements, such as marginalia, which often are set in half-column measures along the left or right margins of the page). In the last few years, many metropolitan newspapers have shrunk the width of the newspaper page to reduce newsprint costs and have switched to a five-column format to preserve a readable line length for stories.

Most newspapers did not move to modular design until late in the 20th century. In modular design, all the elements of a story (headline,

FIGURE 1. *This front page is modular. The page has a dominant visual and a secondary visual as well as some smaller photos. The photos are balanced, and the headlines generally descend in point size from top to bottom. The headlines are in bold or light face for contrast.*

Short headline here

Two lines of text here that refer to a story inside.. .... **Page X**

Short headlline here

Two lines of text here that refer to a story inside.. .... **Page X**

THE FRONT PAGE

A 48-pt. bold head on the strip story

NEW ORLEANS (AP) — A tanker spilled a half-million gallons of crude oil into the Mississippi River on Wednesday, closing a busy shipping route for 26 miles and threatening wildlife.

No injuries were reported, but some pelicans and other animals were found covered with oil, said Roland Guidry, a state oil spill coordinator.

The 800-foot tanker Westchester lost power Tuesday evening and apparently ran aground about 60 miles southeast of New Orleans.

A cargo tank holding more than 2.2 million gallons of Nigerian crude oil lost about 567,400 gallons, or 13,500 barrels, said Virginia Miller, spokeswoman for the ship's owner and operator. The spilled oil would fill about two-thirds of an Olympic-size swimming pool.

The river bottom apparently plugged most of the hole and kept the rest from escaping, Miller said. She said divers were trying to assess the damage while five skimmers and a vacuum unit pulled up the spilled oil.

Modern American tankers are built with two hulls to prevent such spills even if the outer hull ruptures, but the Westchester, registered in the Bahamas and owned by a Liberian company, was a single-hull tanker. Federal law calls for all tankers operating in U.S. waters to be double-hulled by 2015, and the Westchester was scheduled to become double-hulled in 2006, Miller said.

Coast Guard officials said it wasn't clear when or how the tank ruptured. It could have hit something already on the river bottom or its own anchor could have punctured the hull if it became pinned between the hull and river bottom, said Jim O'Brien said an oil spill specialist under contract with the Greek company that operates the tanker, Ermis Maritime Corp. In 15 years of operation, the vessel has had a couple minor spills, never more than one barrel of oil, he said.

By Wednesday evening, patches of oil from the spill floated from just south of Burns, which is 15 miles southeast of the accident site, to Boothville, about eight miles down-river, Miller said. The water was along a three-mile stretch from Fort Jackson to Boothville.

The Coast Guard's halting of traffic on the river stalled more than a dozen vessels and forced others to change their routing waterfowl.

El-Amin said. The Coast Guard planned to open the river to upstream traffic Wednesday evening and to downstream traffic Thursday.

Containment booms were set out to prevent oil from flowing into cuts made earlier this year to divert river water into the drought-depleted wetlands of the Delta National Wildlife Refuge, U.S. Fish & Wildlife Service workers said.

The area is home to pelicans, shorebirds, seabirds, crabs, shrimp and sport fish, as well as more than 100,000 wintering waterfowl.

The area is home to pelicans, shorebirds, seabirds, crabs, shrimp and sport nchored in the Mississippi

36-point four-line headline on this

"On Jan. 20, a President Bush will be ready to take the reins of the government," said top adviser Andy Card — awarding his boss a title that Gore still hopes will be his.

The vice president is trying to overturn official results of the decisive Florida election before the public's patience runs out on the 22-day ordeal. Needing a quick court victory, Gore authorized his divided legal team to ask the Florida Supreme Court to recount contested ballots or order a lower court to do it, two Democratic sources said late Wednesday.

One million ballots were being hand-counted 400 miles from southern to northern Florida, where the precedent-making case has been thrust upon a folksy circuit judge. "Pack 'em up and bring 'em up," Judge N. Sanders Sauls said.

Bush planned to meet Thursday with retired Gen. Colin Powell, his still-to-be-announced choice as secretary of state. The Texas governor also was calling GOP congressional leaders and assigning his staff to call Democratic lawmakers in the vice president struggled to keep his party in line.

With the stakes so high, the Republican-dominated Florida Legislature inched closer to securing Bush a backup plan: Lawmakers were considering naming their own electors to settle the fiercely fought election. Florida Gov. Jeb Bush, the candidate's brother, said he would sign the necessary legislation "if it was the appropriate thing to do."

Still, with the recount case headed to the highest court in the land, Jeb Bush said, "The United States Supreme Court trumps the Legislature." Gore, too, played president-elect as a business meeting with running mate Joseph Lieberman, transition director Roy Neel, Labor Secretary Alexis Herman and Kathleen McGinty, transition waterfowl.

Justices R. Fred Lewis, Harry Lee Anstead, Leander J. Shaw, Jr., Chief Justice Charles T. Wells, Major B. Harding, Barbara J. Pariente and Peggy A. Quince of the Florida Supreme

A 42-point light head

A 30-pt. underline is a secondary head

By RON FOURNIER
AP Political Writer

Al Gore raced between TV interviews Wednesday asking, "Will we count all the votes or not?" while his lawyers urgently sought a court ruling with the answer he wanted. Both Gore and rival George W. Bush pressed forward with separate blueprints for building a presidency.

"On Jan. 20, a President Bush will be ready to take the reins of the government," said top adviser Andy Card — awarding his boss a title that Gore still hopes will be his.

The vice president is trying to overturn official results of the decisive Florida election before the public's patience ran out on the 22-day ordeal. Needing a quick court victory, Gore authorized his divided legal team to ask the Florida Supreme Court to recount contested ballots or order a lower court to do it, two Democratic sources said late Wednesday.

One million ballots were being hauled 400 miles from southern to northern Florida, where the precedent-making case has been thrust upon a folksy circuit judge. "Pack 'em up and bring 'em up," Judge N. Sanders Sauls said.

Bush planned to meet Thursday with retired Gen. Colin Powell, his still-to-be-announced choice as secretary of state. The Texas governor also was calling GOP congressional leaders and assigning his staff to call Democratic lawmakers in the vice president struggled to keep his party in line.

With the stakes so high, the Republican-dominated Florida Legislature inched closer to securing Bush a backup plan: Lawmakers were considering naming their own electors to settle the fiercely fought election. Florida Gov. Jeb Bush, the candidate's brother, said he would sign the necessary legislation "if it was the appropriate thing to do."

Still, with the recount case headed to the highest court in the land, Jeb Bush said, "The United States Supreme Court trumps the Legislature." Florida House constructor or perhaps chief of staff, a job that aides expect would first be offered to campaign manager William Daley.

Florida Secretary of State Katherine Harris, a supporter of Republican Bush, has declared him the winner of Florida by 537 votes out of 6 million cast — handing Gore the steep challenge of nullifying.

A 60-point bold head on the lead

By GENE JOHNSON
Associated Press Writer

SEATTLE (AP) — Broken windows and spray-painted walls in nine Starbucks Coffee Co. stores have left this city uneasy as it marks the anniversary of last year's riotous World Trade Organization protests.

The stores, among dozens of Starbucks outlets in the city, were hit late Tuesday or early Wednesday — with window damage, glass in locks, and walls marked with an encircled "A," a graffiti tag used by anarchists during WTO demonstrations last year.

Authorities hoped the demonstrations scheduled Thursday, including marches, potluck meals and teach-ins, would be peaceful. But the vandalism indicated some protesters might be planning otherwise — even if there was no direct evidence protesters were responsible for it.

"It's disturbing there were anarchist symbols," said Dick Lilly, a spokesman for Mayor Paul Schell.

Starbucks planned to take extra security measures, but refused to say what they were.

Except for extra police, it was business as usual in downtown Seattle Thursday. Partly cloudy skies replaced the rain that fell on the city overnight.

At dawn, 10 to 12 activists gathered at a park next to the Pike Place n. pink and white plywood "cake," decorated with the words, "Happy Anniversary WTO."

Protesters also placed a large anti-WTO banner above the Interstate 90 tunnel leading into Seattle.

Schell urged television stations to broadcast as little of last year's protests as possible, a request that appeared to be ignored on local news.

"We believe the constant repetition of those images simply builds up any tension that might arise this year," Lilly said.

Justices R. Fred Lewis, H taking their seats on

A 2-line head here in 36-pt. bold face

By KARIN LAUB
Associated Press Writer

JERUSALEM (AP) — A senior Palestinian negotiator said Wednesday that he believed a final peace accord with Israel could be reached before Israel's new elections, tentatively set for spring.

But other Palestinian officials indicated that Ehud Barak appeared determined to speed up the process, saying privately that the Israeli prime minister's envoys have told them that he plans to resume talks in hopes of reaching a peace deal before the election.

In a goodwill gesture, Israel on Wednesday resumed the transfer of millions of dollars in tax refunds to the Palestinian Authority. The money had been stopped as one of several punitive steps by Israel during nine weeks of fighting that have more than 280 people dead, the vast majority Palestinians.

Barak on Tuesday cleared to pressure from the hawkish opposition to hold elections, after it became apparent that he no longer commanded backing in parliament to block the initiative.

The elections will probably take place in the spring, two years ahead of schedule, though an exact date will not be set before next week. Opposition leader Ariel Sharon said he wanted to hold the vote before the Jewish Passover holiday which begins April 7, while Cabinet ministers close to Barak said mid-May waters close to Barak said mid-May was a likely date.

Barak was elected 18 months ago in a landslide, on a pledge to negotiate peace agreements with the Palestinians and Syria. Some forces pushing him out of office appeared

Israeli Prime Minister Ehud Barak, right, shakes hand with opposition leader Ariel Sharon

Today's Index

ALBUQUERQUE, N.M. (AP) — Seventeen tapes filled with nuclear science data downloaded by former Los Alamos laboratory scientist Wen

Ho Lee were discarded in the trash, according to a source familiar with the investigation.

FBI agents are combing the muddy, snowy Los Alamos County landfill where the Los Alamos

National Laboratory's trash is buried, and say their search could last weeks.

Agents won't confirm they're looking for the missing tapes, but if the pocket-sized computer cartridges downloaded in the lab's top-secret X Division were thrown in the trash, the 50-acre dump is probably where they would have ended up.

FIGURE 2. *This front page has no dominant visual. Both of the larger pictures are three columns wide, and the lower one is a bit deeper. Both tend to draw the eye, and a reader isn't sure which part of the page to look at first. It also appears slightly imbalanced, with more graphic weight to the right.*

229

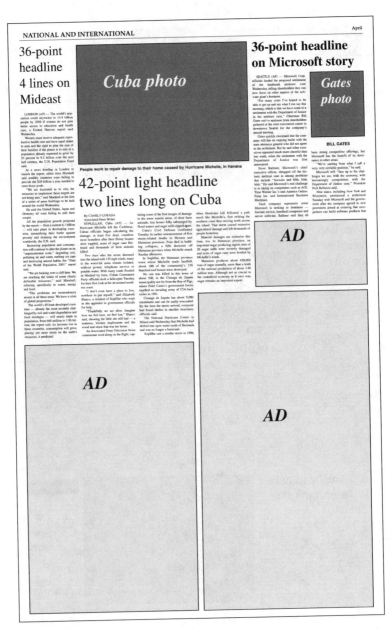

FIGURE 3. The Cuba photo is played three columns wide, which makes it dominant. The other photo is a one-column head shot, which does not compete with the main photo. The Cuba story is not modular because the ads underneath it are uneven. Designers trade off modularity on such pages so they do not have to trim stories to fit into shallow holes.

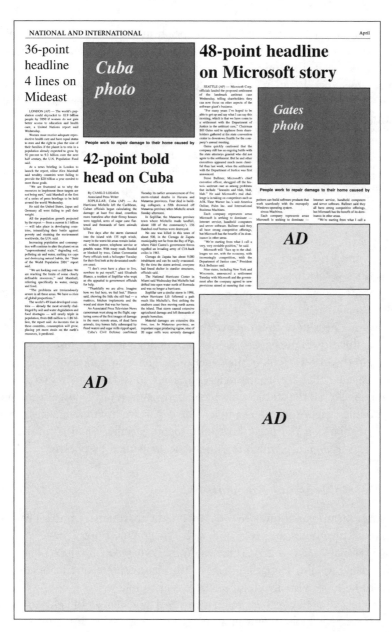

FIGURE 4. *The Cuba photo is played two columns wide. The Gates photo is also two columns wide, which makes it compete for attention with the Cuba photo. The Microsoft story is not modular because the ads underneath it do not square off.*

story, photo, caption, graphic) should appear in a rectangle. The approach can also be used for packages. A story and a sidebar can appear in one module. One of the stories itself might not be modular—it might, for example, have one long leg of type and several shorter ones—but the other elements (sidebar, headlines, photos, etc.) are designed to make the whole package rectangular. Generally, modular design is the best way to make related page elements hang together visually.

Figures 1 and 2 are examples of modular section fronts.

Page designers try to follow modular principles closely on section fronts and other open pages. On inside pages that have uneven stacks of ads, designers sometimes abandon modularity. Designers often try for modularity by working off edges of ad stacks (Figures 5 and 6), but they don't worry if the part of the page that meets the ad stacks is not modular (Figures 3 and 4). Clarity is more important, ensuring that readers can tell what goes with what.

Some papers abandon modularity on section front pages because they want a very large headline, say a six-column banner, at the top but they also want a high story count above the fold. It is difficult to do both and retain modularity. Some papers retain a nonmodular front because they want to retain the historic look of the paper (e.g., The New York Times). Others do it because they feel that single-copy sales considerations require large headlines even if the stories they accompany cannot justify large rectangular modules. Figure 7 is an example. The departure from modularity gets a large headline on the page, but the tradeoff is some visual confusion; it isn't clear at a glance which stories are accompanied by photos.

3. Use Contrasting Elements

Contrast means variation between dark and light sections. Contrast can be created with visuals and text and with typography. Photos have a great deal of visual "weight." So do big headlines. Body type (story text) has very little visual weight. Designing pages with contrasting elements is considered to be more visually pleasing and easier to follow.

One goal of newspaper design is to avoid large masses of light-contrast body type. Such blobs of gray make pages visually unappealing. Contrasting elements, such as subheads, liftout quotes and fact boxes, are often used to break up large blocks of body type. Techniques to solve the grayness problem include:

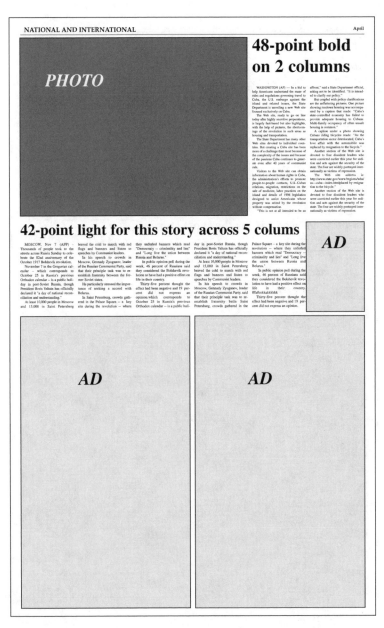

FIGURE 5. *This inside page is modular. The designer placed the five-column story alongside the small ad. The photo is played in columns 1-4 to separate it from the ads, which might also have images within them.*

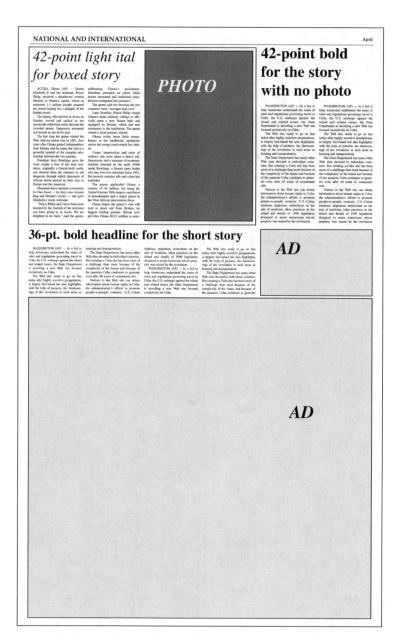

FIGURE 6. *This inside page is modular. The designer placed a box around the story with the photo. If the photo is strongly directional facing left, the box is unnecessary. If the photo is not directional, the box can be used to show which story the photo accompanies.*

Short headline here

Two lines of text here that refer to a
story inside.. .... **Page X**

Short headllline here

Two lines of text here that refer to a
story inside.. .... **Page X**

THE FRONT PAGE

A 48-pt. bold head on the strip story

NEW ORLEANS (AP) — A tanker spilled a half-million gallons of crude oil into the Mississippi River on Wednesday, closing a busy shipping route for 26 miles and threatening wildlife.

No injuries were reported, but some pelicans and other animals were found covered with oil, said Roland Guidry, a state oil spill coordinator.

The 800-foot tanker Westchester lost power Tuesday evening and apparently ran aground about 60 miles southeast of New Orleans.

A cargo tank holding more than 2.2 million gallons of Nigerian crude oil lost

about 567,400 gallons, or 13,500 barrels, said Virginia Miller, spokeswoman for the ship's owner and operator. The spilled oil would fill about two-thirds of an Olympic-size swimming pool.

The river bottom apparently plugged most of the hole and kept the rest from escaping, Miller said. She said divers were trying to assess the damage while five skimmers and a vacuum unit pulled up the spilled oil.

Modern American tankers are built with two hulls to prevent such spills even if the outer hull ruptures, but the Westchester, registered in the Bahamas

and owned by a Liberian company, was a single-hull tanker. Federal law calls for all tankers operating in U.S. waters to be double-hulled by 2015, and the Westchester was scheduled to become double-hulled in 2006, Miller said.

Coast Guard officials said it wasn't clear when or how the tank ruptured. It could have hit something already on the river bottom or its own anchor could have punctured the hull if it became pinned between the hull and river bottom, said Jim O'Brien said an oil spill specialist under contract with the Greek company that operates the tanker, Ermis Maritime

Corp. In 15 years of operation, the vessel has had a couple minor spills, never more than one barrel of oil, he said.

By Wednesday evening, patches of oil from the spill floated from just south of Buras, which is 15 miles southeast of the accident site, to Boothville, about eight miles downriver, Miller said. The worst was along a three-mile river stretch from Fort Jackson to Boothville.

The Coast Guard's halting of traffic on the river stalled more than a dozen vessels and forced others to change their routes, Coast Guard Petty Officer Fa'ig El-Amin said. The Coast Guard planned

to open the river to upstream traffic Wednesday evening and to downstream traffic Thursday.

Containment booms were set out to prevent oil from flowing into cuts made earlier this year to divert river water into the drought-depleted wetlands of the Delta National Wildlife Refuge, U.S. Fish & Wildlife Service workers said.

The area is home to pelicans, shorebirds, seabirds, crabs, shrimp and sport fish, as well as more than 100,000 wintering waterfowl.

The area is home to pelicans, shorebirds, seabirds, crabs, shrimp and sport birds, seabirds, crabs, shrimp and sport **nchored in the Mississippi**

72-pt. head; story is in col. 5, 6

An italic drop head for the lead story

By GENE JOHNSON
Associated Press Writer

SEATTLE (AP) — Broken windows and spray-painted walls in nine Starbucks Coffee Co. stores have left this city uneasy as it marks the anniversary of last year's riotous World Trade Organization protests.

The stores, among dozens of Starbucks outlets in the city, were hit late Tuesday or early Wednesday — with window damage, glue in locks, and walls marked with an encircled "A," a graffiti tag used by anarchists during WTO demonstrations last year.

Authorities hoped the demonstrations scheduled Thursday, including marches, potluck meals and teach-ins, would be peaceful, but the vandalism indicated some protesters might be planning otherwise — even if there was no direct evidence protesters were responsible for it.

"It's disturbing there were anarchist symbols," said Dick Lilly, a spokesman for Mayor Paul Schell.

Starbucks planned to take extra security measures, but refused to say what they were.

Except for extra police, it was business as usual in downtown Seattle Thursday. Partly cloudy skies replaced the rain that fell on the city overnight.

At dawn, 10 to 12 activists gathered at a park next to the Pike Place e, pink and white plywood "cake," decorated with the words, "Happy Anniversary WTO."

Protesters also placed a large anti-WTO banner above the Interstate 90 tunnel leading into Seattle.

McGinty would be a front-runner to head the Environmental Protection Agency under Gore. Herman would be in line for another Cabinet post, while protests as possible, a request that appeared to be ignored on local programs.

"We believe the constant repeti-

Justices R. Fred Lewis, Harry Lee Anstead, Leander J. Shaw, Jr., Chief Justice Charles T. Wells, Major B. Harding, Barbara J. Pariente and Peggy A. Quince of the Florida Supreme Court stand before taking their seats on Wednesday.

A 48-point light face headline

By RON FOURNIER
AP Political Writer

At Gore raced between TV interviews Wednesday asking, "Will we count all the votes or not?" while his lawyers urgently sought a court ruling with the answer he wanted. Both Gore and rival George W. Bush pressed forward with separate blueprints for building a presidency.

"On Jan. 20, a President Bush will be ready to take the reins of the government," said top adviser Andy Card — awarding his boss a title that Gore still hopes will be his.

The vice president is trying to overturn official results of the decisive

Florida election before the public's patience runs out on the 22-day ordeal. Needing a quick court victory, Gore authorized his divided legal team to ask the Florida Supreme Court to recount contested ballots or order a lower court to do it, two Democratic sources said late Wednesday.

One million ballots were being hauled 400 miles from southern to northern Florida, where the precinct-making case has been thrust upon a Friday circuit judge. "Pick 'em up and keep 'em up," Judge N. Sanders Sauls said.

Bush planned to meet Thursday with retired Gen. Colin Powell, his still-to-

be-announced choice as secretary of state. The Texas governor also was calling GOP congressional leaders and assigning his staff to craft Democratic lawmakers as the vice president struggled to keep his party in line.

With the stakes so high, the Republican-dominated Florida Legislature inched closer to securing Bush a backup plan: Lawmakers were considering naming their own electors to settle the fiercely fought election. Florida Gov. Jeb Bush, the candidate's brother, said he would sign the necessary legislation "if it was the appropriate thing to do."

Still, with the recount case headed to

the highest court in the land, Jeb Bush said, "The United States Supreme Court trumps the Legislature."

Gore, too, played president-elect at a business meeting with running mate Joseph Lieberman, transition director Roy Neel, Labor Secretary Alexis Herman and Kathleen McGinty, former head of the White House environment office.

McGinty would be a front-runner to head the Environmental Protection Agency under Gore. Herman would be in line for another Cabinet post, while a job that aides expect would first be offered to campaign manager

**36-point
bold head
on this**

tion of those images simply builds up any tension that might arise this year," Lilly said.

Last year, 50,000 protesters crammed downtown and shut down part of the WTO session. The WTO, a trade alliance of 139 countries, has become a target for a wide range of corporate globalization and takes advantage of the environment and workers.

Overwhelmed Seattle police responded by firing tear gas and rubber bullets. The ensuing riots resulted in 600 arrests, $3 million in property damage, numerous civil-rights lawsuits and the police chief's sudden early retirement.

By all accounts, this year's protests will be smaller because there will be no conference to disrupt.

Generous estimates predicted as many as 5,000 demonstrators, many of whom planned to converge on Westlake Park downtown. Police have asked them not to protest there because they could disrupt shoppers and a holiday event.

Jean Buskin, a 52-year-old Seattle

A 2-line head here in 36-pt. bold face

By KARIN LAUB
Associated Press Writer

JERUSALEM (AP) — A senior Palestinian negotiator said Wednesday that he doubted a final peace accord with Israel could be reached before Israel's new elections, tentatively set for spring.

But other Palestinian officials indicated that Ehud Barak appeared determined to speed up the process, saying privately that the Israeli prime minister's envoys have told them that he plans to resume talks in hopes of reaching a peace deal before the election.

In a goodwill gesture, Israel on Wednesday resumed the transfer of

millions of dollars in tax refunds to the Palestinian Authority. The money had been stopped as one of several punitive steps by Israel during nine weeks of fighting that have killed more than 280 people dead, the vast majority Palestinians.

Barak on Tuesday yielded to pressure from the hawkish opposition to hold elections, after it became apparent that he no longer commanded backing in parliament to block the initiative.

The elections will probably take place in the spring, two years ahead of schedule, though an exact date will not be set before next week. Opposition leader Ariel Sharon said

Israeli Prime Minister Ehud Barak, right, shakes hand with opposition leader Ariel Sharon

FIGURE 7. *This lead story on this front page is not modular. It has a main headline across six columns and a drop headline on two columns. The text is in column 5. It is difficult to tell at a glance which story the dominant photo goes with (it's the story below). Also, the one-column photo in column 6 could go with either the main story or the short one-column story underneath the picture.*

235

- Horizontal page elements—multicolumn headlines with shallow type wraps
- A mix of horizontal and vertical elements
- Additional display type elements, such as summary paragraphs, liftout quotes, fact boxes and logos
- Use of more images, including half-column photos and small charts and other graphics

Figure 1 shows contrast both in the difference between the dark areas (photos) and the light areas (text) and in the difference between headlines of different size and weight.

4. Keep Pages Balanced

Balance in newspaper page design is primarily a matter of separating elements of high visual weight, such as photos and graphics. This is generally easy to do on section fronts, as long as the designer has a variety of photos and graphics to choose from.

Visual balance can be a problem on inside pages because ads may or may not have dominant images. For practical reasons, newspaper designers typically ignore the ads and concern themselves with designing the news hole on a given page. One common strategy is to avoid placing any photo adjacent to an ad because an image within the ad will appear to be related to the news photo if it "bumps" up against it. Sometimes a designer has no choice. A two-column photo on a page that has only two columns for editorial matter necessarily has to "bump" an ad. Sometimes the result is a page that is heavily out of balance, but that is a tradeoff that newspapers accept for the sake of efficiency.

Figures 1 and 7 are balanced section fronts; Figure 8 is not.

5. Have Headlines Descend in Point Size from Top to Bottom

One of the most difficult design decisions for students and novice designers is headline point size. There is no clear set of rules, and the typical mix of horizontal and vertical elements on newspaper pages makes the decision more complicated. The general rule of descending point size is qualified by several visual considerations:

Short headline here

Two lines of text here that refer to a story inside.. .... **Page X**

Short headlline here

Two lines of text here that refer to a story inside.. .... **Page X**

THE FRONT PAGE

A 48-pt. bold head on the strip story

NEW ORLEANS (AP) — A tanker spilled a half-million gallons of crude oil into the Mississippi River on Wednesday, closing a busy shipping route for 26 miles and threatening wildlife.

No injuries were reported, but some pelicans and other animals were found covered with oil, said Roland Guidry, a state oil spill coordinator.

The 800-foot tanker Westchester lost power Tuesday evening and apparently ran aground about 60 miles southeast of New Orleans.

nchored in the Mississippi

million gallons of Nigerian crude oil lost about 567,400 gallons, or 13,500 barrels, said Virginia Miller, spokeswoman for the ship's owner and operator. The spilled oil would fill about two-thirds of an Olympic-size swimming pool.

The river bottom apparently plugged most of the hole and kept the rest from escaping, Miller said. She said divers were trying to assess the damage while five skimmers and a vacuum unit pulled up the spilled oil.

Modern American tankers are built with two hulls to prevent such spills even if the outer hull ruptures, but the

Westchester, registered in the Bahamas and owned by a Liberian company, was a single-hull tanker. Federal law calls for all tankers operating in U.S. waters to be double-hulled by 2015, and the Westchester was scheduled to become double-hulled in 2006, Miller said.

Coast Guard officials said it wasn't clear when or how the tank ruptured. It could have hit something already on the river bottom or its own anchor could have punctured the hull if it became pinned between the hull and river bottom, said Jim O'Brien said an oil spill specialists under contract with the Greek

company that operates the tanker, Ennis Maritime Corp. In 15 years of operation, the vessel has had a couple minor spills, never more than one barrel of oil, he said.

By Wednesday evening, patches of oil from the spill floated from just south of Buras, which is 15 miles southeast of the accident site, to Boothville, about eight miles downriver, Miller said. The worst was along a three-mile river stretch from Fort Jackson to Boothville.

The Coast Guard's halting of traffic on the river stalled more than a dozen vessels and forced others to change their

route, Coast Guard Petty Officer Fa'zq El-Amin said. The Coast Guard planned to open the river to upstream traffic Wednesday evening and to downstream traffic Thursday.

Containment booms were set out to prevent oil from flowing into cuts made earlier this year to divert river water into the drought-deprived wetlands of the Delta National Wildlife Refuge, U.S. Fish & Wildlife Service workers said.

The area is home to pelicans, shorebirds, seabirds, coots, shrimp and sport fish, as well as more than 100,000 wintering waterfowl.

An overline for the box

Justices R. Fred Lewis, Harry Lee Anstead, Leander J. Shaw, Jr., Chief Justice Charles T. Wells, Major B. Harding, Barbara J. Pariente and Peggy A. Quince of the Florida Supreme Court stand before taking their seats on

A 60-point bold head on the lead

By GENE JOHNSON
Associated Press Writer

SEATTLE (AP) — Broken windows and spray-painted walls in nine Starbucks Coffee Co. stores have left this city uneasy as it marks the anniversary of last year's riotous World Trade Organization protests.

The stores, among dozens of Starbucks outlets in the city, were hit late Tuesday or early Wednesday — with window damage, glue in locks, and walls marked with an encircled "A," a graffiti tag used by anarchists during WTO demonstrations last year.

Authorities hoped the demonstrations scheduled Thursday, including marches, potluck meals and teach-ins, would be peaceful, but the vandalism indicated some protesters might be planning otherwise.

"It's disturbing there were anarchist symbols," said Dick Lilly, a spokesman for Mayor Paul Schell.

Starbucks planned to take extra security measures, but refused to say what they were.

Except for extra police, it was business as usual in downtown Seattle Thursday. Partly cloudy skies replaced the rain that fell on the city overnight.

At dawn, 10 to 12 activists gathered at a park next to the Pike Place e, pink and white plywood "cake," decorated with the words, "Happy Anniversary WTO."

Protesters also played a large anti-WTO banner above the Interstate 90 tunnel leading into Seattle.

Schell urged television stations to broadcast as little of last year's protests as possible, a request that

appeared to be ignored on local news programs.

"We believe the constant repetition of those images simply builds up any tension that might arise this year," Lilly said.

Last year, 50,000 protesters crammed downtown and shut down part of the WTO session. The WTO, a trade alliance of 139 countries, has become a target for a wide range of activists who believe it represents corporate globalization and takes advantage of the environment and workers.

Overwhelmed Seattle police responded by firing tear gas and rubber bullets. The ensuing riots resulted in 600 arrests, $3 million in property damage, numerous civil rights lawsuits and the police chief's sudden early retirement.

By all accounts, this year's protests will be smaller because there will be no conference to disrupt.

Generous estimates predicted as many as 5,000 demonstrators, many of whom planned to converge on Westlake Park downtown. Police have asked them not to protest there because they could disrupt shoppers and a holiday event.

Jean Buskin, a 52-year-old Seattle biochemist coordinating anniversary protests, said she expected no violence.

She said the vandalism was a shame because Starbucks has been receptive to activists' arguments and now offers certified fair-trade coffee, which promotes coffee grown in developing countries by small producers. Starbucks has been criticized as a global symbol of American capitalism and a big business helping turn small-town America into a generic

A 48-point light face headline

By RON FOURNIER
AP Political Writer

Al Gore raced between TV interviews Wednesday asking, "Will we count all the votes or not?" while his lawyers urgently sought a court ruling with the answer he wanted. Both Gore and rival George W. Bush pressed forward with separate blueprints for building a presidency.

"On Jan. 20, a President Bush will be ready to take the reins of the government," said top adviser Andy Card — awarding his boss a title that Gore still hopes will be his.

The vice president is trying to overturn official results of the decisive

Florida election before the public's patience runs out on the 23-day ordeal. Needing a quick court victory, Gore authorized his divided legal team to ask the Florida Supreme Court to recount contested ballots or order a lower court to do it, two Democratic sources said late Wednesday.

One million ballots were being hauled 400 miles from southern to northern Florida, where the precedent-making case has been thrust upon a folksy circuit judge. "Pack 'em up and bring 'em up," Judge N. Sanders Sauls said.

Bush planned to meet Thursday with retired Gen. Colin Powell, his oft-si-

be-announced choice as secretary of state. The Texas governor also was calling GOP congressional leaders and assigning his staff to call Democratic lawmakers as the vice president struggled to keep his party in line.

With the stakes so high, the Republican-dominated Florida Legislature inched closer to securing Bush a backup plan: Lawmakers were considering naming their own electors to settle the fiercely fought election. Florida Gov. Jeb Bush, the candidate's brother, said he would sign the necessary legislation "if it was the appropriate thing to do."

Still, with the recount case headed to

the highest court in the land, Jeb Bush said, "The United States Supreme Court trumps the Legislature."

Gore, too, played president-elect at a business meeting with running mate Joseph Lieberman, transition director Roy Neel, Labor Secretary Alexis Herman and Kathleen McGinty, former head of the White House environmental office.

McGinty would be a front-runner to head the Environmental Protection Agency under Gore. Herman would be in line for another Cabinet post, White House counselor or perhaps chief of staff, a job that aides expect would first be offered to campaign manager

Today's Index

ALBUQUERQUE, N.M. (AP) — Seventeen tapes filled with nuclear science data downloaded by former Los Alamos laboratory scientist Wen

Ho Lee were discarded in the trash, according to a source familiar with the investigation.

FBI agents are combing the muddy, smelly Los Alamos County landfill where the Los Alamos

National Laboratory's trash is buried, and say their search could last weeks.

Agents won't confirm they're looking for the missing tapes, but if the pocket-sized computer cartridges

A 2-line head here in 36-pt. bold face

By KARIN LAUB
Associated Press Writer

JERUSALEM (AP) — A senior Palestinian negotiator said Wednesday that he pushed a final peace accord with Israel could be reached before Israel's new elections, tentatively set for spring.

But other Palestinian officials indicated that Ehud Barak appeared determined to speed up the process, saying privately that the Israeli prime minister's envoys have told them that he plans to resume talks in hopes of reaching a peace deal before the election.

In a goodwill gesture, Israel on Wednesday resumed the transfer of

millions of dollars in tax refunds to the Palestinian Authority. The money had been stopped as one of several punitive steps by Israel during nine weeks of fighting that have more than 280 people dead, the vast majority Palestinian.

Barak on Tuesday yielded to pressure from the hawkish opposition to hold elections, after it became apparent that he no longer commanded backing in parliament to block the initiative.

The elections will probably take place in the spring, two years ahead of schedule, though an exact date will not be set before next week. Opposition leader Ariel Sharon said

Israeli Prime Minister Ehud Barak, right, shakes hand with opposition leader Ariel Sharon

FIGURE 8. *This front page is not balanced. All of the photos are in columns 1-4.*

- Column width
- Position on the page
- Depth of type wrap under the headline
- Local option

For example, a long story set in a single column cannot have a very large point-size headline because it would be difficult or impossible to write and would look awkward. A five-column story that has a shallow type wrap (say 2 inches deep) still needs a fairly large point-size headline, regardless of its position on the page. A four-column story with 3-inch-deep legs of type might take a 48-point headline in the top half of a page. The same story at the bottom of the page might take a 42-, or even a 36-point headline. Designers talk of headlines as "carrying the story." This means that stories covering a lot of space on a page generally need larger headlines. Designers should also keep copy editors in mind when they specify point sizes. One tip is to ask whether you could write the headline in those specs. Figure 1 is an example of a front page with headlines in generally descending point size.

Modern computer typesetting allows designers to set type in any size they please (e.g., 15-point, 31-point, 44.5-point). Most newspapers, however, have retained the type-size increments papers typically used in the hot type era (6 points of difference between smaller sizes and 12 between larger). Commonly used headline point sizes are 18, 24, 30, 36, 42, 48, 60 and 72. Preserving those differences enables a newspaper to maintain a consistent look from page to page and from day to day. Some designers and copy editors change point sizes in small increments (say 1 or 2 points) to make headlines fit, but that can degrade the overall look of the paper.

6. Keep Design and Typography Consistent

Many designers favor a limited number of typefaces to provide a consistent look. News should look like news, and features like features. A liftout on one page set in one column should not look different from one set in the same column width on another page. Graphics and charts should have consistent typography and color schemes. Some large papers have design stylebooks, which specify the exact typography to be used in typical elements. For example, a baseball box score should have 6-point Geneva bold headings and 6-point Geneva light text and statistics.

Consistency means that designers don't vary from design standards and typographic norms simply for the sake of variation. Variation may be warranted in special cases, but designers must make sure they are special cases, because variation calls attention to itself. Specially designed center-pieces, for example, might well deviate from the standard typography used on the rest of the page or throughout the paper. Figure 1 has two faces (Times Roman bold and light). Contrast is achieved by that variation and by different point sizes. Figure 9 is the same page with a number of faces that do not complement one another.

Keep internal gutters (the spaces between pictures and text elements) consistent too. On a photo package, for example, the internal gutters should be the same. Some newspapers have specified the widths of gutters in design style guides. If not, a good rule is to use from 1 to 2 picas of space as a gutter. Consistency also is important in drawing and labeling page dummies, which many papers continue to do, even in the era of electronic pagination.[5]

7. Keep Related Elements Together and Unrelated Elements Apart

Readers don't want puzzles. Design should communicate relatedness when things are related (say a story and sidebar), and it should communicate dif-ference when elements are unrelated. Photos and other visuals can be used to separate unrelated elements. They can also confuse the issue. For exam-ple, a photo with a strong directionality (say a profile of a face) should not be designed so that it looks into an unrelated story. The photo will draw the eye, and the directionality will draw the eye to the wrong story.

Try to keep the legs of type under the headline. In some designs, say designs that enclose headline, story and photo in a box, this rule is less im-portant.

DON'TS

Here are a few practices to avoid when designing pages, bearing in mind that some newspapers might not treat all of these as prohibitions.

1. Don't "Bump" Heads

Avoid setting one headline right next to another (Figure 10). In a modular design, a lack of visual elements can sometimes create the need to set sto-

FIGURE 9. *This front page has the same design as in Figure 1, but it uses too many different typefaces, and they clash with one another.*

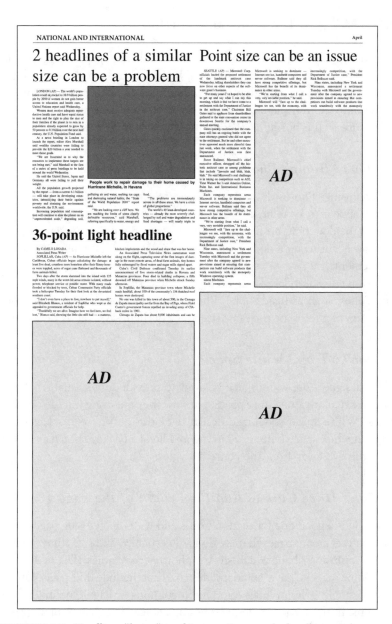

FIGURE 10. *Headlines "bump" on this page. Because the headlines at the top are similar in point size, it is possible to read through them. If headlines bump, they should be in contrasting faces and/or sizes. A solution would be to box the story/ photo element at the upper left and use a one-column headline instead of the two lines of larger type. The photo and the box would visually separate the two stories at the top. Another problem with this page is the weight of the 36-point bold headline on the least dominant story.*

ries side by side. A glance at many different daily newspapers suggests that some papers do not consider bumping headlines to be a design problem. Many, however, do, and they make every effort to design pages without head bumps. Often there is a way to avoid the problem; when there isn't, make sure to use headlines that contrast in size and/or face.

2. Don't "Bump" Photos on Unrelated Stories

It's confusing. Photos draw the eye, and two or more photos placed together appear to be related. Figure 11 is an example. You want readers to look at the dominant art first, then move along to the next. A similar problem can occur when a news photo bumps against a strong image in an advertisement.

Don't use unrelated photos at the same size on a page (except for small ones, such as head shots). Photos provide a visual hierarchy; when two or more photos are the same size, none of them says, "Look here first."

3. Don't "Trap" White Space

Many designers use white space as a way to provide some visual relief on a page, particularly on feature pages, but now they are using it more on news pages. White space should be designed to the outside of packages and pages. If white space is designed in the middle of a package or a page, it will draw the eye away from the content (Figure 12).

4. Don't Have Gutters Run the Length of the Page

This rule is a good one for section fronts and wide-open inside pages. Full-page gutters create pages that are divided vertically, and sometimes the result is confusion about which story a photo accompanies (Figure 13).

Some papers have standard designs that include full-page gutters, such as single-column holes for opinion columns or Page One index/refer columns. In those cases, a designer has no choice. The five-column format many papers have recently adopted seems to be leading to more section fronts with full-page gutters. It is more difficult to design a section front without full-page gutters on five columns, but it's worth the trouble. Dividing pages into vertical segments makes them look static, not active. Solutions include using a horizontal element midway or low on the page or using photos to break the gutters. It is difficult to avoid full-page gutters on

FIGURE 11. *Don't design pages that have unrelated photos touching. The eye will see them as part of the same package. The two-column and three-column photos on this page might appear to be part of the same story even though the two-column picture belongs with the four-column package and the three-column shot accompanies the two-column story at lower left. A good solution would be to move the two- column photo up under the headline and wrap the type below it.*

243

FIGURE 12. *The blocks of white space in the centerpiece package draw the eye because they are "trapped." A better approach is to push the white space to the outside of packages and pages. There it is functional; it provides visual relief.*

FIGURE 13. *This page has a gutter between columns 4 and 5 that runs nearly the length of the page. It creates a segmenting effect and makes the page look static rather than active. It also creates some confusion. Which story does the two-column photo at the upper right accompany? Running the two-column photo at a slightly wider measure would solve that problem and break the gutter. Another easy way to break that gutter is to switch the three-column photo and the two-column story at the bottom. That would also balance the photos better.*

inside pages that have long stories or long continuations from the section front. Many times, it's not important—the ad stacks already segment the page.

5. *Don't Separate the Headline from the Story*

The beginning of the story should touch the headline or summary. Newspaper readers are used to headlines pointing to the start of the story. Don't disappoint them (Figure 14). In smaller page formats, such as those used in many magazines, designers sometimes separate the title and story by other elements, such as photos. This approach can still be confusing, but the danger is generally lower in magazines, which typically display only one story per page.

6. *Don't Break a Leg of Type with Other Elements*

Some papers regularly use one-column liftout quotes or one-column photos in the middle of one-column legs of type. That style, which is often used in magazines, can be confusing on newspaper pages, because unlike magazines newspaper pages have multiple stories. Breaking a leg of type with a visual element can lead readers to mistakenly move to the top of the next leg of type (Figure 15).

7. *Last But Not Least, Don't Get Overly Fancy to Avoid Breaking a Rule*

Some designers sprinkle boxes, liftout quotes, tint blocks and rules throughout routine inside pages to solve design problems, preserve modularity or create contrast. Boxes are probably the most misused design element. Avoid excessive use of any elements that are used in other parts of the paper to communicate something special. If design shows off a story, the story should be worth showing off. In other words, don't advertise a Corolla as if it were a Corvette.

Another idea to remember is that designers often have to make trade-offs, particularly on inside pages. They often have to ignore one principle to follow another. For example, if you have an inside page with a three-column hole and a photo that should be run as big as you can use it, run the picture in three columns even if it bumps an ad. Bump heads if you have to (but make sure to make them contrasting). In other words, follow the rules

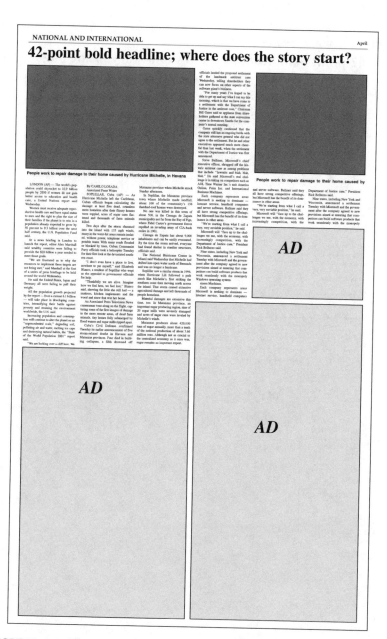

People work to repair damage to their home caused by Hurricane Michelle, in Havana

FIGURE 14. *This page violates the rule that the headline should touch the beginning of the story. Readers will try to begin this story in column 4, then realize the mistake and go back and find the real beginning, which is in column 1.*

42-point bold headline on this one-story inside page

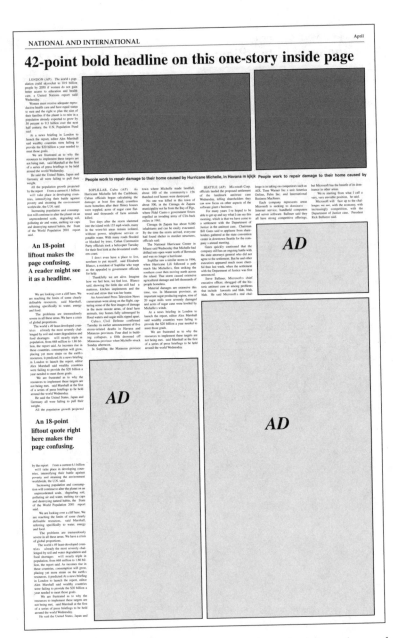

LONDON (AP) The world s population could skyrocket to 10.9 billion people by 2050 if women do not gain better access to education and health care, a United Nations report said Wednesday.

Women must receive adequate reproductive health care and have equal status to men and the right to plan the size of their families if the planet is to rein in a population already expected to grow by 50 percent to 9.3 billion over the next half century, the U.N. Population Fund said.

At a news briefing in London to launch the report, editor Alex Marshall said wealthy countries were failing to provide the $20 billion a year needed to meet those goals.

We are frustrated as to why the resources to implement these targets are not being met, said Marshall at the first of a series of press briefings to be held around the world Wednesday.

He said the United States, Japan and Germany all were failing to pull their weight.

All the population growth projected by the report from a current 6.1 billion will take place in developing countries, intensifying their battle against poverty and straining the environment worldwide, the U.N. said.

Increasing population and consumption will continue to alter the planet on an unprecedented scale, degrading soil, polluting air and water, melting ice caps and destroying natural habits, the State of the World Population 2001 report said.

An 18-point liftout makes the page confusing. A reader might see it as a headline.

We are looking over a cliff here. We are reaching the limits of some clearly definable resources, said Marshall, referring specifically to water, energy and food.

The problems are tremendously severe in all these areas. We have a crisis of global proportions.

The world s 49 least-developed countries already the most severely challenged by soil and water degradation and food shortages will nearly triple in population, from 668 million to 1.86 billion, the report said. As incomes rise in these countries, consumption will grow, placing yet more strain on the earth's resources, it predicted.At a news briefing in London to launch the report, editor Alex Marshall and wealthy countries were failing to provide the $20 billion a year needed to meet those goals.

We are frustrated as to why the resources to implement these targets are not being met, said Marshall at the first of a series of press briefings to be held around the world Wednesday.

He said the United States, Japan and Germany all were failing to pull their weight.

All the population growth projected

An 18-point liftout quote right here makes the page confusing.

by the report from a current 6.1 billion will take place in developing countries, intensifying their battle against poverty and straining the environment worldwide, the U.N. said.

Increasing population and consumption will continue to alter the planet on an unprecedented scale, degrading soil, polluting air and water, melting ice caps and destroying natural habits, the State of the World Population 2001 report said.

We are looking over a cliff here. We are reaching the limits of some clearly definable resources, said Marshall, referring specifically to water, energy and food.

The problems are tremendously severe in all these areas. We have a crisis of global proportions.

The world s 49 least-developed countries already the most severely challenged by soil and water degradation and food shortages will nearly triple in population, from 668 million to 1.86 billion, the report said. As incomes rise in these countries, consumption will grow, placing yet more strain on the earth's resources, it predicted.At a news briefing in London to launch the report, editor Alex Marshall and wealthy countries were failing to provide the $20 billion a year needed to meet those goals.

We are frustrated as to why the resources to implement these targets are not being met, said Marshall at the first of a series of press briefings to be held around the world Wednesday.

He said the United States, Japan and

People work to repair damage to their home caused by Hurricane Michelle, in Havana m kjkjk   People work to repair damage to their home caused by

SOPLILLAR, Cuba (AP) As Hurricane Michelle left the Caribbean, Cuban officials began calculating the damage: at least five dead, countless more homeless after their flimsy houses were toppled, acres of sugar cane flattened and thousands of farm animals killed.

Two days after the storm slammed into the island with 135 mph winds, many in the worst-hit areas remain isolated, without power, telephone service or potable water. With many roads flooded or blocked by trees, Cuban Communist Party officials took a helicopter Tuesday for their first look at the devastated southern coast.

I don t even have a place to live, nowhere to put myself, said Elizabeth Blanco, a resident of Soplillar who wept as she appealed to government officials for help.

Thankfully we are alive. Imagine how we feel here, we feel lost, Blanco said, showing the little she still had a mattress, kitchen implements and the wood and straw that was her home.

An Associated Press Television News cameraman went along on the flight, capturing some of the first images of damage in the more remote areas, of dead farm animals, tiny homes fully submerged by flood waters and sugar mills ripped apart.

Cuba s Civil Defense confirmed Tuesday its earlier announcement of five storm-related deaths in Havana and Matanzas provinces. Four died in building collapses, a fifth drowned off Matanzas province when Michelle struck Sunday afternoon.

In Soplillar, the Matanzas province

town where Michelle made landfall, about 100 of the community s 156 thatched roof homes were destroyed.

No one was killed in this town of about 500, in the Cienaga de Zapata municipality not far from the Bay of Pigs, where Fidel Castro s government forces repelled an invading army of CIA-backed exiles in 1961.

Cienaga de Zapata has about 9,000 inhabitants and can be easily evacuated. By the time the storm arrived, everyone had found shelter in sturdier structures, officials said.

The National Hurricane Center in Miami said Wednesday that Michelle had drifted into open water north of Bermuda and was no longer a hurricane.

Soplillar saw a similar storm in 1996, when Hurricane Lili followed a path much like Michelle's, first striking the island. That storm caused extensive agricultural damage and left thousands of people homeless.

Material damages are extensive this time, too. In Matanzas province, an important sugar producing region, nine of 20 sugar mills were severely damaged and acres of sugar cane were leveled by Michelle's winds.

At a news briefing in London to launch the report, editor Alex Marshall said wealthy countries were failing to provide the $20 billion a year needed to meet those goals.

We are frustrated as to why the resources to implement these targets are not being met, said Marshall at the first of a series of press briefings to be held around the world Wednesday.

SEATTLE (AP) Microsoft Corp. officials lauded the proposed settlement of the landmark antitrust case Wednesday, telling shareholders they can now focus on other aspects of the software giant s business.

For many years I ve hoped to be able to get up and say what I can say this morning, which is that we have come to a settlement with the Department of Justice in the antitrust case, Chairman Bill Gates said to applause from shareholders gathered at the state convention center in downtown Seattle for the company s annual meeting.

Gates quickly confirmed that the company still has an ongoing battle with the state attorneys general who did not agree to the settlement. But he and other executives appeared much more cheerful than last week, when the settlement with the Department of Justice was first announced.

Steve Ballmer, Microsoft's chief executive officer, shrugged off the historic antitrust case as among problems that include lawsuits and blah, blah, blah. He said Microsoft s real challenge is in taking on competitors such as AOL Time Warner Inc. s unit America Online, Palm Inc. and International Business Machines.

Each company represents areas Microsoft is seeking to dominate Internet service, handheld computers and server software. Ballmer said they all have strong competitive offerings.

but Microsoft has the benefit of its dominance in other areas.

We re starting from what I call a very, very enviable position, he said. Microsoft will face up to the challenges we see, with the economy, with increasingly competition, with the Department of Justice case, President Rick Belluzzo said.

AD

AD

AD

FIGURE 15. *The one-column liftout quotes in column 1 might confuse readers. Because they look like headlines, they might lead readers to jump up to column 2.*

unless there's a good reason not to. Like most of editing, design is about making choices. Make good ones—ones that are based in common sense and that will benefit readers.

SOME WEB DESIGN ISSUES

Web designers tend to follow most principles of print design. They too worry about contrast, balance, clarity and consistency. That's not surprising, because most Web designers were print designers first. But there are a few wild cards.

One is navigation. Readers do not use the term, but they are familiar with print "navigation"—indexing, sectioning, packaging, story jumps and the like. Web designers, even after about eight years, do not agree on navigation/design standards involving movement from page to page and approaches to linking. For example, usability professionals tend to take a utilitarian view: Do what makes it easier for users. For example, take the color used for links. Usability expert Jakob Nielsen says that any color is OK for a link as long as it is blue—the default blue color.[6] His approach, which is based on studies of users performing tasks, is that people get used to doing things a certain way and that the link is such a fundamental aspect of Web design that it should look and work the same way from page to page. Some designers have a different view. They use whatever link color they feel works with the other typography and background color on a page. They might use an image as a link with no text. They believe that users are sophisticated enough to figure it out.

Nielsen and others argue for a highly structured type of writing on the Web, including liberal use of bulleted lists and other devices that break type into manageable chunks. He also says the inverted pyramid is a very useful form for Web writing, because it is efficient.[7] Reading on a screen is physically more demanding than reading print, and consequently, Nielsen says, writing should be much tighter. Others, such as Janet Murray, whose background is in computer science and literature, point out that the Web makes many forms of writing possible, including stories that allow readers to take different paths.[8]

To some degree, the choice of navigation and writing styles should depend on your audience. If your site is aimed at a technologically sophisticated group of users, such as graphic designers, artists or college students, you can probably play around with more creative and edgy navigation. If you want your site to appeal to a general readership, it might pay to be more conservative and worry more about usability considerations. If your site is primarily providing information to busy people, you might want to make it segmented and manageable, as Nielsen suggests. If it is aimed at a literary community, you might want a more organic approach.

An important point to remember is that on the Web the relationship between writing and design is much tighter than it is in print. When usability experts maintain that structured messages with visible segmentation are appropriate approaches given how people use the Web, are they talking about writing or design? The answer is both. To be effective, writers for the Web need to know how their work will be displayed.

A FEW SUGGESTIONS ABOUT WEB DESIGN

One navigation strategy suggested by some Web designers is to think of site design as visible and page design as invisible.

In other words, the architecture should be clear, or "visible," so that users will not have problems getting around the site. Confusion still is an all-too-common user experience; users get lost and frustrated. Nielsen, for example, has urged that sites make their file structure visible in a navigation bar across the top.[9] This is an example of visible site design. A reader/user should not have to search for or guess at navigation. That clever image used at the bottom of the first segment of a story might or might not be read as a link to Part 2.

"Invisible" page design means that the design serves the content and does not call attention to itself. In practice, this might mean that the design does not use the "latest and greatest" technology, or that it uses a mild rather than a garish background color.

Headlines that serve as links should be informative. A clever, creative headline that works well with an image in print might not work well at all as a link to the content deeper in a Web site.

Templates that are used to automatically flow type into standard designs are efficient, but they can be a problem. One style is to have the first so many words flow into an index page under a headline that serves as a link to the full story inside. That works reasonably well for inverted pyramid news stories, with clear summary headlines. It doesn't work very well for stories with anecdotal leads or nonspecific headlines.

Another difference is the size of the canvas Web designers work with.

A computer screen is much smaller than a newspaper broadsheet page. In the early days of the Web, the standard design window was small (about 600 pixels wide by 450 deep). The dimensions were based on the typical monitor in use (13-inch diagonal). Now, 17-inch monitors are common, and some people have larger ones, and the typical design width is often 800 pixels or more. On the vertical dimension, a Web designer might be restricted to one typical screen depth, or if the site has a scrolling home page, the design depth might be several screenfuls.

To further complicate matters, Web users can (and do) control the width of the window they use to view the Web. They also can override other design specifications, such as typeface and type size. Design on the Web is still something of a moving target.

Whether you're doing print or Web design, it pays to follow Mario Garcia's three rules:

Make it easy to read.
Make it easy to find.
Make it visually appealing.[10]

14

The Future
of Copy Editing

Students tend to be very pragmatic about what they need to know to launch a career. They typically (and understandably) spend a great deal of time learning the skills required by the job. They spend far less time, if any, reflecting on how the job came to be what it is today and how it might change tomorrow. This chapter provides a brief look at some of the forces that have helped shape the position of copy editor as it stands in the new millennium. Two broad categories, technological and organizational change, both relating to economic changes, have had the most visible impact.

COPY EDITING AND COMPUTERS

Copy editors have had a love–hate relationship with technology for decades. The courtship itself is much older, probably beginning in the late 19th century, about the same time copy editing began to develop as a specialization in U.S. newspapers.[1]

Copy editors have always been the interface between the story and the printing technology of the day. In the Linotype era, they needed to understand metal type and typography so that they could count headlines accurately. They had to understand the technological constraints in the back shop better than others in the newsroom, and they were responsible for meeting deadlines, which in many ways were determined by production constraints.

The character of the job today has a great deal to do with changes that have occurred in the last three decades. The pace of technological change in newspapers quickened dramatically starting in the late '60s and early '70s, first with the shift from hot lead type and letterpress printing to "cold type," which was pasted up, photographed and usually turned into offset printing plates. The introduction of cold type, and, soon afterward, of computer text entry and composition coding, changed the job of copy editor substantially. Strangely, the technological future was in many ways a return to the past. The copy editor became both a journalist and a printer, a blended occupation that would have been familiar to Colonial-era printer Ben Franklin.

Computer technology made it possible (and cost-effective) for newspapers to reduce employment in the back shop and move tasks that had been done by compositors into the newsroom. The transition, which occurred rapidly in the mid- to late-'70s, was anything but smooth, and newspapers found that they could not simply transfer composition coding and proofreading tasks into the newsroom and maintain a high level of quality with the same number of editors. Many newspapers found they had to add copy editors to handle coding and, starting in the early 1980s, to handle the demands of another new technology, pagination.[2]

Pagination, or computer page design and makeup, spelled the end for composing rooms at many newspapers. One effect was a shifting of even more tasks into the newsroom, such as creating the geometry for electronic pages, placing stories and photos onto the pages and adjusting page elements. The overall impact was mixed. Copy editors found that pagination was a two-edged sword. It gave copy/layout editors greater flexibility and enabled them to be more creative in page design. Some said it helped them avoid much of the interdepartmental unpleasantness that they had endured in the days of hot type. They no longer had to rely on sometimes brusque, often uncooperative, compositors to make the last-minute adjustments that frequently are necessary in daily journalism. But many editors also found that the new tasks of page assembly left them less time to do more traditional tasks, in particular editing copy, headline writing and proofreading, which before computer typesetting had been done in the composing room.

When editors became paginators, they became directly responsible for page production, and production pressures often forced their journalistic tasks into the background.[3] Many felt that the traditional aspects of the job suffered and complained that newspapers were accepting lower quality in the interest of cost savings. Others disagreed, saying that quality had not suffered and perhaps had even improved. Chances are both sides were right to a degree, depending on how pagination was implemented at different newspapers and how well staffed a newsroom was to begin with.[4] Several researchers, in surveying copy editors during this period, found high levels of stress and job burnout, and trade journals and professional associations published articles and reports discussing the state of the copy desk and how to make the job more manageable.[5]

Technological change continued through the '90s, with nearly all papers moving to pagination as well as another computer-based production technology: digital imaging.[6] Digital imaging primarily affected photographers and photo editors, but at some papers copy editors learned to use Photoshop and took on some of the image-processing tasks that had been done in the darkroom by photographers or technicians or in the back shop by camera operators and photoengravers.

In the late '80s and '90s, newspapers experimented with a number of organizational changes in part to make better use of computer technology. Some hired technicians to do the more mechanical aspects of page and photo handling; others created design desks and other new structures to both improve design quality and to better manage technological change.[7]

At the new millennium began, most papers had found ways to accommodate pagination and digital imaging. But some of the issues raised about technological change a decade and a half earlier remained problematic. A survey I conducted in 1999 found that many of the criticisms raised by copy editors about pagination in the late '80s, such as time and production pressures, were still problems for their counterparts in the late '90s.[8]

IMPACT ON JOURNALISM PROGRAMS

Technology's impact also has been felt outside the newsroom, in journalism schools. The demand for technologically savvy journalists has led to fundamental changes as well as soul-searching among journalism educators. Some professors complain that it becomes more difficult by the year to find space in the curriculum to introduce students to computer applications such as QuarkXPress and Photoshop while maintaining a strong focus on traditional reporting, writing, editing, photography and page design skills. The demand for computer-based skills is real, as studies in the mid- to late '90s have indicated.[9] Many newspapers expect starting copy editors to already know Quark, and some expect that new hires be comfortable with other computer applications, such as Photoshop and even a graphics program such as Freehand or Illustrator. And professors who want to give their students a leg up realize that those who have little or no experience with the computer applications newspapers use will probably be at a disadvantage when they look for work.

NEW MEDIA

Pagination and digital imaging are old news; the new kid, the 800-pound gorilla lurking outside the newsroom, is the Internet. To be sure, the Internet already is a fact of life in newsrooms; it is heavily used for research and fact-checking and less so for interaction with readers. Among the slowest professions to jump on the Internet bandwagon,[10] newspapers have seen the light and become wired, and copy editors and others in the newsroom have learned to make use of the wealth of information on the Web.

The potential exists for greater change. A growing chorus of voices in universities and in the profession is touting the concept of media "convergence," predicting that newspapers and other traditional information providers will soon lumber off into the sunset as the Web enables them to invent new roles as multimedia information providers.

John Pavlik, for example, insists that news-gathering will change to embrace multimedia technologies, and others, including some in the mainstream newspaper industry, state unequivocally that nothing fundamental ties the information in newspapers to a delivery system based on "crushed trees smeared with ink."[11] Several newspapers, most notably the Chicago Tribune, the Milwaukee Journal-Sentinel and the Tampa Tribune, have experimented with multimedia reporters and with editing desks that combine print, online, TV and radio.[12]

In a parallel development, some professors and administrators have argued that journalism schools should dismantle traditional industry-based sequence structures and revamp curricula to train students to tell stories in whatever medium is most appropriate.[13] In yet another development, some schools are asking whether they are spending too much time on professional skills and not enough on an examination of the role of media in an ever-changing society. In mid-2002, for example, the president of Columbia University suspended the search for a new dean of the journalism school so the school could examine its mission and its place in the university before it brought a new leader aboard.[14]

What are the implications for copy editors? Temporary blips in the employment picture will happen, and they will have an impact on jobs. The tightening of jobs across the country that occurred during the recession in 2001–02 was not the first time students found it difficult to get jobs, nor will it be the last. Like other 21st-century businesses, news organizations react to poor economic conditions by cutting costs, and cutting staff tends to be the chosen path. But there will be no long-term shortage of work for editors.

In online news operations, most staff members are more properly called "editors" than "reporters" or "writers." Some go by the title "producer," which reflects a combination of tasks not too different from the analog title in the broadcast industries, where producers organize elements into packages. The bulk of newspapers' Internet news offerings is still "shovelware," the term used pejoratively to refer to the dumping online of content originally prepared for print. For economic reasons, that situation is not likely to change very soon. It costs money to gather news, and most online news operations have yet to find a way to pay the bills, much less pay for news-gathering. Shovelware needs to be edited for presentation on the Web, and new headlines and captions often need to be written. Such tasks are similar to what most copy editors already do every day.

Some new tasks may emerge. For example, copy editors might be asked to code Web pages, to manage online chats, to moderate discussion lists, to edit audio or video and optimize them for the Web, to interact with online readers, or to do tasks not yet imagined. The job title might even morph into "producer." If this happens, copy editors will need new skills, and if the past is any guide, universities will be expected to provide them.

The demand for multimedia skills among new journalists, however, remains weak, despite the occasional trade journal article touting the need for such new workers. A multimedia reporter for the Chicago Tribune, probably the fastest-moving news organization in pursuing convergence and "synergy," was featured in an American Journalism Review article in 1996. The article described the journalist as carrying a notebook, a video camera and a digital audio recorder so that she could collect information and present it in whatever form was most appropriate.[15] Not long afterward, that same reporter had moved into a traditional print position at the paper and remarked during a panel discussion at an annual meeting of journalism educators in 1997 that the paper had changed its thinking about multimedia reporters. It still collected multimedia information and continued to present it in whatever medium seemed appropriate, but it tended to send video professionals to collect video and print reporters to collect information for print stories.

If two recent surveys are any indication, both professional copy editors and professors place very low emphasis on students graduating with multimedia skills such as the ability to edit audio and video.[16] A recent article in Quill examined the issue, quoting some professors who believe that multimedia training is essential and others who don't.[17] The dot.com crash at the millennium's turn might further delay the need for students to develop those skills. Or it might accelerate the need. It's easy to speculate and difficult to predict, so it's a good idea for aspiring copy editors to prepare for this brave new world by learning what they can about multimedia journalism. Moreover, it's fun to learn how to edit for different media, and lessons learned in one field can often be applied in another. Print, for example, can learn a great deal from television about the importance of writing with images. But it's also wise to keep at least one foot on the ground and pay most attention to traditional skills in a given area. The word at the beginning of the millennium (at least the word coming from the majority of the profession and the academy) is: The jury is still out.

COPY EDITING AND ORGANIZATIONAL CHANGE

Organizational change, sometimes intertwined with technological change, has reshaped the newsroom landscape and had led to the redesign of many traditional copy desk jobs. Perhaps the most widespread change over the last two decades has been the development of design desks and the concomitant professionalization of design.[18] Before the late '70s, copy editors also did page design, known then as "page layout." This task was (and still is) part of a typical copy editor's job at most small dailies, but it also was the practice at many large metropolitan dailies before pagination. That practice began to change, in part because of the demands of pagination. The complexity and high cost of early pagination systems, known as "proprietary" systems, made it more economical to limit the number of editors trained to use the systems. Training was expensive in terms of actual expenditures as well as lost time. The systems were complicated and quirky, and it typically took a long time for an editor to become an expert user. Other forces drove the change as well, including a desire to maintain a more consistent design throughout the newspaper, and to simply raise the paper's standards by placing the best designers in design-desk positions. Creating a separate design desk was a good way to meet those goals.

The result was a change in job descriptions at many newspapers. My own experience as a copy editor reflects that shift. As a copy editor on a 40,000-circulation daily, I laid out pages every day. After I moved to a metropolitan daily, I did no page design in 12 years as a copy editor and copy chief. Small papers continue to rely on copy editors to do most page design, and such skills are considered important criteria in hiring copy editors at those papers.[19]

A parallel development in newspapers that may have an impact on copy editors is the newsroom reorganization movement. Some approaches, such as the team movement, go back a couple of decades, but for most newspapers, newsroom reorganization is a phenomenon of the '90s. Several newspapers began to rethink how they organized staff in response to criticism that the traditional copy flow "assembly line" from reporter to assigning editor to copy editor to page designer was inefficient and a relic of long-outdated technology.[20] Proposals were floated to restructure news processes around design desks, rather than copy desks, or to break apart the traditional copy desk and have copy editors work with design teams or reporting topic teams.[21] The reporting team approach has been gathering steam since the early '90s. It is difficult to estimate the number of newspapers that have teams because the definition of *team* is not consistent. Some, such as The (Portland) Oregonian, have well-defined, long-standing team structures. At the other end of the spectrum are papers that assemble teams on a story-by-story basis.

Copy desk reorganization did not catch on as quickly, and the movement seems to have stalled. A few papers have reported success with the new system (e.g., the [Minneapolis] Star Tribune and the St. Paul Pioneer Press). One of the first to make the switch, the Wichita Eagle, reconsidered its decision after several years and has reinstituted a more traditional copy desk structure.

The potential benefits of having copy editors work side by side with reporters are not trivial. Copy editors who work alongside reporters on teams say they can develop much better rapport and trust, which are important considerations in the reporter–editor relationship. Team copy editors also appreciate the chance to develop expertise in a particular area, such as politics, business or the arts. They also point out that they can get involved in the story process much earlier, have a hand in shaping stories and can spot a serious problem developing before it's too late, as is often the case in a traditional system.[22]

The potential downsides of dismantling the copy desk are also significant, and these concerns have caused many newsroom managers to think twice before implementing such a change. One of the biggest issues is losing the position of "slot," or copy chief, and along with it most of the copy editing training function. Among their many roles, copy chiefs often assume the task of teacher. They act as mentors for new hires, and they serve as a sounding board for questions about editing as well as newsroom policy. Copy editors who report to reporting team leaders might get lucky and develop a similar relationship, but most team leaders have enough to do without having to act as a copy editor of last resort. Moreover, few team leaders are former copy editors, and most could not easily assume the slot's role of teacher.

Another serious problem, perhaps the most serious, is that the new structure might make it difficult for a copy editor to act as a reader representative, as Gene Foreman, former managing editor of The Philadelphia Inquirer, called the role. Copy editors add a great deal of value to stories by virtue of their independence. They can look at a story as a reader would, not as a reporter or an assigning editor who already is close to the story might. Some editors have expressed concern that copy editors who are members of reporting teams might lose that important distance and engage in "groupthink" or that they might not raise serious questions for fear of annoying their immediate supervisor, the team leader. In a traditional copy desk system, rim editors report to copy chiefs, who typically report to higher-level newsroom managers. Copy editors are insulated from reprisals from assigning editors.

A third concern is more operational. Several papers that have experimented with copy editors on teams have found that they do not have enough staff to cover breaking stories that occur after the teams go home, or that there are not enough copy editors to meet the needs of all of the teams and still have resources to fill in for vacations and illness. A few papers, for example, The (Portland) Oregonian, have created hybrid systems to try to reap the benefits of both. At The Oregonian, some copy editors are members of topic teams, but most are assigned to traditional slot–rim desks. Team copy editors essentially report to two supervisors: the team leader and a copy chief. The structure is difficult to visualize in an organization chart, but it seems to have worked pretty well.[23] On balance, it's probably wise that more papers have not adopted the copy editor/team model, but copy editors entering the field may find this approach, or some variant of it, gaining ground in the future. What is a safe bet is that other ideas for organizational change will continue to appear. Management consultants have finally captured the attention of newspaper editors, and new ideas that they propose might be rooted in technological or organizational considerations or both.

TIPS AND STRATEGIES

The most effective strategy for dealing with the increasing burden of technology is to hire more editors, but copy editors are not in a position to do that. What they can do is keep an eye on quality and point out that inadequate staffing can affect quality and ultimately credibility. If copy editors have built a reputation for hard work and dedication to quality, their observations should carry some weight with newsroom managers, the people who do have a role in hiring.

But that may be a tough sell. Publishers have squeezed about as much cost saving out of technological change as they can, and increased pressure from Wall Street for bigger profit margins has led to budget tightening even in relatively good economic times. The result is an unwillingness to increase staffing. In bad times, the pressures to let positions go unfilled and to actually cut positions is much greater. Some observers have accused the industry of shortsightedness in making cuts to and freezing positions on copy desks. The American Copy Editors Society has raised this issue often in annual meetings. But little change appears to be on the horizon.

• Pay attention to changes in the newspaper industry, particularly in the area of media convergence. Read trade journals, such as Editor & Publisher, presstime and Quill, the magazine of the Society of Professional Journalists. Industry groups such as the American Society of Newspaper Editors and the Associated Press Managing Editors association also publish periodicals. Many of the articles in these journals are written by journalists on the front lines of change.

• Try to keep your skills current and look for opportunities to expand those skills. Consider attending a conference or workshop or taking a class in an area that might be useful. Many universities and community colleges have "community education" programs, which allow non-degree students to take classes.

For the newspaper industry and those who want to pursue careers in it, change is clearly in the wind, but whether and how soon it might appear in more than a few pioneer newsrooms is anyone's guess. Looking at the technological future, the cliché is accurate: The only constant is change. In organization, look for new approaches and more team experiments. And for new media, look into the crystal ball. The economics that support on-line news operations still don't add up, and until they do I would expect to see traditional industries maintain their position as the dominant information providers of the early 21st century. But stay tuned.

15 ▗ ▖ ▗ ▖ ▗ ▖ ▗ ▖ ▗ ▖ ▗

Pursuing Excellence

Copy editors who would like to make the leap from good to excellent can pursue two main strategies: formal training or self-improvement. One should be able to follow both paths throughout a career, but, unfortunately, newspaper managements too often see training as expendable. Formal training, whether onsite or offsite and paid for by the paper, often is the first expense to be cut when the economic picture worsens. Observers of the news industry long have criticized it for short-sightedness about staff development, pointing to other white-collar fields that invest substantial resources in staff development.

Some companies—individual newspapers and chains that maintain their commitment to training even in down times—are notable exceptions. A few examples are The Seattle Times, the (Minneapolis) Star-Tribune, The New York Times and the St. Petersburg Times. They continue to send staff members to development programs offered by The Poynter Institute, the Freedom Forum and the American Press Institute, and they support staff members' applications to midcareer fellowship programs at top-notch universities. Some also bring in outside experts to provide one- or two-day workshops in reporting, writing, editing and design. Some pay to send staff members to national and regional professional conferences.

A few have even developed in-house "universities," where staff members can pursue advanced training in a variety of areas. The Detroit Free Press and The (Portland) Oregonian are two examples. Unfortunately, the reality at most papers is that little formal training is available unless a staff member does it on his or her own time and dime.

Regardless, a career in journalism means lifelong learning. Indeed, many longtime journalists—reporters and editors—tell students that they stayed in the business so long because it offered them the opportunity to do something different every day and to keep growing. But it's difficult to learn without teachers or mentors. Some broad strategies can help.

Get as much training as you can while in school. The opportunities for technical training are typically greater in a university setting than they are in the industry. Learn QuarkXPress, the overwhelming desktop publishing choice of small to midsize newspapers, and, if possible, learn some Photoshop. Take a class in online journalism if your institution has one, and if not, teach yourself HTML. Most people using HTML and teaching it are self-taught. It isn't difficult to produce basic and even fairly complicated Web pages. Play around with nonlinear video editing. Your school probably has at least one student lab outfitted with video editing software.

Technical know-how can help you get that first copy desk job, and it can help you change jobs. But keep in mind that what gets you much farther in your career as a copy editor is the ability to edit well and to write good heads even in bad counts. At the largest and most prestigious papers, copy editors do not even do page design, and pages are typically not even designed in Quark.

Once in the profession, you should continue to pursue training, but remember that training is a very low priority at many news organizations. A 1992–93 Freedom Forum report called "No Train No Gain" listed three major findings:

1. Almost all journalists want professional training.
2. Regular training does not reach most journalists.
3. The training gap hurts newspapers.

The gap, the study points out, indicates that three major problems—quality, morale and retention—can be linked to the shortage of professional training. The situation has not improved in the decade since the report appeared.

CONTINUING EDUCATION: OFFSITE

Opportunities exist, but copy editors are competing with others in the newsroom for offsite training. Organizations that offer continuing education for professional journalists include the American Society of Newspaper Editors (ASNE), the Associate Press Managing Editors (APME), Investigative Reporters and Editors (IRE) and the group's National Institute for Computer Assisted Reporting (NICAR), the Society of Professional Journalists (SPJ), the Society of Environmental Journalists (SEJ), and the Society for News Design (SND). Demand is high to attend programs offered by these organizations, and others, and training resources typically are scarce.

The best organization for copy editors is the American Copy Editors Society (ACES), founded in 1997. The Web site is www.copydesk.org. The group, which numbered more than 700 members in 2003, is composed primarily of newspaper copy editors or their supervisors. It includes a smaller number of magazine and online editors, as well as professors who specialize in the teaching of editing. The group, which is dedicated to improving the profession of copy editing and to attracting talented people to the field, stages a national conference that is well worth attending. Sessions are extremely practical, focusing on topics such as headline writing, personnel management, libel, technological challenges, time management, managing one's career, and many other copy editing issues.

Every year during a plenary session at the national conference, an ACES officer asks how many attendees have paid their own way, and a surprisingly high percentage raise their hands. Many of them work for newspaper corporations that can well afford to send a staff member or two from a given newspaper. Newspapers that do not spend the money to send copy editors to such events run a risk of losing copy editors to papers that do, and that is penny-wise, pound-foolish behavior. ACES also has been developing regional chapters, which schedule workshops that are less costly to attend. It also offers several scholarships for students who are interested in copy editing careers.

The Society of Professional Journalists is another good organization for copy editors to join. SPJ has many student chapters based at universities, and these chapters are a good opportunity for copy editors to get involved, to learn about issues affecting all journalists and to help develop sessions of greater value to copy editors.

Other offsite training is periodically available at the American Press Institute (API) in Reston, Va., and The Poynter Institute in St. Petersburg, Fla. API offers some workshops specifically geared toward copy editors and the challenges they face; Poynter tends to bundle design and copy editing into occasional workshops focusing on the concept of WED (writing, editing and design), which it pioneered. State and regional press associations also often provide training sessions at their annual meetings and at other times.

The Associated Press sometimes runs regional workshops, and the Society of News Design offers what it calls "flying short courses" around the country that offer advanced training for designers and other editors who ·play a role in design at their papers. Some university journalism schools offer short workshops for newspapers in their regions or states.

CONTINUING EDUCATION: ONSITE

Some papers offer periodic training sessions in-house, and at other papers copy editors have taken it upon themselves to set up training sessions or discussions such as brown-bag lunch bull sessions. Unfortunately, many papers do nothing of the sort, and, as the Freedom Forum report noted, the desire for ongoing training is largely unmet and is one of the key morale problems in U.S. daily newspaper newsrooms.

If you find yourself working for a newspaper where such opportunities are lacking, don't spend more than a year or two there. It's difficult to improve without role models or ongoing training, so find a paper that pays attention to (and spends some money on) continuing education for copy editors. The recession of 2001-02 made it difficult for journalists to move to other papers, but over the long term copy editors should remain in sufficient demand that any dedicated professional willing to work hard and improve should have options.

Similarly, if you would like to have the opportunity to advance into middle management or higher or to switch to reporting, find a paper that allows such movement. Many of the best papers in the country view the copy desk as a breeding ground for news editors, assignment editors, topic team leaders and assistant managing editors.

TIPS AND STRATEGIES

• If you're a student, take the Dow Jones test. Take it when you're a junior, and if you don't do well enough to land an internship, take it again in your senior year. This competitive program places more than 100 copy editors a year at dozens of the nation's newspapers. The program includes a two-week copy editing "boot camp" at one of several centers for editing excellence throughout the country.

Some students are placed at small papers; most go to midsize and larger dailies. The Newspaper Fund also offers internships for copy editors who are interested in working for online news operations. There is no better entry into the profession of copy editing than this internship program. You can find Dow Jones Newspaper Fund alumni at most major newspapers throughout the country and at many midsize and smaller papers. The internship sometimes leads to a job offer at the newspaper where a student interned, and even when it doesn't, it often opens doors at other publications. Each year, the program distributes a list of students who did well on the test but not quite well enough for an internship. Papers that need copy editors sometimes call those students seeking job applicants. Ask your academic adviser for details, or contact the Dow Jones Newspaper Fund (http://djnewspaperfund.dowjones.com/fund/).

- Don't overlook other copy desk internship opportunities. They number far fewer than reporting internships, but sometimes a newspaper that does not typically accept copy desk interns will take one on if a student asks. Sometimes a student can negotiate an internship that includes both reporting and copy editing. Models for such internships exist; one example is the University of Kansas program, which places students at many newspapers in the country.

- Find experts. College papers or community dailies can invite a faculty member from a local journalism school or ask an experienced copy editor or copy chief from a metropolitan daily to come in for a short session. Good contacts are editors who had worked at the paper beforehand and might come in for free—or maybe for the price of a lunch. On a bigger budget, try consultants. Many papers bring in writing coaches, primarily to work with reporters, but editing consultants and coaches also are available. Look to retired editors and to professors to provide such training.

- Form a group. Reporters create writers groups that provide them more feedback than they often get from their assigning editors. Copy editors can do something similar. Peer-to-peer criticism can be valuable; a desk of editors typically represents a wide range of experience and ability in a variety of areas. For example, some copy editors are better wordsmiths. They can help the others improve those skills. Some write sharper headlines. They can help the others do a better job. Some are better at meeting deadlines. Others are better at page design, Quark, HTML or Web searching. Tap into the talent sitting next to you. Share the expertise.

- Build a file. Copy editors and others in the newsroom can create training materials on an intranet or on the Internet. Encourage all editors and reporters to offer suggestions. Some news organizations have developed excellent sites. The Detroit Free Press site is one of the best (http://www.freep.com/jobspage/).

- Find a mentor on staff. Some papers have formalized the mentoring process. Most have nothing of the sort, but it is still possible to connect with an experienced editor whom you respect and who can teach you skills that will be valuable at your current paper and prepare you for advancement. I worked with a wire editor at my first newspaper who became a mentor. We had a mutually beneficial relationship. She was an experienced editor who taught me a great deal about news judgment and headline writing. I was also the computer systems manager, and I helped her deal with the new technology of the mid-'70s. This strategy can also work at a college newspaper.

- Look for opportunities. Offer to work as a supervisor, say as a fill-in for a vacationing copy chief or news editor. Such experience will enhance your career within a publication and improve your resume when you seek your next job. Supervision requires different skills, particularly people skills, and news organizations value those skills.

- Set sound priorities. Copy editing is both craft and production. Copy editors must learn to edit well, but also edit quickly, because they also have to get pages out in time to meet deadline. Remind yourself often that you're a journalist first and a production worker second. Admittedly, focusing on the journalism can be difficult when the minutes are ticking away and the pages are not out, but it's an important attitude to maintain. When it comes time to make one of the many unavoidable tradeoffs between production demands (Is that caption spacing a little off?) and editorial demands (Is that headline a little misleading?), put the journalism first.

ATTITUDE

Having a good attitude is probably the most important strategy. A belief in the value of what you're doing is crucial. Copy editing is important work. At times, it is thankless work. It's often underappreciated work, and much of the time it's simply too much work. But it can be satisfying to help writers say what they want to say and tell stories that people need or want to hear. Copy editors can justifiably feel that they are doing some good. It's the same motivation that drives other journalists—only the execution is different.

A career in copy editing isn't for everybody. In fact, it won't be the first choice of most aspiring journalists. But if you have the interest and the ability, copy editing can be wonderful.

Notes

CHAPTER 1

1. Trinity University in San Antonio, Texas, the University of Minnesota, the University of Nevada–Reno, Brigham Young University, the University of Kansas and Indiana University are several that have moved in the direction of non-industry-specific and multimedia journalism education. See Christ, William G., McCall, Jeffrey M., Rakow, Lana and Blanchard, Robert O. (1997), Integrated Communication Programs. In Christ, William G. (Ed.), *Media Education Assessment Handbook* (Mahwah, N.J.: Erlbaum). Also see McCall, Jeffrey (1999), Student Occupational Concerns in a Liberal Arts Program. In Christ, William G. (Ed.), *Leadership in Times of Change* (Mahwah, N.J.: Erlbaum), 279–293. For a different view, see Medsger, Betty (1996), *Winds of Change: Challenges Confronting Journalism Education* (Arlington, Va.: Freedom Forum).

2. Auman, Ann E., Fee, Frank E. Jr. and Russial, John T. (2002), Noble Work but Undervalued: The Status and Value of Copy Editing in Journalism Schools, *Journalism and Mass Communication Educator*, Summer, 139–151.

3. Russial, John (forthcoming), Pagination and the Copyeditor: Have Things Changed? *Journalism and Mass Communication Quarterly*.

4. This is a concept pioneered by Gene Foreman, former *Philadelphia Inquirer* managing editor and executive editor.

5. Harrower, Tim (2002), *The Newspaper Designer's Handbook* (New York: McGraw-Hill).

CHAPTER 2

1. *Examining Our Credibility: Perspectives of the Public and the Press* (1999) (Reston, Va.: The American Society of Newspaper Editors).

2. More than 30 years ago, one or two members of the usage panel assembled by the editors of the *American Heritage Dictionary* said they would drop the word *whom* altogether "as a needless refinement," and some would eliminate the distinction between the restrictive *that* and the nonrestrictive *which*. See Bishop, Morris (1969–1973), "Good Usage, Bad Usage, and Usage." In Morris, William (Ed.), *The American Heritage Dictionary of the English Language* (Boston: American Heritage Publishing Co., Inc. and Houghton Mifflin Co.), xxiv.

3. *Examining Our Credibility.*

4. Gibaldi, Joseph (1999), *MLA Handbook for Writers of Research Papers* (New York: Modern Language Association), 68.

5. Bernstein, Theodore M. (1995), *The Careful Writer* (New York: Atheneum).

Bremner, John B. (1980), *Words on Words* (New York: Columbia University Press).

Brooks, Brian S., Pinson, James L. and Gaddy, Jean (1999), *Working with Words*, 4th ed. (New York: Bedford/St. Martin's Press).

Strunk, William Jr. and White, E. B. (2000), *The Elements of Style*, 4th ed. (Boston: Allyn & Bacon).

Fowler, H. W. (2000), *The New Fowler's Modern English Usage*, rev. 3rd ed. R. W. Burchfield, ed. (New York: Oxford University Press).

Kessler, Lauren and McDonald, Duncan (2000), *When Words Collide: A Media Writer's Guide to Grammar and Style* (Belmont, Calif.: Wadsworth).

CHAPTER 3

1. The Dirksen Congressional Center, *http://www.dirksencenter.org/featuresBillionHere.htm.*

CHAPTER 4

1. *100 Questions and Answers about Arab Americans* (undated) (Detroit: The Detroit Free Press), 19.

2. *A Guide to Religion Reporting in the Secular Media* (2002) (Westerville, Ohio: Religion Newswriters Foundation), 39.

3. *A Guide to Religion Reporting in the Secular Media*, 40.

4. Paulos, John Allen (1990), *Innumeracy: Mathematical Illiteracy and Its Consequences* (New York: Vintage Books); Paulos (1995), *A Mathematician Reads the Newspaper* (New York: Basic Books).

5. This quote appears many times in printed material and on the Web, but Dirksen might never have said it. (See Chapter 3.)

6. Reprinted in Hart, Jack (1993), *Second Takes: Monthly Reflections on The Oregonian* (February).

7. Reprinted by permission.

8. Zinsser, William (1998), *On Writing Well*, 6th ed. (New York: HarperPerennial).

9. Miller, Casey and Swift, Kate (1988), *The Handbook of Nonsexist Writing*, 2nd ed. (New York: HarperCollins).

10. Wilhoit, G. Cleveland and Weaver, David H. (1990), *Newsroom Guide to Polls & Surveys* (Bloomington: Indiana University Press); Meyer, Philip (1991), *The New Precision Journalism* (Bloomington: Indiana University Press).

CHAPTER 5

1. Clark, Roy Peter and Fry, Don (1992), *Coaching Writers* (New York: St. Martin's Press).

2. Wilhoit, G. Cleveland and Weaver, David H. (1990). *Newsroom Guide to Polls & Surveys* (Bloomington: Indiana University Press).

3. Zinsser, William (1998), *On Writing Well*, 6th ed. (New York: HarperPerennial); Kennedy, George, Moen, Daryl and Ranly, Don (1993), *Beyond the Inverted Pyramid* (New York: St. Martin's Press).

CHAPTER 6

1. Pember, Don (1999), *Mass Media Law* (Boston: McGraw-Hill), 127.

2. Goldstein, Norm (Ed.) (2002), *The Associated Press Stylebook and Briefing on Media Law* (Cambridge, Mass: Perseus Publishing), 342.

3. The First Amendment Handbook, Reporters Committee for Freedom of the Press, *http://www.rcfp.org/handbook/viewpage.cgi?0101*.

4. Pember, 151–152.

5. *The Associated Press Stylebook*, 352–358.

6. *The Associated Press Stylebook*, 347.

7. The Society of Professional Journalists Code of Ethics, *http://www.spj.org/ethics_code.asp*.

8. The First Amendment Handbook, *http://www.rcfp.org/handbook/viewpage.cgi?0109*.

9. Sloan, Wm. David, Stovall, James C. and Startt, James D. (1989), *The Media in America* (Worthington, Ohio: Publishing Horizons Inc.), 409.

10. Pember, 138

11. *The Associated Press Stylebook*, 348.

12. Bernstein, Theodore M. (1965), *The Careful Writer* (New York: Atheneum), 33.

13. Pember, 147.

14. Pember, 147.

15. Pember, 289.

16. The Society of Professional Journalists Code of Ethics, *http://www.spj.org/ethics_code.asp*.

CHAPTER 7

1. E-mail interview with Dick Moss, copy chief, *Rochester Democrat and Chronicle*, July 19, 2002.

2. Frank E. Fee Jr., who teaches at the University of North Carolina–Chapel Hill, was the originator of the panel idea.

3. McIntyre, John, post to ACEStalk@topica.com, Aug. 12, 2001 (reprinted by permission).

4. Clark, Roy Peter and Fry, Don (1992), *Coaching Writers* (New York: St. Martin's Press), 28.

5. Metzler, Ken (1996), *Creative Interviewing*, 3rd ed. (Boston: Allyn & Bacon).

6. Clark and Fry, 4.

7. Russial, John and Bentley, Clyde (1998), Newsroom Rewards, *Presstime*, April, 52.

8. Clark and Fry, 155

9. Clark and Fry, 156–157.

10. Clark and Fry, 159.

11. Clark and Fry, 4.

12. Michael Roberts, post to newscoach-l@freedomforum.org, April 22, 1999.

13. Clark and Fry, 14.

14. Clark and Fry, 15.

15. Shoun, Brenda (2000), 22 Things Never to Say to a Newspaper Designer, *The American Editor*, April.

16. Zelizer, Barbie (1995), Words Against Images: Positioning Newswork in the Age of Photography. In Hardt, Hanno and Brennan, Bonnie (Eds.), *News Workers* (Minneapolis: University of Minnesota Press), 135–159.

17. Moss, Mary Jo (1994), Lost Among Pixels: Who's Minding the Store, *News Photographer*, February, 10–11.

18. Reason, Ron, Things Never to Say to or About a Photojournalist (*http://www.ronreason.com/personal/photonever.html*).

CHAPTER 9

1. Hoopes, James (Ed.) (1991), *Peirce on Signs* (Chapel Hill and London: University of North Carolina Press), 180–185.

2. Sloan, Wm. David, Stovall, James C. and Startt, James D. (1989), *The Media in America* (Worthington, Ohio: Publishing Horizons Inc.), 202–203.

3. Thanks to Chris Frisella, news editor for *The Register-Guard* of Eugene, Ore., for some of the specificity examples.

CHAPTER 10

1. Bendinger, Bruce (2002), *The Copy Workshop Workbook* (Chicago: Copy Workshop).

2. The title comes from the precomputer era, when the copy desk at many papers was U-shaped. The supervisor, or "slot," sat in the inside of the U—the slot of the desk—and physically handed paper copy to the copy editors and took it back for a second look. The copy editors sat around the outside, or the "rim," of the desk, making editing changes by blue or black pencil and handwriting head-lines on scraps of papers, or sometimes typing them. Computer editing, which was introduced into many newspapers in the '70s and the rest by the mid-'80s, elimi-nated the need for the U-shaped desk, but the positions and the names remained, though many papers call the supervisor a "copy chief" now. In some cases, the ac-tual U-shaped desk stayed in the newsroom too.

CHAPTER 13

1. Harrower, Tim (2002), *The Newspaper Designer's Handbook* (New York: McGraw Hill).
2. Barnhurst, Kevin (1994), *Seeing the Newspaper* (New York: St. Martin's Press), 193.
3. Garcia, Mario. Garcia.Media. (*http://www.garcia-media.com/resources/032002.html*).
4. Barnhurst, *Seeing the Newspaper*, 189.
5. Pagination has eliminated the need for a page dummy, or sketch, at some papers but not others. Some newsroom computer systems do not make it possible for copy editors to view electronically drawn pages. Page dummies are either printed out or hand-drawn so that copy editors will know what the page looks like and what headline size to write.
6. Nielsen, Jakob (1996), Top 10 Mistakes in Web Design, Alertbox (*http://www.useit.com/alertbox/9605.html*). Nielsen reaffirmed the use of nonstandard link colors as a mistake in 1999. See Top 10 Mistakes Revisited (1999) (*http://www.useit.com/alertbox/990502.html*).
7. Nielsen, Jakob (1996), Inverted Pyramids in Cyberspace, Alertbox (*http://www.useit.com/alertbox/9606.html*); Nielsen (1997), How Users Read on the Web, Alertbox (*http://www.useit.com/alertbox/9710a.html*); Nielsen (1997), Be Succinct: How to Write for the Web, Alertbox (*http://www.useit.com/alertbox/9703b.html*).
8. Murray, Janet (1997), *Hamlet on the Holodeck* (Cambridge, Mass.: MIT Press).
9. Nielsen, Jakob (1996), Rise of the Sub-Site, Alertbox (*http://www.useit.com/alertbox/9609.html*).
10. Garcia, Mario, Garcia.Media (*http://www.garcia-media.com/resources/032002.html*).

CHAPTER 14

1. Solomon, William Samuel (1985), Technological Change in the Work-place: The Impact of Video Display Terminals on Newspaper Copy Desk Work, Doctoral dissertation, University of California, Berkeley.

2. Russial, John (1989), Pagination and the Newsroom: Great Expectations, Doctoral dissertation, Temple University; Brill, Ann (1994), Pagination and the Newsroom: A Study of Implementation of New Technology, Doctoral dissertation, University of Minnesota.

3. Russial, John (1994), Pagination and the Newsroom: A Question of Time, *Newspaper Research Journal*, Winter, 91–101; Underwood, Doug, Giffard, C. Anthony and Stamm, Keith (1994), Computers and Editing: The Displacement Effect of Pagination Systems in the Newsroom, *Newspaper Research Journal*, Spring, 116–127.

4. Russial, Pagination and the Newsroom: Great Expectations.

5. Cook, Betsy B., Banks, Steve R. and Turner, Ralph J. (1993), The Effects of Work Environment on Burnout in the Newsroom, *Newspaper Research Journal*, (14, 3&4), 123–134; Adcock, Beryl (1995), Attention, Please, for Some Words from the Copydesk, *The American Editor*, October, 34–35; To America's Top Editors, From Your Copy Desks: How We Can Help Each Other, *The Human Relations Committee of the American Society of Newspaper Editors*, 1995–96.

6. Russial, John and Wanta, Wayne (1998), Digital Imaging Skills and the Hiring and Training of Photojournalists, *Journalism and Mass Communications Quarterly*, Autumn, 593–604. Russial, John (2000), How Digital Imaging Changes the Work of Photojournalists, *Newspaper Research Journal*, Summer, 67–83.

7. Russial, John (1995), Pagination and Digital Imaging: A Contrarian Approach, *Newspaper Research Journal*, Fall 42–56.

8. Russial, John. (forthcoming). Pagination and the Copy Editor: Have Things Changed? *Journalism and Mass Communication Quarterly*.

9. Russial, John (1995), Mixed Messages About Pagination and Other Skills, *Newspaper Research Journal*, Winter, 60–70; Russial, Pagination and the Copy Editor: Have Things Changed?

10. In the mid- to late '90s, many reporters and editors could not read their own newspapers on the Web at work because they lacked Internet access in the newsroom.

11. Pavlik, John. Information Technology: Implications for the Future of Journalism and Mass Communication Education. (*http://newmedia.Colorado.EDU/links/pages/24.html*).

12. See, for example, the package of articles in *The American Editor*, July 2000, on convergence at the *Milwaukee Journal Sentinel* and the *Tampa Tribune*. Stories available at *http://www.asne.org/kiosk/editor/00.july/convergence1.htm*; Auletta, Ken (1998), Synergy City, *American Journalism Review*, 18–35.

13. Christ, William G., McCall, Jeffrey M., Rakow, Lana and Blanchard, Robert O. (1997), Integrated Communication Programs. In Christ (Ed.), *Media Education Assessment Handbook* (Mahwah, N.J.: Erlbaum), 23–53. Also, McCall, Jeffrey (1999), Student Occupational Concerns in a Liberal Arts Program. In Christ, William G., (Ed.), *Leadership in Times of Change* (Mahwah, N.J.: Erlbaum), 279–293.

14. Farrell, Elizabeth F. (2002), Columbia U.'s President Halts Search for a Journalism Dean While Reviewing School's Role, *Chronicle of Higher Education online*, July 25, (*http://chronicle.com/free/2002/07/2002072502n.htm*).

15. Harper, Christopher (1996), Doing It All, *American Journalism Review*, December, 24–29.

16. Fee, Frank, Russial, John and Auman, Ann (2003), Back to the Future: Teaching Copy Editing in Changing Times, *Newspaper Research Journal*, Summer.

17. South, Jeff and Nicholson, June (2002), Cross Training, *Quill*, July–August, 10–12.

18. Auman, Ann (1994), Design Desks: Why Are More and More Newspapers Adopting Them? *Newspaper Research Journal*, Spring, 128–142.

19. In surveys asking what skills are important in entry-level copy desk hires, editors at small papers rank page design and Quark skills just below traditional word-editing and headline-writing skills. Editors at large and midsize papers do not consider those skills as important as traditional word editing and headline writing. See Fee et al., Back to the Future: Teaching Copy Editing in Changing Times.

20. Miller, Edward D. (1992), Where Is Design Leading Us? *Quill*, September, 24–25.

21. Ryan, Leland "Buck."(1991). Goodbye Copy Desk, Hello Display Desk, *ASNE Bulletin*, April, 7–12. Weaver, Janet S. (1996), Wichita Is Doing Fine Without a Copydesk, *The American Editor*, January–February–March, 14–16.

22. Russial, John (1998), Goodbye Copy Desk, Hello Trouble? *Newspaper Research Journal*, 2–16.

23. Russial, John (1997), At The Oregonian, It's Easy Does It: Portland Paper Is Changing Its Copydesks One Step at a Time. A Return to Quality Editing, American Society of Newspaper Editors Human Resources Committee report, 10–11.

Index

About the Author

John Russial has taught editing, writing and new media courses at the University of Oregon School of Journalism and Communication for 11 years. He spent 17 years working for daily newspapers, the last 12 at The Philadelphia Inquirer, where he was Sunday copy chief. He is active in the American Copy Editors Society and occasionally leads professional workshops for copy editors and reporters.

Russial has a bachelor's degree from Lehigh University, a master's from Syracuse University and a doctorate from Temple University. He studies how technology and organizational change affect copy editing and newspaper quality.